D0385793

DEATH
of the
DARK HERO

DAVID SELBOURNE

DEATH

of the

DARK HERO

Eastern Europe, 1987–90

JONATHAN CAPE
LONDON

First published 1990
© David Selbourne 1990
Jonathan Cape Ltd, 20 Vauxhall Bridge Road,
London SW1V 2SA

A CIP catalogue record for this book
is available from the British Library

ISBN 0-224-02792-1

The following photographs are reproduced with
permission: 1, 2, 3, 4, 5, 6, 7, 8, Laurie Sparham/Network;
9, 10, 11, 22, 23, 24, Mike Abrahams/Network; 12, 13, 14, 15,
16, 17, Witold Krassowski/Network; 18, 20, Mark Power/Network;
19, Popperfoto; 21, Rex Features; 25, Martin Argles, *Guardian*;
26, Paul Lowe/Network; 27, Christopher Pillitz/Network.

Maps © Malcolm Porter 1990

Photoset by Rowland Phototypesetting Ltd,
Bury St. Edmunds, Suffolk
Printed in Great Britain by
Mackays of Chatham PLC,
Chatham, Kent

Contents

'Communism is the secret name of the dread antagonist setting proletarian rule with all its consequences against the present bourgeois regime. It will be a frightful duel. How will it end? No one knows but gods and goddesses acquainted with the future. We know only this much: Communism, though little discussed now and loitering in hidden garrets on miserable straw pallets, is the dark hero destined for a great, if temporary, role in the modern tragedy . . .'

Heinrich Heine,
Paris, 20th June 1842

Acknowledgments

I have more debts than I can pay to those who helped me in my journeys in eastern Europe, who gave me contacts, advice and information, and who assisted me in the writing of this book. I would especially like to thank Pavel Bratinka, Alena Hromadkova and Jan Urban in Czechoslovakia; Gaspar Tamas in Hungary; Mariana Celac and Andrei Plesu in Romania; Violeta Stoichkova in Bulgaria; and Marta Sienicka in Poland, for their help and friendship. I am also grateful to the trustees of the Jan Hus Educational Foundation, and its secretary Barbara Day; to Assen Novatchkov of the Bulgarian Embassy in London; to Marek Matraszek, secretary of the Jagiellonian Trust; to Nora Beloff, for her generosity with journalistic contacts; to Mark Almond of Oriel College, Oxford, Karel Kyncl of Index on Censorship and Chris Mititelu of the Romanian Service of the BBC for answering my queries; to Perry Worsthorne, Paul Barker and Alexander Chancellor for early encouragement of my writing on eastern Europe; to Mike Abrahams, Witold Krassowski and Laurie Sparham of Network for their company and professional enthusiasm as photographers on some of my journeys.

More personal thanks are due to Lord Goodman, for his advice and moral support in a difficult period; to Hugo Young, for his friendship and journalistic example; to my daughter Emilie and son Raphael for help with research and the collation of information; to my wife, Hazel, for her advice, company – in Yugoslavia, East Germany and Czechoslovakia – and knowledge, at all stages.

To Tony Colwell at Cape I owe a special debt, for his constant support of my work as a writer.

Introduction

This is an account of the new reformation in eastern Europe. I count myself privileged to have seen what I saw during the last three years, and to have known the people who appear in these pages. After twenty-five years and more of wrestling with the theory and practice of socialism, I record in this book my experience of what has been one of the greatest of all historic revolutions: a democratic, and essentially anti-socialist revolution, the effects of which will continue long after its actors, and their observers, have disappeared from the scene. It will be a match for 1789.

By the nature of it, this is a personal chronicle as well as a more general history of the period from 1987 to 1990. That I found myself in eastern Europe in the first place I owe to the fortuitous circumstances of being unable to continue teaching at Ruskin College, Oxford, after I had written an article in *The Times* in March 1986 during the Wapping dispute. I was 'punished' by student boycotts and pickets, and accused of 'provocation', and much else besides. The College failed to defend my academic freedom, and I was forced to withdraw from the College and start legal proceedings against it, which were ultimately successful.

During this time, I began to travel in eastern Europe, released by chance from my long thraldom to the world of the British left and British Labour – a world as suffocating, sterile and authoritarian (in its own way) as the world I began to encounter in eastern Europe. I found myself witnessing, in country after country, the quickening to new life and hope of moribund political cultures; spoke, in country after country, to varieties of dissident and heretic, men and women of heroically independent minds who made my own puny dissent a trivial matter. I met those who would turn out later to be shaping, and even leading, their countries, and entered into debate with people for whom the moral issues which concerned me intellectually were a life-and-death matter.

Much of this experience was purest joy – the joy of participation, even if vicarious, in what I knew from an early stage to be a revolutionary process. I found myself cross-examining with exhilaration apparatchiks who were politically on the run, sharing the ideas of persecuted freethinkers at the very moments when their prison doors were about to open, and in the end seeing liberated citizens stream into the streets and squares in their hundreds of thousands. There were darker moments also; memories of a benighted world, a grey world of wrecked lives and grubby falsehoods, of tanks in the street and nothing much in the pockets.

This book is my third on the long discomfiture of the left. The first, *Against Socialist Illusion*, an analysis of socialist wishful thinking, was written in 1983-4, and was published at the beginning of 1985. The second, *Left Behind: Journeys into British Politics*, published in 1987, tells of the left's inability to outgrow its own narrow traditions in Britain. Now, yet more rooms in the Utopian mansion of socialism have fallen. Proletarianism, East and West, and the politics pursued in its name, has proved to be one of the world's curses. Labour and the politics of labour, not capital, has been shown – from Wapping to Warsaw – to be the true fetter on the forces of production. It is capital, not *Das Kapital*, which the States of eastern Europe require in order to release the pent-up energies of their people.

Few are glad to be relieved of the burden of their illusions. For me, too, the idea that the net historical balance of socialism's record has been to hold back human development was difficult to acknowledge, and required several separate efforts in the 1980s. It was (and remains) a hard truth for me that Marxism has turned out to be an intellectual apostasy which almost undid the emancipatory legacy of the French Revolution. It was not an easy matter to accept that the imposition of the left Utopia upon human aspirations in all their variety required, and was bound to require, both lies and violence.

Why was it so difficult for me finally to come to terms with these truths? Mainly because of fears, legitimate fears, of the right's own capacity for evil doing. Indeed, for millions, this has always been the principal sanction against abandoning left positions. They are positions which provide, so we think – and for long have thought – a bulwark against 'reaction', and, at worst, against fascism. It was for me a bitter discovery that those who have experienced the full weight of the socialist incubus will generally wish, sooner or later, to unburden themselves of it. Moreover, the 'sophisticated' distinctions between right and left totalitarianisms which I had learned (and taught) had turned out, in the real world, to have diminished substance; especially for the victims.

It was after my first visits to eastern Europe in 1987 that I saw that the left, for wholly progressive reasons, ought to have been actively working – if necessary alongside the right – for the downfall of regimes which so lacked legitimacy in the eyes of their depressed peoples. The installation of plural liberal-democratic systems, founded upon parliamentary accountability, a freed market and the overthrow of the State socialist order, far from representing the triumph of anti-socialist reaction, would represent a new historical form of anti-socialist progress.

The western left, I saw, even had a moral duty to offer its old (discredited) 'fraternal solidarity' to those whose lives had been blighted in the name of socialism. They had a duty to those whose hopes and liberties had been lost, their intellectual and spiritual energies sapped, their labour exploited, while party élites ostensibly pursued the 'socialist' chimaera. I came to see that the western left's vicarious idealism – at a safe distance from such realities – had in fact been a kind of intellectual treason for all these decades: a betrayal not merely of the truth but of real people.

While I saw and thought these things, I also began enquiring how it was that after a century and more of huge western intellectual investment in the theory and practice of Marxism, its latter-day exponents – of whom I had been one – had barely a single honest word to say on these matters. My friends (and foes) on the left appeared to feel not the slightest obligation to tell the truth, explain themselves, or offer a *mea culpa* for intellectual and political errors which they would acknowledge in private.

Obviously enough, the left was bound not to be able to say, even when it could see, that the restoration of capitalism in eastern Europe (and the Soviet Union) would be historically progressive. But the reasons for silence and confusion are deeper. The intellects of the left, especially of the Marxist left, are wounded intellects. That is, as Milan Simecka brilliantly explained to me in Bratislava, thought-damaging intellectual harm has been done to all those whose permanent inclination is to reduce the many-faceted *homo sapiens* to the single-faceted, class-bound *homo economicus*; whose deepest instinct is to deny the vice and virtue of human nature; whose narrow categories of understanding seek to tyrannize over the riches of human belief and expression. These left categories of understanding are, in general, *low-grade*. Yet they present themselves – fatal flaw – as being of a superior explanatory power to all others.

The disabling consequence has been a mixture of intellectual arrogance and foolish certitude, now defeated, yet unable to acknowledge its own dilemma. Having read the wrong books, my friends on the left found themselves caught by surprise at events in eastern Europe. That is, they were intellectually unprepared for an anti-socialist revolution. Now, far from re-evaluating their own nostrums, they appear still to be huddled around them, silently warming their hands at the embers.

What's left, so to speak? In Prague, I was told by Vanek Silhan – who for a brief while in August 1968 replaced Alexander Dubcek as the Czech Communist Party leader, after the latter had been abducted to Moscow – that 'the left in the world will have to transcend attitudes which have more to do with authority *over* society and with personal competition between themselves than with the genuine development of humane social thinking. There is no future', Silhan declared, 'for this "left style" of practice.'

But this too is illusion. Such attitudes are the very essence of 'left practice', and are universal. I do not believe they can be transcended, or transcended for long, in any socialist order or organization. So what is left? 'Being social,' Milovan Djilas told me in a banal reduction of aspiration. 'Democracy, choice, social justice,' said the editor of a Bulgarian Party paper in Sofia, vaguely covering the political spectrum, right, left and centre. Indeed, after the pains through which eastern Europe has passed for forty years, the dream of Utopia has been reconstructed: it is now composed of a mixed economy dominated by the free market, large-scale foreign investment, reduced welfare provision, parliamentarism and a benignly utilitarian coalition of interests. As for the apostles of genuine workers' power, they are doubtless biding their time for the next historical phase of the class struggle in eastern Europe and the Soviet Union.

Meanwhile, we for our parts have begun to coddle ourselves with new illusions about this post-Communist order, as if under the skin the Latvian nationalist or Romanian peasant shared the world view of the average reader of the *Independent*. It will doubtless be another painful awakening to discover that this is not so. Indeed we must now live, in East and West alike, with the consequences of Gorbachev's belief – brave or foolhardy – that 'freedom of choice' is a 'universal principle which allows for no exceptions' and 'applies equally to capitalist and socialist systems'. It is a belief which has served as the catalyst both for the reunification of Germany and the undermining of the Communist Party of the Soviet Union. Nevertheless, that in eastern Europe the dissolving socialist system should have gone so far as to restore free parliaments and free markets, under popular pressure, is a great undoing. It is an historic reformation of socialist error, whatever its further outcome.

EASTERN EUROPE

Baltic Sea

Berlin ■

EAST
GERMANY
(GDR)

Warsaw ■

POLAND

USSR

WEST
GERMANY

Prague ■

CZECHOSLOVAKIA

AUSTRIA

■ Budapest

HUNGARY

ROMANIA

Belgrade ■

Bucharest ■

ITALY

YUGOSLAVIA

Adriatic
Sea

■ Sofia   BULGARIA

Black
Sea

ALBANIA

GREECE

TURKEY

miles
0   300
0   300
kilometres

Mediterranean Sea

1

Czechoslovakia, February 1987: Still-life

On an icy Prague morning a pale and acne-spotted youth, in jeans and a quilted ski-jacket emblazoned with the words 'Parmalat World Ski Series', picks his way among the heaps of blackened and refrozen slush. O the dreary pain of life, too cold for rage, in such a sullen setting – with cardboard fixed to car-radiator grills, blank-eyed army officers carrying flat brief-cases into a freezing wind, its cyanosed lips, its plodding solemnity, its inertia. Even the wind seems grey, *comme il faut* in eastern Europe.

On the 119 bus to Leninova there is a crowded silence; in the Metro, again silence (pasty-faced and in fur-lined bootees), seemingly without energy or tension. Here is a dusty window full of tinned sardines, or biscuits in Cellophane; there, a silent queue of asexual and classless *hausfraus* – snug in their fur, some of them – waiting for Cuban grapefruit, frost-bitten cabbage, tinned Vietnamese pineapple juice or acorn-like coffee. Brown sausages (for there is meat here) lie coiled on a white plate in another dusty window: is the shop closed, or open? From one (aesthetic) angle, this might be a still-life; from another, *nature morte*, lifeless.

*

The silence of winter in what used to be central Europe: Prague, its pavements frozen, is a city in waiting, its atmosphere that of a European capital which has been long vacated. Within sight (almost) of the bright lights of the West, it seems all grey orderliness, unhurried stolidity – or docility – and low spirits. 'At the present time, Czechoslovakia is passing through the phase of building an advanced socialist society', says the official handout, given to me at the Czech

Embassy in London. The citizens I pass in the street, well enough fed and shod but dowdy, avoid eye-contact.

Despite the signals from Moscow, where Gorbachev now speaks of the socialist ideal as one of 'free labour and free thought in a free country', it is as if nothing new were stirring in Prague beneath the surface appearance of things; as if there were no possibility of a new Prague Spring coming to flower.

'All mouths are turned down,' says the philosopher-turned-janitor in his book-lined flat – with its old farmhouse furniture, bowls of dried flowers and Victorian bric-à-brac – below President Gustav Husak's Hradcany Palace, home of the ancient kings of Bohemia. 'When I go out, my mouth turns down also.' '*Il est très, très triste ici,*' his wife added.

*

But what beauty of Viennese baroque, garlanded rococo, and arabesque art nouveau there is in this domed and turreted city – together with its Stalinist, or neo-Fascist, bunkers in concrete, or granite. Prague is a city-of-all-the-architectural-graces; where Mozart came to write *Don Giovanni*, where the poet Rilke was born, but where you cannot find a text of Franz Kafka, a non-person since the early 1970s.

'All major cultural facilities – theatres, film, press, radio, television, etc. – come under the state administration in one form or another. The State also has charge of publishing activities and the book market, and has given cultural life a new content, while the creativity of progressive artists reflects the mainstream of socialist art,' declares my handout. In consequence, there is no Kafka. You can, however, get yourself a consolation copy of *The Speeches and Writings of Gustav Husak*, published in English by Pergamon Press, and its ex-Czech owner, Robert Maxwell.

Today's dispirited dissenters – liberal democrats, Christians of left, right and centre, 'independent socialists' – inhabit and make the best they can of a wasteland; 'the land of forty years of the Stalinist personality cult', as they put it, 'but without personalities.' In a previous generation, the Czech writer Karel Capek spoke with dismay of the 'peculiar gloom of Communism', and invented the word 'robot'.

But this is also the land of the Good Soldier Schweik, who escaped the clutches of authority by pretending to be, or perhaps being, feeble-minded. 'Caution', he told an agitated fellow-prisoner in police detention, 'is the mother of wisdom. Just sit down quietly if you don't want to hang yourself, and wait to see how things turn out.'

The tide of life seems to be barely moving, and a leaden silence descends upon Prague in the darkness. It is a city where the pulse-rate slows to the pace of the general depression; and where visiting delegations of Iraqi trade unionists with flapping brown suits and 12-noon shadow are greeted like conquering heroes. 'In the Czech Socialist Republic, all power is in the hands of the working people,' my handout explains.

Yet something is stirring, despite it.

*

'This barbarian, Bolshevik regime', she [Alena Hromadkova] says (not wanting her name or occupation mentioned), 'is corrupt, helpless and a political fake.' Strewn on the floor among her papers are copies of the *TLS*, Hayek's *Constitution of Liberty* in a *samizdat* translation, and past issues of *Encounter*. 'It has no conception of legality, not in the sense that you understand it. It has an obsolete ideology only, and the arrogance of what it calls "socialist culture"' – 'its own absurd clichés and traditions' is how she puts it – 'in which no one believes any longer.'

'In the 1920s there was a rich co-operative and trade union life in Czechoslovakia, and a strong sense of law also. These had to be broken down and physically destroyed to create Stalinism in this country. Such terms as "liquidation of the bourgeoisie" or "class struggle" – which you leftists in the West use so lightly – have a real connotation for us. They were a real, physical experience. Now, we are gradually rediscovering our roots, our own history, and many of us are going back to conservative traditions.'

The room is dark, lit by a single table-lamp. It is 10 p.m.; outside there is silence. She is a devout Christian. What effect is Gorbachev having? I ask her. 'Most people find it hard to believe that anything of importance will ever change here. Many younger people do not even know that the situation in Czechoslovakia is not normal; 1968 was nearly twenty years ago.'

She means, I take it, that these pale youths with dazed eyes will not set the River Vltava on fire, unlike their predecessors.

'I too sometimes think, when I am depressed, that the demoralization and apathy in Czechoslovakia will never be overcome. For instance, people are absolutely habituated to working only 20 to 30 per cent of what is possible, although they make every effort to be *observed* working.' It is what she calls a 'general social reaction'. To what? 'To the socialist system. Very few people know how to do more than the necessary minimum. It is true of everybody, the police included.'

But what about the regime? What has Gorbachev's effect been on the apparatus? 'We dare not hope,' she answers, her hands folded chastely in her lap. 'At the moment, the apparatchiks are in a state of panic. They have panicked,' she repeats, laughing (briefly) with pleasure. 'In fact, they are so self-preoccupied with the problems of totalitarian reform' – 'these brutal pragmatists' she calls them, with fastidious distaste – 'that we non-Communists have recently had a period of relative freedom.

'Even so, in Czechoslovakia you are always invaded by their plebeian culture,' she says, weary; her eyes are dark-shadowed. 'It is hard to defend yourself against such a culture. How to keep your standards of truth and when to compromise: these are the everyday choices and struggles.' Outside in the street the silence is as profound as ever. You can hear a clock in the next room ticking, ticking.

*

After the fall of Alexander Dubcek to Warsaw Pact armies in August 1968, this became the land of born-again Stalinism. It has a secure basis in the violence and cruel vendetta of 1948, when the Communists took over; in the purges and executions (for 'Trotsky-ism', 'Titoism', 'revisionism' and god-knows-what besides) of the 1950s; in the imprisonments, job dismissals and exile of tens of thousands of Dubcekites in 1969 and 1970 – reminiscent of the exiling of almost one quarter of the urban population during the seventeenth-century counter-reformation; and in the hounding since 1977 of Charter human rights signatories, persecuted for upholding the principles of the Helsinki Agreement.

You don't have to look far in Prague for the consequences of the last two decades of reprisals against reformers. It has made physicists into caretakers, writers and historians into stokers and bricklayers, and theologians into nightwatchmen; Dubcek himself became a modest State employee in Bratislava. Even President Husak, in an earlier turn of the wheel, received a life sentence in 1954 as a 'bourgeois nationalist', and did a six-year stretch before his release and 'rehabilitation'. In 1968, during the Prague Spring's heady moments of freedom, Husak spoke of the 'brutal and violent interrogations' to which he had been subjected. 'All-round socialist development', as the London Embassy handout calls it, obviously has its dangers.

No wonder, either, that your average Prague burgher or his red-faced country cousin, trudging through the gelid streets, is cautious. Even Good King Wenceslas was murdered (in AD 929) by his brother, in the old fraternal Czech tradition.

*

Lying on the bed, leafing through my collection of grey handouts. '". . . A part of our youth is showing an incorrect attitude to work and the results of socialist construction, putting their individual interests above all-society ones. Many of them behave in a way which is alien to socialist morality. Some young people do not have the principles of class consciousness, socialist patriotism, proletarian internationalism, and socialist collectivism sufficiently well rooted in their minds, refus-ing to go to work where society needs them most. These elements are incompatible with the socialist life style," Comrade Josef Harlin, central committee secretary, declared at a meeting of educationists in Uhersky Brodo. "Pedagogical skill must be used to make people understand the advantages and complexities of the construction of advanced socialism," Comrade Harlin stated. "Low working morale among students has . . . " ' At the hotel window, snow-flurries.

*

'He is tough, he has been through a lot', was their description of him before he arrived. Vaclav Slavik, a Charter 77 signatory, was one of six Party secretaries under Dubcek and a member of the central committee; he remains a 'close friend of Alexander'. An old-time Party apparatchik, Slavik has spent the years since Brezhnev's tanks swept away the 1968 Prague experiment as a bulldozer-driver on building-sites, and in a construction gang building the Prague Metro.

'I helped to build Leninova station,' he said to me, the young men in the room, Charter activists, laughing at the whimsy of it. Later, when he had gone, they described him as 'very naive and old-fashioned in his thinking, but he knows the people in power'; he described himself as 'still a socialist, despite eighteen years [since 1969] of quite hard experience.'

In what sense a socialist? I had asked him. 'I am not a Utopian,' he had answered, 'but I still believe in the possibilities of socialism.' What possibilities? 'That it can catch up with and overtake capitalism in production,' he had answered.

'Gorbachev's speech to the Moscow plenum a fortnight ago [on 27 January 1987] was followed with great attention here,' he declares. 'It was published in the Prague press, and on that day the newspapers sold out quickly. The day after, when I went to the kiosk to buy the Soviet papers from Moscow, people were queuing in the street for them; two working men who did not know Russian followed me in the street, asking me to tell them what was in *Pravda* and *Izvestia*. Gorbachev's speech touches exactly the same questions which we raised in 1968. It was we who said first, in 1968, that there should be changes of the kind which Gorbachev is preparing, for example to open up the electoral system. To us, Gorbachev's speech is a rehabilitation' – that word again – 'of our politics of 1968.'

Two weeks ago, says Slavik, while Gorbachev was addressing the Moscow plenum, a meeting was also being held in Prague of top technocrats, economists and central committee members. 'I have learned that at this meeting Lubomir Strougal [the prime minister] stated that, as far as economic reform was concerned, we had been "too shy" in 1968, and that we "should have been bolder". Strougal is not saying who wrecked things in 1968 – he is still talking too vaguely about that period – but at least he is not repeating all the old slogans: such as calling the Soviet invasion "international solidarity help", and so on. There is a cloud nineteen-years-old over our affairs,' the elderly Slavik adds, 'but this is a step forward.'

This is also the voice of grey-haired defeat, thankful for small mercies. Later I hear a different version from another informant, who asks me not to identify him, of strange goings-on at the official CTK news agency on 27 January, after the text of Gorbachev's Moscow speech had come through on the wire and the full extent of its radicalism had become apparent. Late at night and into the early hours of 28 January, Strougal's own speech to 'top technocrats' was in part rewritten by agency staff. 'We had to match the atmosphere of Strougal's speech to the new line from Moscow,' my informant told me.

Slavik, rough-handed from his post-1968 labours and now in his seventies, was educated in the old days at Prague's French lycée; his French is fluent. He is one of a group of forlorn (and sometimes heavy-drinking) Dubcekite veterans – whom Slavik calls 'those active in the 1960s and now retired' – which meets regularly in Prague. Emboldened by 'Gorbachevism', they have been pressing the present Czech central committee (by writing letters) to tell them what it proposes to do about reform.

'We are saying to them, some of you claim to be in favour of the new Soviet policy, Strougal for example. But what are you doing about it, how are you going to solve Czechoslovakia's problems? People are starting to speak more openly, writing to *Rude Pravo* [the Party daily newspaper], writing to the central committee, writing also to Moscow.' Which people are writing to Moscow? I ask Slavik. 'Many, including people coming from families with strong socialist traditions, families which were founders of the Czech workers' movement in the last century.'

Yes, but who, and what are they saying? 'I don't want to personalize it,' Slavik answers obliquely. But the rumour in Prague, where rumour magnified can turn into a fantasy from the pages of Kafka, is that Dubcek has even *been* to Moscow to seek help in his efforts at 'rehabilitation'. 'They are complaining to Moscow about two things. One is that nothing real is happening here. The other is that people who have shown their socialist dedication, an historic dedication, are still working outside their qualifications' – Slavik's ex-Stalinist euphemism for all the stoking and bricklaying. 'They are protesting that there is a generation in Czechoslovakia which is still paying for having the same views that Gorbachev holds now.' Such as? 'That socialism is impossible without democracy,' he answers.

Slavik goes further. 'Dubcek is (or was) a man of the same style as Gorbachev. They are both creative socialists,' says Slavik. 'It means Gorbachev and Dubcek both know that in the real world a plurality of forms of life exists, a plurality of ideas and interests, and that socialism must respect and articulate them.

'From my last meeting with Dubcek, I can say that not only has he read Gorbachev's speech in the newspaper very carefully, but that his copy of the speech is full of notes and underlinings. But our people coming from Moscow' – again he draws a discreet veil over their identity – 'say that Gorbachev's position is not yet so strong. They tell us that his ideas are not being received as favourably as we would like. They are worried that he is taking too many risks with the KGB and the army.'

After Slavik had left the young men talked fitfully about him. 'What he says is what Dubcek is saying,' one of them declares. There is a silence. 'These old men are getting more confident that the wheel will turn again,' says another, 'you can see the change in them. Before they die they want to see their truth winning.' 'Like when the good guys win in the last act of a drama,' a voice added.

Outside, the pavements were as icy as ever.

*

A group of 'dissident intellectuals' is gathered around the midnight table. They laugh ironically at the circumstances of my own case of heresy: denounced as a 'provocateur' and 'traitor', told by my militant left students to 'repent or resign' for my actions, abandoned by colleagues of twenty years' standing at Ruskin, formally condemned by the College's governing body of trade unionists, and all for writing an article in *The Times* – or 'crossing the picket-line' – during the Wapping dispute. 'So you know a little about Czechoslovakia,' says Rudolf Kucera, a Catholic historian-turned-bricklayer.

*

Browsing, you may find Sidney Bechet and Ray Charles, and even Bill Haley and the Comets on an imported Polish label. The sleeve-note, in Polish and English, declares that 'what used to express the revolt of teenagers in the 1950s – "Blue Suede Shoes", "Whole Lotta Shakin' Going On", etc. – have by now become classical numbers, described in serious encyclopaedias.'

Or, if you prefer, there is Dickens's *Barnabas Rudge*, Evelyn Waugh's *Sestup a Pad*, and a biography of Einstein; and in the second-hand shop near Karlovy Bridge, Margaret Cole's *Life of Beatrice Webb* for 18 crowns.

This is a market under (dusty) wraps: offering a dour but steady commerce of basic needs, with its diversions carefully managed and its bootleg pleasures thinly scattered.

*

'Before', Jan Urban says, 'I couldn't nail a picture into the wall. I had an absolute fear of manual and technical work.' He is a tall, handsome fellow with an upright bearing; his surprisingly thickened hands are dusty from the day's labour. Son of a diplomat (an ambassador in the Dubcek period), Urban was once a schoolteacher. A Charter signatory and awkward customer, he is now a jobbing builder.

'To me, like to others in the socialist intelligentsia, the proletariat seemed dirty, uneducated, passive and selfish. But suddenly I had to shovel shit myself, and learn to live with people I had only read about before, or observed from a distance. I discovered they were no different from anyone else: some would steal your last coin, others would give you the last penny they had in their pockets. My problem was that I couldn't afford to show how weak I was.'

Why not? 'Because the apparatus wanted to break me, and I was determined not to let them. At the same time, I learned how easy it is in a system like ours to break anyone. After 1969, many crawled to avoid manual labour, and half a million left the country. Some of my friends who stayed started drinking, and even began weeping. They felt that 1968 had been their last chance and that their whole way of thinking and living had been defeated. Many of them are now very tired; they consider that they have paid for their views with years of their lives.

'To avoid this kind of self-destructive feeling, a man must go on believing in his own truth. But that is not enough in itself. You have to show everybody that you can live through it, and, for yourself, try to learn something from your labours.' He looks at his own hands, turning them from side to side. And how about the average man and woman in the streets? I ask him. How do they survive?

'They survive', Urban answered, 'by being grey and inactive. For most people it is the only way to live through the social tragi-comedy of this system.' (This was truly Schweik-like.) 'Everyone is so tired that not to give in under the obstacles of daily existence is enough of a struggle for the average person. In Czechoslovakia being scared – even without reason – makes people behave the way they do. They are used to it; the whole nation might collapse if it got its freedom. People daren't demand their rights. They are even frightened of their duties,' he added, laughing, or grimacing. 'This is why the economy runs at such a low level. Some are also afraid of hoping, as if to hope were forbidden. The real moment of danger could come when things really begin changing. I'm very afraid of what could happen.'

Why? 'Nearly everybody has lived for decades with fear at their backs, betraying themselves just in order to keep going. Hardly anyone is "clean". All of us, in one way or another, are guilty. Some might seek revenge for these years of self-betrayal. They might try to silence their own consciences by punishing other people. But if they turn to revenge, it could be the end of the nation.'

What kind of moral state do you dream of? I asked him. 'A state of intelligent normality,' the man with the dusty hands answered. 'A state where there is the possibility of being decent in an ordinary way. We have lived long enough on ideology, counting all the time.' Counting? 'Who is who, who is on our side, who is on theirs, and how many.'

Outside, in Thunovska Street, a small video camera is fixed high on the crumbling stucco wall of the unmarked police station. It has Urban's visitors covered. 'When change comes, I want to have clean hands,' he anxiously repeated.

*

Earlier in our conversation, I had asked Urban if Gorbachev was making any difference. 'Gorbachev', Urban had answered, 'is an excellent Machiavellian. But he can't do the job for us, he can't teach us democracy, he can't undo in a generation a thousand years of Byzantine politics in Russia – and someone may kill him. He is good for us merely by existing, even though there is no one in our gerontocracy who could or would carry out a genuine perestroika in

Czechoslovakia. After Husak, there may be quite a long time of interregnum. But we already see more open space in front of us. This year is a crossroads. The active are being less punished.'

*

The Pariz Hotel, with its restored blue-green and gold *fin de siècle* mosaics, conjures up the world of Gustav Klimt and the Vienna Sezession; that is if you ignore the grey streets outside and their as-if-sightless figures, most of whom pay you no attention in order not to attract it.

There are not many shining eyes in the Pariz, and no elegant chatter. It is a place of whispers, dissident assignations, and the off-stage sound of plates, rattling somewhere in the distance.

*

'He may be the cleverest Russian leader since Lenin, but even he will not be clever enough,' says Ladislav Hejdanek, referring to Gorbachev. Hejdanek – mathematician, philosopher and redoubtable Evangelical theologian – spent eight months in prison in 1972, and has subsequently worked as a stoker and nightwatchman, himself under constant surveillance.

'To tell you the truth, most people have not much interest in Gorbachev here,' he says coldly. 'And, even when they are interested, few people have faith in Gorbachevism. How can they, when the most open-minded intellectuals in Czechoslovakia have lost their sense of social direction? You in the West see Gorbachev as a kind of liberal. This is an error. His policy is imperial, not a policy of liberalization. It is essentially a new and complex way of making Soviet propaganda. You can see it less clearly, because he is the first Soviet leader to be Europe-orientated. He is skilfully, or I should say cunningly, turning his face towards the European powers, especially towards the Germans but also towards you English. Mrs Thatcher may be a strong woman, but Gorbachev is much more sophisticated.' Even his apologetic smile is wintry. 'I, as a Czech, am able to see him first of all as a Russian. He is a Russian nationalist who knows that the USSR has to be reformed, that its economic tempo must be quickened if it is to become a stronger world power.'

Hejdanek's flat is characterless, and these blank judgments of his are chilling. 'Gorbachev's gamble is risky for him, a dangerous project. But, at first, most of the apparatchiks here were pessimistic.

They were afraid of his cleverness – he is much cleverer than Dubcek – and unsure what to do about him. At first, they thought they were facing a new 1968 in Czechoslovakia. But now I think they are convinced that if they can hold on for a few more years they have nothing to fear from Gorbachevism.'

On the bookcase behind him is a photograph of his friend and fellow Protestant theologian, Jan Dus, whose trial on a charge of subversion is imminent. 'Of course, if they should come under pressure from Moscow to reform, I am sure they will be ready to make certain changes. But these changes will be to gain time for themselves and will be only formal.'

Sceptical about the possibilities of a new Reformation in Czechoslovakia, for Hejdanek the dispersal of the Stalinist *ancien régime* which presides over Prague from the heights of Hradcany will take more than a liberal wind blowing from Moscow.

He sat in his armchair, silent, musing without expression. 'Despite what I have said, Gorbachev is the only hope for us,' he added suddenly.

★

These are still winter's depths, but with the first hint of a thaw dripping here and there from broken gutterings. Might not there be a new Thirty Years' War (1969–1999) in subterranean progress, which will one day turn out to have been more successful than its disastrous seventeenth-century anti-Habsburg predecessor? After all, the Czechs always seem to have been engaged in long-term struggles for their national identity and political freedom: struggles against each other, against Rome, against Vienna, against Budapest, against Moscow. (Most notable of all were the Hussites – named after Prague University's rector Jan Hus, burned at the stake in 1415 and the subject of a biography by Mussolini – who stood against virtually the whole of Europe from 1419 to 1434, in defence of their premature attempt at reforming the late-medieval church.)

'Russia', said Jan Masaryk, the liberal democratic foreign minister in the first Communist government of 1948, 'is like a big fat cow. Its head grazes in Prague, but it has its udders in Moscow. I am hoping to turn it round.' In those days he never got the chance; 'falling' to his death from his third-floor window in the Czernin Palace, a mere three weeks after the Communists took power.

The Czechs have had other picturesque ways of getting rid of their leaders, but ageing Party General Secretary Husak, whose days are numbered, will be elbowed aside – not defenestrated – perhaps with a note from the palace doctors. In neo-Stalinist Prague, this kind of thing must be counted progress.

*

The old Jewish quarter of the glacial city, in early morning sunshine. Here the Jews first settled in AD 906; died at the hands of the First Crusade (in 1096), were burned at the stake in 1336, and were murdered – 3,000 of them – in the 1389 pogroms. Supporters of the reforming Hussites from 1421, they were plundered for it; were expelled from Prague in 1541, and returned; and in the Thirty Years' War were taxed and mulcted to exhaustion. Decimated by the Plague of 1680 and the Great Ghetto Fire of 1689, and expelled (once more) in 1744 by Maria Theresa, they returned to live peaceably in Prague until the exterminations (of 77,300 souls) in Terezin and Auschwitz.

The quarter had its own Town Hall once, designed by Renaissance Italian architects; its clock-face numerals are Hebrew. There is also a thirteenth-century synagogue where a few last survivors still gather in their dark cloisters, and where a small memorial light has been set upon a wall for 'Dr Fr. Kafka'. The Town Hall is now a museum. Here are ancestral synagogue silks and velvets of the Renaissance, heavily-brocaded bridal bonnets from Moravia and embroidered table-coverings for the bread of the Sabbath; dear relics.

And in the tumbled cemetery are ancient grey and grey-pink tombstones, some bearing carved hands upraised in a silent freezing benediction.

*

Outside St Salvator's, beside the Karlovy Bridge, you can hear the baroque sounds of the Sunday organ and of full-throated singing. Inside, the unheated church is full. The responsa are firm, or dogged, breaths funnelling white in the cold, the candles a-flicker. When the communicants crowd to the altar, they are young and old, men and women; some hobbling forward on sticks, others waiting on their knees, eyes closed in prayer.

*

Vladimir Kadlec, a former professor of economics, was Dubcek's minister of education. He says, restlessly, that 'everybody recognizes that these ideas of Gorbachev's are the same as they were here in 1968. People can see the affinity.' But he describes his political generation as 'all over sixty, disappointed and frustrated because we know we will not take part in building the new system.'

Beached by the nineteen-year-old turning of the tide since he held power – 'so many years of apathy and lethargy for Czechoslovakia' – he sits in his spartan flat, worrying; concluding that the upheaval of any new reform in Prague might create even worse economic problems, including an inflation in prices and expectations.

His is yet another lost life, its anxious energies wasted. His younger visitors you can see are sorry for him, simultaneously respectful and embarrassed. 'So many people in this country don't work much but are reasonably well paid for it. Such people are not very keen on reform,' he says, speaking very rapidly, and from within some deep well of isolation. 'They fear that labour discipline would be tightened, that they might be paid less and have to work harder.'

Or perhaps this intense kind of agonized depression of his is central European. 'We, our generation, want to see discredited politicians – Bilak [the Czech regime's veteran ideologist], Husak and so on – removed. History will judge them harshly. For us socialists they have devalued the very concept of socialism, especially in the eyes of the younger generation.'

The shy young people in the room (who no longer even speak of socialism) shift uneasily, for fear that he might ask them questions. 'What Czech youth really thinks about socialism I no longer know', Kadlec says, ignoring them and speaking as quickly as ever, 'but I think it has been so discredited that whether they will want to take the path of democratic socialism in the future, or socialism at all, is an open question.

'At least some things are changing,' he continues in a depressed torrent of words. 'People used to cross the street to avoid me when they saw me approaching. Now, they come up to me to tell me the latest rumours. It reminds me of an old proverb, you have it also in English, about what happens when ships are sinking.'

He pauses for breath, the young people – suddenly unguarded – looking at him as if in horror, their mouths open.

*

The spires and blackened towers of medieval Prague are of soaring German Gothic. On a cold morning, water dripping in the old courtyards and cobbled alleys, their gold-tipped pinnacles and spiky turrets – as in a frightening tale by the Grimm brothers – seem like crowns of thorns placed upon the heads of a generation of martyrs.

*

He reads the *Spectator* whenever he can get hold of it, speaks the most fluent English, and talks of the time when 'we will all be free'. Pavel Bratinka is a leading Catholic layman in his mid-thirties. A witty fellow, with fine hands and a somewhat Wildean manner, he was once a physicist and member of the Czech Academy of Sciences.

In October 1977, after signing (with 54 others) a Catholic petition calling for religious freedom, he was given one hour's notice to leave his job at Prague's Institute of Technical Development. He is presently shovelling coke to heat the managers' offices and workers' changing-rooms at an excavation site for the Prague Metro.

'We cannot believe our eyes', he says, 'when we see the peace demonstrations and all those mad women at Greenham Common.' Mad? 'If you were to protest at a missile-base in Czechoslovakia you would be immediately arrested for espionage. The absurdity of these ladies is too much for us.' Why? 'Because they are protesting at things which help to guarantee their right to protest in the first place. You have to be a profound Stoic, or a devout Christian, not to hate them.'

There is a 4-foot high wooden crucifix on the wall of his study; his is a voice from the 'right' of the dissident movement. And change in Czechoslovakia? 'This regime has no room for manoeuvre. Even if they wish to make concessions, they cannot do it,' he chuckles. Why not? 'Because any infinitesimal change would be seen by the public as throwing in the towel. It is impossible to change things in Czechoslovakia, and impossible not to change them. It is an interesting position,' he added, laughing.

*

' " . . . Do you believe in the end of the world?" Schweik was asked by his interrogators. "I shall have to see it first," Schweik replied in an offhand manner . . . '

*

To the courageous younger dissidents, gradually growing in number, their most immediate concerns are with the imprisoned Jazz Section organizers Karel Srp and Vladimir Kouril, charged with 'economic crimes', the trial of Protestant theologian Jan Dus, and the arrest in Brno of Chartist Peter Pospichal, charged with incitement and subversion for 'establishing active contacts with the Polish hostile grouping, so-called Solidarity'.

'Even Marx,' the dissenters say, 'would have ended up under interrogation in Czechoslovakia, if he had opened his mouth in public.' Their own *samizdat* declarations speak a language which has long buried the *Communist Manifesto*. As for the Good Soldier Schweik, 'he wouldn't have been able to live here,' said Jan Urban. 'In Prague, to get by without trouble, you have to be both stupid and silent, and Schweik couldn't keep his mouth shut. I won't believe in change', he added, 'until I see the people in the street changing.'

Fur-wrapped, they avoid your glances; perhaps dreaming of shopping-trips to Vienna, and minding their own business.

2

Hungary, April 1987:
'We are on the way'

In the fashionable streets of Budapest – Vaci Utca, for example – the shops are full of silks and Sonys. At prices far beyond the reach of the Hungarian proletariat, there are Lacoste shirts, Wrangler jeans and tools by Black & Decker; Aiwa 'music centers', Yves St Laurent perfumes and bottles of Martini. The stout owner of the Nina Ricci couture shop wears a skull-cap; you can pay for his merchandise with American Express, Visa or Soviet roubles.

Working the passers-by, gipsy beggar women, dark as Indians, carry swaddled infants in their swarthy arms, their underskirts ragged. Behind them, in the glittering windows, pale dummies stand in svelte poses, dressed in the best Italian knitwear.

*

It could be a representative sample of the British middle-class left in Kentish Town and Camden, but this is Budapest and they are all Hungarian members of the 'democratic opposition'. Just over a month ago they marched through the city, with 2,000 or 3,000 other dissidents, on the anniversary of the 1848 uprising against the Habsburgs, singing the 'Marseillaise' and demanding 'freedom', 'democracy' and 'national independence'.

'You can't even imagine', says a black-bearded, English-fluent figure, lighting up a Cuban cheroot, 'how obsolete Marxism is here. When I still had my job' – Gaspar Tamas used to teach philosophy at the University of Budapest, until he was sacked in 1982 for 'oppositional activity' – 'I asked my first year students to name any work by Marx. They could only think of *What is to be Done?*' (Is he joking?) 'But that is by Lenin. In such an ideological vacuum, which used to be filled by the Party, any madness could happen,' he adds.

Above our heads there is a small patch of recently renewed plaster in the ceiling.

We are at the historian Ivan Baba's place; he, his wife Judit (an ecological activist), Tamas, Sandor Szilagyi – a member of the editorial board of the dissident journal *Beszelo (Talker)* – and I are sitting at the post-prandial table. Tamas claims, cigar in hand, that Marxism as the doctrine of the State has completely disappeared; 'Party people have lost their Marxism,' he repeated later, as of a faith lost by believers. 'It was never popular in any genuine sense', he continues, 'but it had a profound effect on people's minds. Marxism provided a kind of ideological corset. Take off the corset, and what have you?' he asks with a rhetorical flourish. 'Ugly protruding flesh,' he answers. With his cigar between his teeth, it is hard to tell whether he is smiling.

The others let him hold the floor, fingering their coffee cups. 'Kadar [the Hungarian Socialist Workers' Party general secretary since 1956] is a mere symbol, no other leading figure has emerged, and reform rhetoric is everywhere. But the decisive steps towards pluralism are not being taken. The regime is in complete disarray. They talk of the need for reform on Tuesday, and the perils of reform on Wednesday. This is a dangerous situation in a country where proletarian dictatorship has destroyed the notion of the citizen. In the absence of Marxism, we cannot survive without an intelligible civic ideology, without some other kind of national doctrine. Instead, we have an ideological vacuum, which used to be filled by the Party. The Party "knew everything". Now, the situation is chaotic.'

'You know, this is also a psychologically very unhealthy society,' says Judit Baba, interrupting him. 'On the outside, it seems good-looking. On the inside, it is pathological. We are very materialistic, we have the world's highest suicide rate' – at over 45 a year per 100,000 people in recent years, it is 5 times the British rate, 4 times the American and nearly 3 times the Japanese – 'and we have more paranoia than any other nation.' They laugh together, with a strained gusto.

'Any political madness could happen,' says Tamas. 'We could head towards an authoritarian State combined with a free market', which he calls 'the Chilean situation'. 'Or we could get a rather unpleasant type of Hungarian nationalism. It would be very different from the patriotism of western Europe. Many people here have a great nostalgia for the "faith and order" of the inter-war period,' adds Tamas, whose mother is Jewish. 'It is as strong as the desire of other people for democratic changes.'

Tamas came to Budapest early in 1978 as a refugee from Cluj-Napoca, in the Hungarian-dominated region of Romania where he was born, the son of Communist parents; his father was a writer and theatre manager. Co-editor of a Hungarian literary weekly in Cluj, Tamas was silenced after refusing to write a panegyric of Ceausescu for the journal. To get employment he had to leave the country.

His head is wreathed in cigar smoke. 'The other day, Karoly Grosz', whom Tamas describes as a 'neo-Stalinist' member of the Hungarian politburo, and who is first secretary of the Budapest Party Committee, 'announced that "some people are trying to sell our country to the international financial mafia".' So what? 'We can read the codes here,' Tamas answers. 'These are the old antics of Bolshevik anti-semites.'

There is a moment of uneasy silence; Sandor Szilagyi discreetly sips his coffee. Apart from Marxism, I ask, what has happened to the idea of socialism? There is condescending (and relieved) laughter around the table. 'Nobody uses the word here, or wants to argue for or against it,' replies Ivan Baba. (This was untrue.) 'The question of socialism as a set of moral values is a dead issue. Take a term like "common property",' Baba says, beneath the patched ceiling. 'It no longer has a meaning. It is State property, and the State is the politburo, and the politburo is merely thirteen people.' ('Cheating and stealing' he later called 'part of the daily routine'.) 'Our problems are immediate, material.'

'No one is being coherent at the moment,' interjects his wife. 'In the Party there is only a kind of short-term speculation, with a few ideological fragments of the old beliefs scattered around in messages to the people. In any case, everyone is sick of ideology. In the past, it was an art to read between the lines of the official press. Everyone had to know the art of reading, in order to master the symbols and allusions. It was one of the special arts and crafts of socialism. Now it is becoming easier to understand what they are saying, by normal methods.'

She pours more coffee. 'The difference between us', Tamas says with sudden impatience, pushing his cup aside, 'is that we have been through this damned thing of socialism. To you it is theory, to us practice.'

'The question of socialism is a matter of absolute indifference to us,' Baba repeats calmly.

Tamas leans across the table, gesticulating with his cigar stub, and speaking with his voice raised. 'You cannot find anyone who takes it seriously, not even in the Party.' ('There is a lot of indifference, even about a complete change of the system,' says Judit Baba, *sotto voce*.) 'There are so few Communists left here', Tamas declares, 'that anti-Communism will soon become obsolete also.' There is another outburst of strained laughter, the laughter of intellectuals, under the newly-plastered ceiling.

Then why should anyone care if the country becomes capitalist? 'From the point of view of ideology or moral values, no one in Hungary would care,' answers Szilagyi, stirring out of his silence. 'It matters only to the leaders of the Party.' Why? 'Because it is a question of power.'

There is a bleak silence. 'The police called me in recently,' Tamas says quietly. '"Why are you sacrificing your own interests by your activities?" they asked me. "For my moral faith," I answered. They simply couldn't understand it. "You may be right," one of them said, "but why don't you speak less loudly?"'

★

Hungarian Communist 'unhealth' is bred in the bone. In the November 1945 election – 'the only free election ever held in modern Hungary' – the Hungarian Communist Party (HCP), as it was then called, gained 17 per cent of the vote. No less than 57 per cent went to the Smallholders' Party. But the result could not prevent the HCP's ruthless use (under its general secretary Matyas Rakosi, and with Soviet tutelage) of the 'salami tactics' which then began to slice away at post-war Hungary's newly democratic political institutions; HCP placemen were installed in them, the better to undermine them. In the elections of August 1947 the HCP was able to secure only 22.3 per cent of the vote, even with the aid of ballot fraud. But it had become, at least on paper, the strongest political party; and the consolidations of the Communist takeover followed.

The years from 1949 to 1953 were times of forced industrialization, collectivization, deportation of 'class enemies' to the countryside, and so forth; times during which whirlpools of violence swept away both tormentors and their victims, and even the very architects of the 'People's Republic'.

Moreover, under the 'unlimited authority' of the Stalinist Rakosi – 'those who are not with us are against us' was his sinister slogan – 'a huge army of grassroots activists, trusties and informers penetrated the entire social fabric, and took root in each institution and agency, even in individual apartment buildings', according to the Hungarian-born political historian Hans-Georg Heinrich, 'The top-Party bodies', Heinrich reports, 'were staffed with individuals who owed loyalty and allegiance to Rakosi personally'; Rakosi, in consequence, 'could rely on the ambitions and the anxieties of his protégés, who were strongly opposed to change because this could mean the end of their careers'.

The violent convulsions almost beggar description. In the rigged trials of the period, Laszlo Rajk, for example – who had himself been minister of the interior – was charged with 'Titoism', tortured and executed. Janos Kadar, who had participated in the conduct of some of the trials, was himself in turn imprisoned (as were his earlier eighteenth-century counterparts in the France of the Great Terror); only to be later released, in April 1955, by Imre Nagy, the then Party general-secretary. When Kadar in turn took power – after the Soviet-organized crushing of the 1956 Hungarian revolution – he repaid Nagy with betrayal, with execution in June 1958, and with burial in an unmarked grave for having 'betrayed the working classes'.

Nagy himself, before he went under to Kadar and in the style of these things, had had Rajk not only 'rehabilitated' but ceremonially reburied on 6 October 1956. These were the heady early days of the Hungarian uprising for 'democracy, neutrality and independence'; revolutionary events in which – in a further grotesque twist – the turncoat Kadar for a while had himself played a supporting role. It is an irony not lost on this generation of Hungarian dissidents that Nagy's aborted 1956 programme had included free elections, a multi-party system and the recall of Soviet forces. But it was a Soviet invasion – four days after Nagy, on 31 October 1956, had announced the withdrawal of Hungarian forces from the Warsaw Pact and declared Hungary neutral – which broke the rebellion.

Or, in the Party version of events, 'the Soviet Union, faithful to the Leninist principles of proletarian internationalism, granted the request of the Hungarian revolutionary workmen's and peasants' government, and came to the help of our country.' Discredited official figures insist that '3,000' people were killed in the fighting – the real figure may have been as much as eight times higher; some 150,000 were injured; and 200,000 left the country. In Kadar's mopping-up operations, euphemistically termed 'normalization', it is believed that 20,000 were arrested, 2,000 executed and thousands deported to the Soviet Union.

Under Kadar, who optimistically reversed Rakosi's slogan to read 'those who are not against us are with us', the phase of violent repression was followed by a period of 'consolidation' (or stasis) to 1962; the ideology of the state, behind its rhetoric, boiled down to little more than *'ez van, ezt kell szeretni'*, or 'this is what you have, so like it'. Then came gradual 'decompression' (1962–68) and, after 1968, a cautious process of Party-controlled liberalization. During the latter period, Kadar was attempting – in vain – to secure the Party's re-legitimization after the 1956 bloodbath: by pragmatism, by the securing of political stability, by the granting of certain freedoms, by the achievement of a measure of economic progress, by limited decentralization and by making piecemeal concessions – in fits and starts – to the market.

But the mouldering Nagy's grim fate remains a taboo subject; or another skeleton in the stinking Hungarian cupboard.

★

Madonna, with her blonde halo, lithe body and red lipstick, is in the city centre record-shop window; around the corner, a head-high poster of the 75-year-old Kadar grimaces from a roundabout's bed of red tulips. In the Budapest night-clubs peroxide dancers in glittering G-strings (courtesy of the Hungarian State Tourist Bureau) do the splits for Japanese and Italian tourists.

Here, a three-star army officer in Ruritanian uniform can walk the boulevard, proudly toting his sports-bag with its precious Adidas logo; there, prostitutes can openly ply their trade in the chandeliered hotel lobby. This is the mixed economy with a vengeance. At the four-star, State-run, Beke Hotel, the management charges the women $60 a day for the use of a hotel room, double the normal guest-rate. Three blocks away down a side-street is the old dowdiness; the pinching hardship which no spangles can cover.

*

There is a weary scepticism at Ivan Baba's place about what is going on. To them – are they not too cynical by half? – it is a case of a Communist Party facing deep economic crisis and a crisis of legitimacy, which is beginning to offer to reform everything while changing nothing, or very little; to them, reformist and neo-Stalinist interests, market and anti-market lobbies, are at political deadlock in a struggle which could go on for ever. Not even the recent announcement of the establishment of a nudist beach at Lake Balaton is persuasive. 'We do not share the western left's illusions about the possibility of something called "socialist freedom",' said Tamas flatly.

But then it is only nine months ago that the Hungarian politburo – attempting to hold the line, the Party line, against excessive reform pressures – was talking, secretly, about the 'activities of enemy opposition groups'. A resolution of July 1986, leaked to dissidents, roundly declared that 'efforts must be made to prevent these enemy groups from seizing the initiative', and called for a 'consistent, principled stand against all anti-socialist and anti-Marxist phenomena. It cannot be tolerated', the resolution continued, 'that enemy viewpoints . . . should seep into the press. The response to hostile actions and manifestations must be open and aggressive. Nor can it be tolerated that members of the Party should maintain contacts with members of enemy groups, without the prior permission of the appropriate Party organs.'

No wonder there is today's confusion. For what Tamas calls 'unofficial dialogues' between dissenters like himself and Party reformers in the politburo and central committee – such as Imre Pozsgay, who has called for an extension of the Hungarian Parliament's powers – are continuing in private. At the same time, these very members of the 'enemy opposition' are being denied official publication of their works, or remain banned from public employment as counterrevolutionaries and subversives.

What manner of people are these Party reformers? I ask Tamas, who is toying in irritation with a spoon on the table between us. 'There are social democratic supply-siders, strong free-marketeers very sympathetic to Friedman, civil libertarians, populist democrats – some much more nationalistic than others – and old fashioned authoritarians.' A strange bunch, he calls them.

At a recent informal meeting which Tamas attended – 'a good meeting, though the differences between us and them are deep ones' – 'we agreed on many substantive issues, above all on the need for greater political freedom. But we told them', says Tamas, 'that we were not interested in getting licences from the Party. We said to them outright, "This regime of yours cannot be reformed from inside. You think it can. Whatever the Party decrees", we said, "will not legitimize your regime in our eyes. However deep the transformations you try to carry out, you cannot create from inside or from above a genuine liberal democracy, but only a greater space for your political and economic manoeuvres. Even if we have to support you tactically, you cannot produce our idea of a good society, our idea of a lawful regime, or our idea of real freedom."'

Hasn't Imre Pozsgay recently said in public that 'genuine political change demands that the Party takes action against itself'? I asked. Isn't that a step forward? 'He is a clever man, with good speechwriters,' said Baba. 'These are democratic antics,' said Szilagyi. 'In the long run he is a careerist', said Tamas, 'who seeks power for himself as the most advanced democrat in the Party.'

These sentiments were complex and corrosive. 'It depends on the World Bank what they put in their shop window,' Tamas added for good measure.

*

The ghosts of 1956 – ghosts of the murdered past – stalk every such conversation. 'There were Russian tanks under our window,' she says, holding back the curtains and pointing. 'Over there, in the building opposite, there were revolutionaries sleeping. It was like a bad dream. Tanks didn't suit this street. They didn't fit, the street is too narrow.

'But people were so happy at that time. They were ready to put everything at once into the common resources. There had been frustration for two generations; suddenly, the best qualities of people came out as from a well, quickly. My own parents were out in the streets all day. I pleaded with my father to let me go out too, so that when I became a grandmother I might have something to tell my grandchildren. My father would argue with my mother in German about it. Eventually, he let me come out with him, telling me to do what he did: to lie down on the pavement when there was firing, to press myself against the walls, to jump into gateways. There was so much concentration then,' is the way she puts it.

More than thirty years later, there are estimated to be between 65,000 and 80,000 Soviet troops in the country, in 40 separate garrisons. The 1848 revolution against the Habsburgs was put down in August 1849 by the Emperor Franz Joseph, also with the help of the Russians. Then, too, the leaders of the revolt were executed, or, like Lajos Kossuth, fled into exile. 'The younger generation is sceptical about the future,' she adds. Why? 'Because they know that even with the greatest efforts of 1956 we were unsuccessful.'

*

But isn't the genie-of-the-market out of its bottle, and beginning to escape the clutches of the planners? At the weekend, columns of cars – not only Russian Ladas, but Renaults, Fords and Fiats and even an occasional Hungarian-registered BMW – head out of Budapest, past the Shell service-stations, towards the Danube and its hillside dachas, two-thirds of which were built by private contractors.

There is already an embryo private capital market in being; VAT and personal income tax are in the offing; cuts in welfare provision are under discussion; and public sector enterprises are now being permitted to go bankrupt and lay off workers. The shape of the Hungarian economy is beginning to seem familiar. To the more sceptical, however, this kind of thing does not represent the irreversible passing of the old socialist order, but is still no more than a 'shadowy market system'; even a 'pseudo-capitalism', overseen by Party cunning, whose purpose is to pluck the socialist brand from the fire with the aid of western investment and credits.

'Do you know why the bees have a queen?' goes a Budapest joke. 'Because if they had a central committee, there would be no honey.' Here such patter, which could have fallen off a Friedmanite hawker's barrow, raises no laughter. It is black humour, still; or, the humour of the black market.

*

Perhaps it is right to take nothing for granted here, above all the prospect of a future 'liberal' dispensation. Yet, unlike in Czechoslovakia, dissenters are no longer treated as entire outcasts. There is also a relatively free flow of information and no general censorship, foreign radio stations are not jammed, there is relative freedom of travel, religious services are broadcast and today's Hungarian State even prints Bibles.

Then why the anxious, dark edges to every political conversation? 'Because', says Tamas, 'we know that the totalitarian mentality has very deep roots in Hungary, apart from the problem of 1956. The one original contribution of central Europe to the history of political thought was Fascism. From 1918 to the present, liberalism has played no role in the politics of Hungary whatever.'

First came Bela Kun. Revolutionary son of a Jewish clerk – and later to be both the target of Lenin's *Left-Wing Communism, An Infantile Disorder* and victim in 1939 of Stalin's Great Purge of the Soviet Union, where he had taken refuge – he was the leader of Hungary's abortive 133-day Bolshevik revolution of 1918-19. Following him came Admiral Miklos Horthy, White Army commander, who rode into Budapest on a white horse in 1919 to save the nation and restore order. By the mid-1920s, Kun's rebellion had become known as the 'Jewish-Bolshevik Revolution'; worse still, the 'Horthyite-Fascist' regime, as Hungarian Communists came to call the Admiral's dispensation, was popular enough – especially among the peasantry and upper middle class – with its combination of a limited suffrage, use of corporal punishment, and anti-Jewish discrimination.

The period from 1932 to 1936 was more fascist still, under Gyula Gombös; while the Hungarian Nazi Party, the Arrow Cross, had gained the support of the majority of the Hungarian working class by the time of the 1939 elections. In the Second World War, Hungary was an Axis power. And then, during the briefest non-totalitarian post-war interregnum, came Communism's salami tactics and the 1947 takeover. Rakosi, and the rest of it, followed.

*

Even the mesmerizing gazes of the portrait figures in the National Gallery – by Dürer, by Giorgione, by Goya – seem, in such a dim light, ambiguous; intent and steady at first glance, unsure a moment later.

*

Do not multi-candidate elections and other measures of electoral reform beckon on the political horizon? 'We have already had multi-candidate elections in the 1985 general election' is Baba's dismissive answer. (It is as if no change, and certainly no merely interim measure, can escape this kind of reflex censure.)

In 1985, the Party allowed what it called 'Independents' to contest its 'Official' candidates, but the process of selecting the 'Independents' was entrusted to the Party's own front organization, the People's Patriotic Front (PPF). Set up under the 1972 Constitution to 'galvanize the social forces in the construction of socialism', it has now some 4,000 local committees, and is chaired by Imre Pozsgay. (A 'good-for-nothing organization' it is nevertheless called, at this table.)

Doubting Tamas takes up the story. 'The Party decided that branch meetings of the PPF could be open to local electors, with the right to nominate "Independents" by a vote from the floor. I put myself forward in the Budapest constituency of the foreign minister, Peter Varkonyi.' 'There was a very fascistic atmosphere at the nomination meeting,' Baba says. 'Tamas challenged Varkonyi to open debate about Hungary's foreign policy and other matters. The scene for us was unprecedented.' ('A real political scene', he also called it.) 'For a while, Varkonyi was forced to behave in a democratic way, and argue openly with Tamas. But the crowd of about five hundred people – most of them had been brought in by Budapest Party organizers – became restless, and began shouting, "Why do we have to listen to him? Beat him! Beat him!"'

'It became very ugly,' adds Tamas. The crowd accused him, among other things, of provocation, for having a Polish Solidarity badge in the lapel of his jacket. Who was doing the shouting? 'Proletarian stalwarts', he answers, 'yelling at a middle-class intellectual. Isn't it typical?' he asks wrily.

Nevertheless, a total of thirty-four 'Independents' was elected that year, the 'fascistic atmosphere' notwithstanding.

*

The 'contradictions', as Marxists used to call them, are deep ones. Take 1968, for example. In that year Kadar, to the manner born, contributed Hungarian forces to the crushing of the Prague Spring. But from the same year the outlines of a new, more 'liberal' economic order began to be established in Budapest, in the teeth of a Stalinist command economy's traditions; providing the model, so it is said, for the subsequent 'Gorbachev turn' in the Soviet Union.

The consequences are the even worse economic toils in which Hungary now finds itself; bringing together inefficient State planning with the anarchy of a reviving market, and combining reliance upon the Soviet Union for energy supplies and basic raw materials, with dependency upon western banks and governments for funds to finance its laggard technological modernization.

There is some tragedy in this too, which can only be understood historically. The collapse in 1918 of the Habsburg monarchy – the 'dual monarchy' of the Austro-Hungarian empire – led to Hungary's dismemberment. Its land area was reduced from 325,000 square miles to a mere 92,600; the main losses were of Magyar-dominated territories in Slovakia and Transylvania (now Romania). Indeed, Hungary's population today, at around 11 million, is still only half of what it was in 1918. More important, economically, is that Hungary was left after 1918 with its major manufacturing centres intact, but without adequate natural resources. Oil, gas and iron ore, electric power, and even timber have to be imported, mainly from the Soviet Union.

Today, contradiction is heaped upon contradiction. An increasing scale of private entrepreneurism – there are already more than 35,000 private companies, many of them in the private sector – is sustained by the growing availability of personal credit; a metropolitan bourgeois culture and a huge black economy co-exist with the grimmest Stakhanovite symbols of the old proletarian-socialist order. The facts of widening class inequality challenge the flagging rhetoric of public and collective interest; and, most dangerous of all, a slow but steady fall in the real wages of the Hungarian working class has coincided with a growing appetite for consumption.

An official team from Budapest has even visited the Department of Employment in London, seeking advice on how to improve Hungarian efficiency and restructure the labour force. If this chaotic situation is depriving most people (the dissenters included) of their political bearings, it is beginning to give unprecedented economic opportunities to others. The rich and privileged now include not only doctors, lawyers, engineers and party officials, but building contractors, private artisans, black market hustlers, and car mechanics. Whether these phenomena are the by-products of Hungary's 'long march back to capitalism and pluralism' remains an open question. That they are *not* the 'contradictions of a higher stage of socialism', according to the Marxist canon, is absolutely certain.

*

The glittering Budapest hotel lobby: a place of thick-pile, uniformed deference, and stiletto heels on marble. In ten years this will be a capitalist country, I ventured. 'I hope so,' said the sleek young manager on the desk – an Hungarian flash-Harry – out of the corner of his mouth, while attending to another guest's enquiry. 'There is no other way,' he added, as the phone rang; and, hand-over-the-mouthpiece, 'Well, there is another way, but it goes downwards.'

He was jocular when he put the receiver down; his finger in many pies, his accent American, his haircut stylish. 'You have a good President, Thatcher,' he said, making a strong-arm gesture and feeling his own biceps. Is the structure, the system, changing? 'We'll change our structure for yours. Everything, if you want, you can have it. You take Kadar, we take Thatcher,' he added, dropping his voice.

But is anything really changing? I repeated. 'We are on the way,' he answered, winking.

*

'It is not so simple,' says Tamas, sitting at a large table heaped with books and papers in his cavernously gloomy and unkempt nineteenth-century apartment; this once-elegant, barn-like drawing-room, with its gracious double doors, dusty parquet and unpainted corniced ceiling, once belonged to gentry in faded Habsburg times. Now, another kind of privilege – that of dissidence, fastidious to its intellectual finger-tips – is installed here; but still (Tamas says) under surveillance. It was long past midnight.

'On the one hand, serious organized resistance within the Party to reform is dying out,' he declared, getting down to brass-tacks, and one of the best-informed in the city. 'But, on the other hand, the reformers are not securing reforms of substance. A central committee communiqué has just declared openly, for the first time, that it "could not arrive at a decision" on new tax measures. This is unprecedented, incoherent,' he added. (His is, perhaps, a superior form of scoffing.) 'The Party reformers are also complaining that certain reforms which had been agreed are not being implemented, and that the apparatus is trying to pick and choose between them.' On what basis? 'In favour of the short-term changes, and against the structural measures,' he answered.

Isn't their dilemma a real one, even tragic? I asked. How can old-guard Hungarian Communists like Kadar and his apparatchiks – or Husak in Czechoslovakia – launch modern market reforms and liberal democratic changes, even if they wanted to, without confusion? 'It is Hungary's situation which is tragic,' Tamas replied, irritated. 'And what "dilemma" are you talking about? Don't you understand why Thatcher is so popular, even among the hardliners in the Party? It is because they all have the same late-Victorian petit-bourgeois approach to things, now that they have lost their Marxism. These people have the prejudices but no longer the faith of "old fashioned Communists", as you quaintly called them. They are in any case being forced by economic circumstances to launch market reforms; everyone knows that there is no choice in the matter.'

Then why the deadlock as you see it? 'It is very complex. We are being told that the private arguments they are having among themselves in the politburo do not yet represent the clash of intelligible ideologies. They are still a confused business of personalities, prejudices, and atavistic feelings. A genuine dialogue could only take place if these people were speaking their minds. Here they cannot. The debate is not yet open.'

What do you mean? 'Look,' he replied with asperity, 'no one on the so-called anti-reform side of the politburo will accuse somebody of being a pro-market Friedmanite.' Why not? 'Because at the moment there is a general reluctance to speak out about such matters. That is what we hear.' What are they afraid of? There was a silence, as Tamas got up to rummage among his papers, his shadow rearing up on the bare expanse of wall behind him. 'They don't yet want to admit, even to themselves, how far their rethinking is taking them.'

The subterranean conflict paralysing the Hungarian Party is over how to dismantle the aims and apparatus of socialism without appearing to be doing so; in the Soviet Union also. But aren't all these agonizings, I asked Tamas – as he continued to rummage – the concern only of intellectuals? 'Which agonizings?' he asked testily, fumbling with the lid of a cigar-box. Both in the Party and among the democratic opposition, I answered.

'No,' he said. 'People in the street are also worried about what is going on. I hear them almost every day. They say, "We don't know who to trust." Soon, out of this confusion, if the politburo does not move faster, will come the desire for a strong leader and an authoritarian message. This is Hungary,' he added, lighting up. '"Give me something at least to believe in" is what they start thinking,' he said, exhaling. 'A leader with a strong national ideology, and a tough position on the Hungarians in Romania, could whip up real fervour in the lower strata.'

Aren't you being too impatient? Why don't you give them the benefit of the doubt? The questions again irritated him. 'The situation can look promising enough here, compared with Czechoslovakia or Romania. But why don't people like you start comparing us with Austria? Weren't we once part of the same monarchy? Who do you think the man-in-the-street, the average Hungarian, compares himself with?' His voice, harsh in the bareness, sounded increasingly angry. 'He measures his conditions against conditions in the West, not the East. To us', he said scornfully – with a fierce, dismissive gesture – 'Romania, Bulgaria and Poland are backward areas, absolutely irrelevant to our situation!'

Poland, too? 'Even working-class people I know couldn't understand why I, as a dissident, sympathized with the Polish Solidarity movement. Most people here see this old kind of trade unionism, and a stodgy, proletarian type of fellow like Lech Walesa, as obsolete, backward. To us it is a kind of reactionary, clerical anti-Communism.' (There was radical snobbery in this even; an old familiar.) 'We see in Poland', he continued, 'not our future, but our past. The Solidarity movement, to us, is like a Polish cavalry charge. For a few it is quite touching, but for others something laughable, quite ridiculous. Only a tiny minority feel sympathy for it.'

He drew on his cigar amid the mounds of books, the barely-lit room all shadows. There was a long silence, his eyes closed in his own exhalation. 'The basic reason why you don't understand the situation', he eventually said, 'is that you have illusions about Gorbachev. You are typical of the western left, which is trying to invent new hopes for itself in the Soviet Union.' This was mordant,

Mephistophelean. 'He wants things, you know, to be freer, nicer and more fun in Russia,' Tamas jeeringly added. 'This is how people like to see it. But who knows what goes on inside his head? Do you know? No one knows, yet the idea of Gorbachev's "grandeur" has already become scripture in the West, even in the State Department and Foreign Office. Everybody has begun to depend on the image of him they have constructed,' he said, shaking his head over the folly of it.

*

Sunday morning Mass has just ended in the dark baroque church at Szentendre; the smell of incense is fragrant, the verger quietly putting away candles and tapers, the young priest removing his cassock.

Outside, beneath the tall horse-chestnut trees in the churchyard, churchgoers dressed in their Sunday best stand talking, in a dappled deep-green shade. These are old pieties; part in shadow, part in the sunshine of early summer.

*

Every six months, the 120 judges of the Budapest high court system assemble to listen to a lecture, part of a compulsory State study-programme for the judiciary: 'We are summoned, ordered to attend,' she said to me. She is a mousy woman in her mid-forties, living in a cramped flat – little more than a bedsitter – who talks in anxious whispers.

The last six-monthly lecture, given behind closed doors and unreported, was held three days ago. The speaker was Istvan Horvath, one of the six secretaries of the central committee. In a one-and-a-half hour speech – which 'seemed serious' she said, whispering – Horvath told the assembled judges that the Party had taken the decision that henceforward 'two power centres', Parliament and the Party, were needed, and that 'Parliament should stand higher'. ('These are Pozsgay's ideas,' she added timidly.)

On her bookshelves are Pushkin, Goethe and Lukacs; and she has a tiny kitchen, barely bigger than a broom-cupboard. 'His theses were clear and logical in themselves', she continued pallidly, 'but they were all mixed up with other things.' What other things? 'Mainly quotations from Marx,' she replied, with a wintry smile.

Horvath had revealed to the judges that the question of abolishing the Presidential Council – a 21-member decree-making body which has effectively usurped the existing Parliament's legislative functions – was also being 'debated within the Party'. 'It would be a great step towards parliamentarism if it were to happen,' she said softly; 'these are radical things for us.' In his speech, Horvath had hinted too at what she called 'even larger changes', roundly declaring to his audience that 'our electoral system must be perfected'.

How were your fellow judges reacting while Horvath was speaking? I asked her. 'Horvath has always been regarded as a strong conservative, not a liberal, so it was more surprising. But what he was saying is becoming the new Party line, and he is a careerist.' She hesitated. 'In fact, he apologized in the middle of his speech if some of his ideas were "astonishing to some comrades who are a bit conservative".' She was still whispering. But how were they responding? I repeated, also lowering my voice. 'Some of the younger judges, especially those who are Party members, seemed disturbed by what he was saying. There were others whom I heard afterwards saying cautiously to each other, "These ideas are interesting." But while Horvath was speaking their faces had absolutely no expression.' And you? She became even more timid. 'It's what I am praying for,' she answered.

Do you think these changes are going to happen? 'The main question is whether Parliament will be given real power to initiate legislation. I am not sure if Horvath can be trusted. No one has touched the leading role of the Party before. But if Horvath did not mean what he was saying,' she asked nervously, 'why did he say it? Was it only opportunism, or was he floating the ideas to us, as part of some inner party struggle?'

And if he meant it? 'If he meant it, and these things happen' – she seemed to startle at the prospect – 'how is the Party going to stop Parliament exercising its rights in any way it chooses, once it has been given the powers?' She sat in a meek, anxious silence, her hands working together. On the wall beside her bookshelves my eye caught a tiny 'Solidarnosc' sticker. 'And how can we have parliamentary democracy without a free press and other freedoms?' she whispered, brow furrowed. 'Are they playing with reforms, or are they real? But if they are real, what happens if the Party apparatus resists them?'

She smiled anaemically, as if there were no answers to her own questions. 'It is very unpleasant for us', she said in an undertone, her eyes lowered, 'when everyone is talking about the need for fundamental changes in our institutions.' Don't you welcome it? 'It

is becoming very difficult to exercise judicial authority, compared
with previous times. Judges are leaving the bench, retiring early, or
returning to practice.' Why? 'Because there is a political vacuum in
Budapest, but no judicial independence. How can we know where
we are going?'

There was a bleak silence. 'It is very unpleasant,' she said again;
a solitary person in a dowdy setting, wrestling with her problems.

*

The hostilities of the irreconcilable opponents of the regime, with
their taut hatreds for Communism and all its works, are unremitting.
The dapper Sandor Szilagyi, with his clipped manner, is one such;
it is as if there were a coiled spring of loathing in him. A literary
critic who had his passport confiscated after a visit to Poland in 1980,
Szilagyi describes Hungary astringently as an 'occupied land', and
the one-Party State as 'a taboo which cannot be broken. When people
last asked fundamental questions thirty years ago, they were shot,'
he says fiercely; in his abrasiveness is something which is itself like
violence.

'It is very similar here to the last years of Franco', he continues,
'but with one difference. Spain was an independent country. What
is Hungary? And what are these bloody Romanians doing with our
brothers?' (There is a 1.7 million-strong Hungarian minority living
in Romania, many of them in the old Hungarian region of Transylvania.) 'I am afraid for our nation. Look at Yugoslavia, it is a
terrible warning. Here, they think they are getting smarter. They are
changing the slogans of the 1950s: from red to pink, to grey, to green,
to any colour. To them, it does not matter. We have been paralysed
by our own leaders,' he adds, seeming to recoil with distaste at the
mere thought of them.

Here, an historic viciousness, as well as pessimism and inertia, lies
close below the present surface. I tell Szilagyi that I have seen gipsies
being roughly treated by police in the modish Vaci Utca. 'Gipsies are
hated,' he says briskly. (There are from a quarter to half a million
gipsies in Hungary, an estimated 40 per cent of whom are illiterate,
and 25 per cent jobless, in a population of around 11 million.) 'They
are our blacks, our Sikhs and Pakistanis. But at least they speak
Hungarian,' he added sardonically.

And the Jews? 'The Jewish background of most of the Hungarian
Communist leaders in the past – Bela Kun, Matyas Rakosi, Laszlo

Rajk, et cetera – is a touchy question for us. A really touchy question,' he repeated.

*

'We have reached some kind of half-way stage,' says Ivan Baba. Above us was the patched ceiling. 'We are not in the Czech position. The Hungarian Party is more cynical, with a better understanding of realpolitik, and more intellectual; the Czech Party is cruder and more aggressive. Our problem is the new level of manipulation.'

What do you mean? 'I mean the Gorbachevian way of thinking. It is more cunning.' I begin to demur; Baba brushes aside the objection. 'First manipulation', he continues, telling them off on his fingers, 'is to say in Hungary, and also in the Soviet Union, that dictatorship and the one-Party system are "not the necessary components of socialism", but some kind of error. At the same time, second manipulation, the reformers are threatening the Stalinists that only if their so-called socialism "democratizes itself" will the Party and the apparatus be able to keep their monopoly of power.

'Third manipulation' – his fingers held up before me – 'they are promising everybody democratization, liberalization etc, etc. At the same time, fourth manipulation, they are telling the apparatchiks quietly that this can be achieved without going as far as a multi-party system.' He laughs, despite himself, at what he takes to be the duplicity of it.

The trouble with his argument, I tell Baba, is that the Hungarian reforms, embryonic and fitful as they are, lead in a non- and anti-socialist direction. Moreover, each new measure of reform, in Hungary as in the Soviet Union, leads logically to another, whatever the manipulations. The real question is how much of this can go on before socialism itself has to be openly abandoned.

'Even to the Party, I have already said to you, this issue about socialism is of no interest. Do you think they will worry to make the market the controlling factor, if it helps them to get out of their economic crisis and to prevent another Poland?' Another Poland? 'They know that if the Party doesn't change its entire method of operation, they will get themselves into the Polish situation: the desolation of the social structure, a destroyed economy, a destroyed Party.'

How can they avoid this, while retaining a one-Party system? 'I think we will get something more democratic. I told you that we have reached a kind of half-way position. But it will also be a manipulation. A liberal democracy, as you understand it, we will not get, of course not, not for a long time,' he said, shrugging away the prospect.

So what will you get? 'I think we will have a relatively democratic parliamentary structure. We will have freer elections. We will have greater powers [given] to local administration. But it will be a limited democratization, organized from above by one means or another. Everybody knows that the Party has all the structures to remain a parallel government, whatever is decided on the democratic surface.' He raised his eyes heavenwards.

Above our heads were the clumsy signs of the electronic eavesdropper, who had recently done a botched job of repairing the floor in the upstairs apartment. His drill had come through the ceiling.

*

It might, at first sight, be a Lancashire 'Whit-Walk' in the early 1950s, when the eager girls wore white shoes and ribbons, the mill women in their floral prints had had their hair permed, and the pale men walked stiffly in their suits to the sound of brass-band music, their heads brylcreemed and their boots polished. Here, on a hot May Day morning, the procession is more listless; a ragged column slowly tramping towards Heroes' Square and the reviewing dais, carrying chaplets of paper flowers and crucifixes, red flags and national tricolours, and (here and there) patriarchal portraits of Marx and Engels. Passing you are factory floats and sombre, perspiring men with grey faces and loosened collars; small girls in frilly frocks looking like Christmas-tree fairies; stout women fanning themselves with their bouquets; and pale young men in cheap suits carrying heavy, ribbon-bedecked maypoles.

The band is far away in the distance now, its music lost in the sounds of low voices and trudging feet, some still trying to keep in step with its imagined rhythm. The fag-end of the procession – strollers sauntering idly across its tracks, licking ice-creams – walks by in an embarrassed silence; the once-martial clangour of the massed proletariat, marching to socialist triumph, reduced to these last footsteps scuffing the asphalt.

3

Romania, November 1987:
Darkness

Tirana airport. There is not a sound. A small group of dark-clad travellers stands together, without speaking. With a dusty shelf to itself in a cheaply carpentered display case, and resting on a curling grey-white doily, is a single packet of twenty Marlboro; the shelf above contains (also standing on a paper doily) a bottle of Cinzano, its once bright label bleached and faded.

The small 'transit-lounge', overseen by a framed portrait of Enver Hoxha – who died in 1985, after 41 years in power – is a scatter of utility armchairs on lino. The building is of single-storey concrete; a few shrubs can be seen struggling in a cold wind beyond the metal frame window. There is also a bar. Leaning against it and lost in an Albanian reverie is a plump, middle-aged waitress in a thick cotton blouse, shapeless black skirt – worn shiny around the buttocks – clod-hopping shoes, and what look like surgical stockings. Her chipped nail-varnish is no more than a red smudge at each nail-bed.

'Forty years ago', the tousled barman (a local patriot) says to me in broken Italian, 'Albania was nothing. *Niente*,' he repeated, his voice resonating in the dimly-lit silence.

*

It is a Biggles-like flight from Tirana to Bucharest in a four-engined Ilyushin 18 of the Romanian airline, exhaust soot streaking the wings, propellers whirling. The coffee tastes like Camp, the aircraft sounds like a bomber, and Romanian reads like Esperanto – the *Instructiuni de Salvare* show you how to blow down a tube in order to *umflare* your *vesta*. But then Romania was settled by Trajan's legions, and the air-hostess herself looks like a jolly Italian mamma with hair on her upper lip, glitter on her eyelids, and very fat fingers.

A little smaller in area than Britain, Romania's present-day territories, composed essentially of the historic provinces of Wallachia, Moldavia and Transylvania, have been ruled in their time from Rome, Constantinople – Turkish suzerainty was established in the fifteenth century – Budapest, Vienna and Moscow; its 23 million hybrid inhabitants are made up of 'ethnic Romanians', Hungarians (at 1.7 million they constitute around 7.5 per cent of the population), Germans, Ukrainians, Jews, Serbs and Bulgarians.

In the second century AD this outpost of the Roman Empire in the north Balkans was known as *Dacia Felix*; in the second century after Marx, it is *Romania Infelix*, very. The amount of kilowattage twinkling from the ground as you land at night in Bucharest – in these 'years of light', as they call the socialist era – is comparable with a provincial town in northern or central India. Hyderabad easily outshines it.

★

The taxi's rackety doors are closed, and we move away down the forlorn airport approach-road, bleakly lit, on to a broad highway without traffic. The silent taxi driver puts his foot down, the chassis creaking; the engine knocks as we bowl along in the darkness towards a city of 2 million. A solitary banger passes us in the opposite direction, showing sidelights only. A few dim street-lamps eventually herald the approach of the night-shrouded city; around each of them is a foggy, cold penumbra.

The night-staff are wearing coats and thick scarves in the freezing hotel lobby. I can see my own breath as I put down my suitcase. At the reception desk the dark handsome girl with black curly hair has a blue thin-bridged nose peeping over the folds of a muffler swathed about her; she enters my particulars in the register with her pen held in a fingerless mitten.

*

The November city-centre streets at midnight, beyond the parted curtains, are deserted. In a cold, spartan bedroom, an Amnesty report does not make pretty reading, with its references to the use of torture to extract confessions, the forced emigration of dissenters, religious persecution, and the worsening treatment of the Hungarian minority – to say nothing of the handing out of sentences, under 'Decree 153/70', for 'parasitical conduct'.

Included in the definition of such conduct is 'the forming of groups which, by their behaviour, show that they have a parasitical or anarchist view of life running counter to elementary rules of decent behaviour, and to whom the principles of socialist coexistence are alien'.

Outside, in the frost-covered boulevard, the silence is abyssal.

*

Men and women, shopping, are in a hurry by 6.30 a.m., already late for the queues and moving quickly in the foggy, grey morning. The police are patrolling everywhere, warm in their greatcoats. (Tomorrow I will be told that for the last week in Bucharest – a 'Citadel of Science and Technical Progress', according to the Ministry of Tourism – there have been no eggs, no cheese, no fruit save apples, very little fish, and no potatoes to be found for love or money.)

At 7.30 a.m., outside the Unic Supermarket in Boulevard Balcescu, there are already ninety people waiting; the queue stretches round the corner of the block and out of sight. For sale is a consignment – contained in large cartons being broken open by assistants, as the crowd presses on them – of frozen chicken heads-and-necks, feet and wings. The torsos are most likely to be in the Soviet Union under a meat-for-crude-oil barter deal which every year takes thousands of tonnes of Romanian meat to Moscow. Romania is said to be the Soviet Union's principal foreign meat-supplier.

Out of each box comes a solidly impacted mass, some three-feet square, of congealed chicken pieces; you can see blue eyes staring bleakly from within these icebergs, white scraggy wings black-spiked as if with splinters, and a tumble of feet, yellow talons curled and stiffened. At noon, when I passed again, the queue was longer, the press at the counter as intense as ever. By then, the chicken-blocks had begun to melt into a half-frozen flux of meat. The mess was being manhandled, with purple fingers, from collapsing, sodden cardboard into plastic bags, juices dripping.

Not far away, in a shoe shop doorway, at mid-afternoon, there were seventy people clustered like a bee-swarm. Round the corner, they were queuing on one side of the street for lingerie, being sold direct from boxes stacked on the pavement; on the other side, a queue was buying small frozen packets of 'Neapolitan' ice-cream gateaux – selling like hot cakes – and stamping its feet as the day grew colder. And when a refrigerated truck appeared, muddy from its long journey (from where?), a sudden crowd closed in, pushing and shoving to see, as the rear doors were opened.

But here, amid the headscarves and buxom dowdiness, were also several women seemingly bourgeois in style of dress and manner. They were 'well turned out', *soignées* even, in Latin fashion; although God knows how, in a place so forsaken. At 6.30 p.m. in the Boulevard Balcescu there was also a woman in her seventies carrying multiple bags and swathed in many layers of clothing (in the universal way of the homeless) wordlessly begging, hand extended.

By 7 p.m. the streets had begun to empty. By 8 p.m. they were almost deserted, an out-of-petrol car being pushed into a black side-street. Even in the main boulevards I could barely see the faces of the few people who passed close by me. But if I could not see them, they could not see me, as I went about in my own cloak of darkness.

*

This most tightly-controlled, centralized, conservative and secretive country of eastern Europe is also the poorest. Its hardships are worsened by Ceausescu's harsh austerity programme – Bucharest's street-lighting, for instance, was reduced in 1979, and cut off altogether in most country towns and villages – which is designed to clear Romania's hard currency debt to the West by 1990. It involves paring imports to the bone, exporting basic foodstuffs, and letting the people go hungry. Only the grapevine is heavily-laden: with rumours of provincial unrest, further energy cuts, or a new round of sackings of scapegoats.

The pattern of Romania's economic development and decline is now a familiar one. In the 1950s and 1960s, there was substantial heavy (and top heavy) industrial growth – organized by the State apparatus, yet funded by ever-larger foreign credits – which saddled the country with grandiose, and ultimately uneconomic, white elephant prestige projects, for example in petrol-refining capacity. In the 1970s and 1980s came the mounting difficulties: of the obsolescence and inefficiency of Romania's Soviet-built 'smoke-stack' industries, of world recession, of the oil glut, of Romania's rising debt burden, of growing waste and inertia, of increasing dependency on the Soviet Union for imports, and the deteriorating competitiveness (or unsaleability) of Romania's own poor quality industrial products.

Burdened by the overriding priority being given to external debt clearance, the result is a regime of 'police socialism', imposing long hours – even May Day is a working day for many Romanian proletarians – low wages, inadequate food, and hard labour. Ceausescu, *à propos* of Polish Solidarity, has not surprisingly denounced 'so-called independent trade unions'; the purpose of Romanian trade unions, under Section 165 of the Labour Code, is merely to 'mobilize the masses for implementing the programme of the Romanian Communist Party'.

Similarly, economic restructuring on the Gorbachevite 'market-socialist' model was dismissed by Ceausescu, in April 1987, as a 'capitalist' sell-out. Those of Gorbachev's political measures of which Ceausescu claims to approve – in the direction of 'new democratic structures', multiple candidacies in elections, 'participation' in decision-making, 'devolution' and so on – he falsely claims to have carried out in Romania already. Ceausescu's reforms have been described as 'simulated'; that is, they are reform without change, to match the development without progress. Even prices in the 'open', 'free' market are fixed by the State in Romania; and Ceausescu rules, despite his 'new democratic structures', by presidential decree, without the need to submit his decisions for the approval of any State body.

Yet Ceausescu sees himself – and presents himself to the Romanians – as the archetypal modernizer, and architect of Romania's continuing 'transformation'. For this is a 'multilaterally developing socialist society', which under its current Five Year Plan is 'passing to a new and higher stage of development in all fields of activity'. The eggs, meat and potatoes will come later.

*

There is a small, grey knot of people outside the Italian Cultural Institute, raptly studying the photographs on display there – of the newest Alfa Romeo, of sailing boats on Lake Como, of the latest Italian fashions. They gaze, in muffled awe, at Gina Lollobrigida, wide-eyed and heavy-breasted; in winter gloom like this, hers seems a dazzling summer radiance.

Not far away on the same pavement, is another display cabinet about 35-foot long and 7-foot high, containing colour photographs of Ceausescu. One shows him standing in a field of maize, in built-up cream shoes and ill-fitting off-white safari suit, with baggy trousers; the prize cobs are being pinched between the stubby presidential fingers. Other photographs are of Ceausescu and his wife Elena, leaving from and arriving at airports; addressing (to 'stormy' applause, doubtless) serried ranks of the faithful; stepping, he dead-eyed, she elegant, into and out of curtained black limousines, waving. Swaddled against the cold, the citizens hurry by, with faces averted.

*

I ring a contact at the appointed hour. He sounds panic-stricken. 'What is your problem?' he shouts several times, pretending not to understand me. 'OK,' I say, retreating. 'OK,' says he, putting the phone down quickly. I never met him.

*

Born in January 1918 and protégé, or place-man, from the age of thirty-six of the previous dictator Gheorgiu-Dej (general secretary of the Romanian Communist Party from 1944 to 1965) Nicolae Ceausescu is described by the Ministry of Information as 'the greatest Romanian in history'. Political heir both to the Emperor Trajan and Vlad the Impaler, the shoemaker from Scornicesti is also the Pooh-Bah of Romania: president of the Republic since March 1974, general secretary of the Party since 1965, supreme commander of the armed forces, president of the Council of State, chairman of the Socialist Unity Front and chairman of the National Defence Council, *inter alia*.

His wife, two sons, six brothers, brothers-in-law (two of whom have been prime minister), nephews and cousins, together with remote relatives by marriage, have most of the other key jobs covered, including the Ministries of Defence and the Interior, the Council of State, and the State Planning Commission. By presidential decrees, Ceausescu has awarded many of them with gongs and honorifics. These include an Order of Labour (first class) for his son Nicu – regarded in Bucharest as a playboy and the family's *gauleiter* in the city of Sibiu in Transylvania – and an Order of Labour (second class) for his daughter Zoia.

Marxism-Leninism may be the official term for Romania's ideology of State; Marxism-nepotism, the unofficial. 'Socialism in one family' you could call it. Indeed, the Romanian State is a very private business – a matter of clan, not class, struggle – from which the ordinary citizen keeps his distance. He needs to. Under the Romanian penal code 'insulting' Ceausescu counts as 'anti-socialist propaganda' and is tantamount to treason.

But lest anyone should think that the dictator is all political muscle and no intellectual substance, take a look in any Bucharest bookshop. What an *oeuvre* in one short lifetime! For Ceausescu has penned dozens of texts – the cover-portraits those of an eternally dark-haired and smiling forty-year-old – on Dialectics, on Ideological Activity, on Cadre Politics, on the Qualitative Transformation of Romanian Economic Development, and on one damned thing after another. There are also four volumes of the cobbler's *Selected Speeches* bulging in the window; and, beside them, a new celebratory tome, two feet square, entitled merely *Omagiu*, which expresses the 'love, friendship and deep gratitude manifested by the whole Party and people to Comrade Nicolae Ceausescu'. Alongside these are books by his brother-in-law, Manea Manescu (former prime minister and vice-chairman of the Council of State); by his brother, Ilie Ceausescu (deputy minister of defence) on military strategy; and by his wife, Elena (the deputy prime minister) on polymer chemistry and other scientific subjects.

'To the ear of an educated person, Ceausescu speaks a very primitive Romanian,' I was told. 'He uses perhaps 800 stereotypical words only in his speeches, organized in the same repeated phrases.' 'Strips of words, gummed together', George Orwell called this kind of thing; but then he would have understood Romania in an instant. 'I know a man', runs a Party anthem, sung in chorus, 'whose eyes are like the sun after the tempest, I know a man whose mind is broad as the horizon, I know a man whose soul is fire. That man', the choir thunders, 'is Nicolae Ceausescu.' It is the bootmaker's apotheosis.

★

The windowless, tiled soup kitchen in the Calea Victoriei, one of Bucharest's main streets, is crowded at 11.30 in the morning, very dark – too dark to see across – and very cold. Here, some of the poorer eat. At the dimly lit and unheated counter, a long queue stands, coat collars turned up, in stoical silence; moving forward slowly for its not even lukewarm mess of pottage. On the other side of the counter, cooks, downcast and puffy-faced in their kerchiefs, stare blankly into the gloom out of their own limbo.

On offer for 7p (at the black market exchange-rate offered by furtive street dealers), there is a thin soup – served in a small metal bowl – which has the appearance of greasy dishwater, mantled with a pink film of tomato; an unnameable brown stew of fatty gobbets and gristle, at 18p; yellow polenta and a grey 'mushroom' sauce, but without mushrooms, also at 18p: a small piece of fish, the size of a pilchard, in a dark, cold batter, and sold by weight, at 11p per 100 grammes; and small dishes of pickled tomatoes. There are no fresh vegetables, no greens, no fruit, no potatoes.

There is not much more sound than that of shuffling feet and coughing. Here are young workers in balaclavas and dusty overalls from the nearby building site; weary, elderly shoppers setting down their bags after hours of queuing; shop-girls in their lunchbreaks, bright-eyed in the darkness; and unshaven old men in caps – one clutching his head in both hands and slumped at the table – who seem derelict. The table surfaces are filthy, and for some reason there are no knives; thick fingers dip into the plates and pull at the gristle, sopping up the slops with bread.

Compared with this, Moscow thirty years ago was positively booming. The dreariness is suicidal; the blood, like the body politic, as if frozen solid into stasis. What they are eating in here would have caused a riot even in a Victorian workhouse.

★

Ceausescu is an eccentric Stalinist. Thus, he refused in 1968 to take part in the Warsaw Pact invasion of Czechoslovakia, he maintains amiable relations both with Albania and Pinochet's Chile, he permits no Soviet forces in Romania (they were withdrawn in 1958), and he has recognized both the PLO and Israel, refusing to break off links with the latter even after the Six-Day War in 1967.

Gorbachev, when he visited Bucharest at the end of May 1987, is said to have denounced 'nepotism', 'conservatism' and the 'personality cult' in the cobbler's presence. But the Russophobic Ceausescu is alleged to have made it plain that, despite Romania's dependence on the USSR for its fuel oil imports, he would not tolerate Soviet pressure. Anti-Russian feeling has a long historical pedigree in Romania: not only did it 'lose' its provinces of Bessarabia and northern Bukovino to the Soviet Union in 1940 – Romania's claims to them were formally renounced only in September 1965 – but since 1711 the Russians have invaded the territory of Romania on thirteen separate occasions. Indeed, Russia traditionally considered the Danube, which runs for a thousand kilometres through southern Romania to the sea, as her own ideal southern border.

International disfavour has not deterred Ceausescu; internal critics, such as they are, are swiftly and effectively silenced. Ministers – eighteen during a three-month period of 1987 alone – are regularly purged, and apparatchiks put on trial as scapegoats for economic failure and public hardship. Against all these pressures has stood Romania's 'disciplined' Communist Party, whose membership of between 3 and 4 million, in a population of 23 million, makes it the largest 'vanguard of the working class' in proportion to population in eastern Europe.

Together with the membership of the Party's front organizations and secret service apparatus, the Securitate, as many as one in three adult Romanians, possibly more, have been enrolled in Ceausescu's pretorian guard, and huge private army.

*

He makes what he calls dangerously a 'double living', as official state guide and as hustler, changing money on the black market at roughly three and a half times the official exchange rate. In a dark street he says, 'This place is like a tomb. We have no voices.' Fluent in several languages, and a university graduate in his mid-thirties, he will not talk about politics. 'I have a wife and young children. Such talk can get me twenty years in prison. It is not worth it.' But having illegal foreign currency could itself earn him a life sentence.

There was a frozen silence as we walked along the deserted back street. Only in his car, parked in the unlit darkness, would he allow the name 'Ceausescu' to cross his lips. 'There is nothing special about his nepotism and corruption,' he said casually. 'Everyone is like that in Romania. He did not start it.' I could see his dark shape crouching over a wad of banknotes, which he kept hidden at the back of the glove compartment. 'That is how it is in our socialist republic,' he said wrily, flicking through them with the dexterity of a croupier.

★

Romania, like Hungary, has a significant fascist tradition. It arguably provides the historic basis upon which Ceausescu has been building his own grotesque Utopia. The Russian revolutionary Pavel Axelrod, Lenin's political comrade-in-arms, once said – pointing to Romania's 'national peasant character', and the way in which its intelligentsia was perceived as alien – that 'not even the greatest optimist would dare entertain hopes that modern socialist ideas could take root in Romania.' Its turbulent parliamentary history, which goes back to the late nineteenth century, was characterized by unstable bouts of reforming ardour, rigged elections, and arbitrary erosions of its authority by Romania's monarchs.

In the inter-war period Romania pursued essentially corporatist policies in which the State assumed increasing control over the economy and society. At the same time, demagogy grew fond of using the minorities, especially the Jews and Hungarians, as scapegoats for Romania's troubles. By 1938, the country was ruled by a pro-fascist royal dictatorship under King Carol II, until Marshal Antonescu – land-reforming, anti-bourgeois, anti-semitic, anti-Hungarian, and fervently nationalist – seized power in 1940. The Romanian army assisted in the Nazi invasion of the Soviet Union, helping to carry out the infamous annihilation of the Jewish population in nearby Odessa.

In August 1944, Antonescu was himself arrested and ousted by the successor monarch King Michael, supported, among others, by the Romanian Communist Party (RCP). At that time the RCP was very small – preponderantly Hungarian, Jewish and German, rather than ethnic Romanian – with no more than 1,000, or perhaps 2,000, members. It was quickly to build up its strength, including by the recruitment into its ranks of many former Iron Guardists, among them one of their leaders, Nicolae Patrascu. Eugen Cristescu, head of the Romanian fascist secret police, also joined the RCP; and even high-ranking army officers who had taken part in the Nazi invasion of southern Russia were admitted into the Party.

By March 1945, the Communists, using their familiar 'salami' methods, had taken over, although they did not force King Michael to abdicate formally until the end of 1947. The equally familiar, and ghastly, Stalinist routines then unfolded, conducted under the aegis of the ex-electrician Gheorgiu Dej, the leader of the ethnic Romanian element in the RCP. They included: forced industrialization and collectivization, the unleashing of terror in the countryside (some 80,000 kulaks, whom Dej used to call the 'mortal enemies of socialism', were arrested), and the usual purges, as Party treason and plot were 'unmasked' by paranoia.

Up to 40 per cent of the Party's members, many of them its 'non-Romanian' intellectuals, had been expelled by the 1950s; there were executions, or 'liquidations', of 'deviationists', 'zionists', and so forth, typically succeeded in the late 1960s by the posthumous 'rehabilitation' of some of the victims. What had been achieved was the effective 'Romanianization' of a Party largely foreign in its original composition.

Today, the stony-faced leader-worship to which the RCP's ethnic Romanian cadres have been trained, coupled with Ceausescu's proletarian anti-intellectualism and his skilful exploitation of popular atavistic feeling against the Hungarian minority, fit comfortably enough with tradition: providing a mixture of nationalism and socialism – or 'national-socialism' – under a dictator with absolute powers, who is also much given to mythologizing the ancient Dacian past of Romania. 'Partidul-Ceausescu-Romania!' cry the hoardings; 'Romania-Ceausescu!' shout the Party-assembled crowds, at the little grey cobbler's every appearance.

*

Inside the Romanian Orthodox Church of St Nicolas in Academiei Street there is a clock ticking in the silence, and fresh flowers have been placed in the vases. Directly facing, across the road, a huddled queue stands outside the foodstore champing at the bit, rubbing its hands, and chafing in a wind which has become icy.

The walls are blackened and hung with icons, the embroidered altar cloths covered with plastic and the floor with Turkish carpets. A creaking door opens and shuts every few moments to admit a procession in single file, which seems never-ending, of all manner of people; genuflecting, buying small brown tapers to commemorate their *morti*, and posting carefully written prayers – pens scratching on paper – into what looks like a ballot box on a side table.

Waiting for an hour in St Nicolas's, I watched young married women kneeling prettily (until I saw that one was flushed and weeping) on cushions before their favourite Madonna; aged men, caps in hands and temporal arteries knotted, standing, heads bowed, for a pious or vague moment; well-heeled young men, carrying briefcases and brisk from some office, their lips placed intently to the dark icons; old women in headscarves, shopping bags in hand, making their practised round of the saints, each by the same route and according to the habits of another epoch.

Here, the incubus of the State is momentarily lifted, and the shoemaker's exhortations forgotten. Here, one daily rite is exchanged for another: in devout kissing, in sighing messages written to the Almighty, in the touching by fingertip of the holy, and in contemplation.

*

Some estimates put membership of the pliant Orthodox Church, which has seen many of its churches bulldozed, at 70 per cent of the population. The old Uniate sect of Catholics, members of the Byzantine rite and loyal to Rome, was outlawed in 1948 – when all the churches were expropriated without compensation – and forced into unification with Romanian Orthodoxy. Around 1,400 Uniate priests, together with their bishops, were arrested, many dying in prison, although the sect has a continuing underground existence. As for the Roman Catholic Church, it is estimated to have some 1.2 million followers, most of them of Hungarian and German extraction. Also savagely repressed in the late 1940s and early 1950s, its priests, monks and nuns were exiled, sentenced to forced labour, and executed. Today, when all the churches are administered by the State through a department of cults, it is the Baptists – perhaps half of them ethnic Hungarians – who are particularly persecuted.

*

The frozen city recalls photographs of Berlin in the winter of 1945; and in some districts of Bucharest there are enough empty lots and mountains of rubble – from demolition of acres of old buildings, including churches – to conjure up memories of wartime bombing.

Alternatively, there is the Ministry of Information's Orwellian version, in which a 'new urbanistic upsurge' is 'systematizing' the streets of the city. But there is no ground for alarm; 'the Romanian government shows steady concern for restoring the foremost monuments of the past, thus preserving carefully the most outstanding values of the Romanian creative genius'.

And on what does this 'steady concern' rest? Why, nothing less than 'the Romanian people's innate feeling for harmony, their permanent aspiration to live according to the ineffable laws of the beautiful'. Yet here are grey-haired, elderly *babushkas* on their knees in the freezing cold, laying new turf (now, at this season?) around another neo-Stalinist bunker, while handsome young men, in their twenties and thirties, oversee the grey shapes kneeling before them.

Here, once, were the prettiest of the nineteenth-century streets of the 'Paris of the East'. Here, now, the Boulevard of the Victory of Socialism is being constructed. But what will be done with all these bunkers, when the cobbler's world collapses in ruins?

*

'The repressive system here is very rigorous,' he [Andrei Plesu] says – a former research academic, now eking out a poor living as a reprisal for his opinions. 'Protest movements are quickly put down and their leaders liquidated.' What will have happened to the leaders of the Brasov riot two weeks ago (November 15), when thousands of workers suddenly took to the streets in violent protests over their wages and living conditions – unreported in the Romanian media, and as suddenly suffocated – he does not know and can only imagine. In the past, such agitation has led to long terms of imprisonment, forced exile, 'disappearances'.

Thus in 1977, when 35,000 Romanian miners – who are frequently restive – went on strike over poor housing, food shortages and inadequate pensions, 4,000 were sacked and thousands transferred out of their areas. Their leaders, Ion Debre and G. Jorca, were officially said to have 'died in accidents', but are alleged by miners to have been murdered.

'Sometimes we hear from one man to another', as he puts it, 'of a strike, or a demonstration, or of some poor worker trying to do something on his own, and being liquidated. These things happen spontaneously, but they are not typical and they are inefficient. We can't discuss them because there is no real information, only rumours and fragments.' (Not even *Pravda* and *Izvestia* are available in Bucharest; the word 'glasnost' is unheard, and Gorbachev's speeches go unpublished.) 'So far, such actions have been a form of self-sacrifice. People do these things', he says, spreading his hands helplessly, 'and disappear next day. There is no news of a trial, and usually no one knows who the leaders were, where they have gone, whether they are alive or dead or have left the country. Things happen here', he adds laconically, shrugging, 'which are not normal even in eastern Europe.'

How do you cope with it? 'Someone who has spent many years in jail in Romania told me he had met three main types of prisoner in his prison,' he answers. 'First, those who were irritable, fought with their guards and responded strongly to humiliation. Usually they did not survive. Then, those who discussed politics the whole time, what should have been done in the past, what will be done in the future and so on. They behaved as if they were in Parliament. These people in general survived physically, but after approximately two years of such fantasies they became ridiculous and also mentally unstable. The third type exchanged their knowledge – some languages, some history, some philosophy – and tried to give a meaning to their existence in prison. Generally, they survived physically and mentally, and also made life possible for themselves afterwards.

'The only way for me is to succeed in the third way, to continue to learn, to write, to think as if everything was all right, in our prison. This', he says, 'is also a form of endurance'; but there is a despair in his eyes, which belies what he is saying. 'It is a very special place,' he continues, not looking at me. 'There is no chance for you to understand it unless you live here. This is not Hungary, or even Czechoslovakia. Romanian socialism', he says quietly, 'is something different, very special. Ceausescu has survived because no Romanian will give solidarity to another, unlike in Poland. Here, there is no such psychology. Here, people simply feel terrified. They are so terrified that they think nothing practical can be done about the situation they are in, nothing whatever.

'I have heard', he goes on calmly, 'that people outside ask why we don't do anything to free ourselves. But to create even an informal group for private meetings is out of the question. If we had such a meeting, it would be the first and the last one. In your case, it was my obligation to inform the Securitate, to say to them, "This Englishman has made contact with me." They would reply, "If he comes to your house, one of us must be present." There is simply no trust here. Everyone is isolated. So many people are involved in surveillance, maybe millions. Even when we meet for purely social reasons in a house, with three or four friends, everyone is thinking [tapping his forehead] that it could be dangerous. People are afraid even to go to church to pray together.'

Once a year, like everyone else who owns a typewriter, he has to register it with the police, leaving them with a print-out, or type-out in duplicate, of what he calls a 'stupid piece of official prose'; the peculiarities of any piece of typed *samizdat*, or even of a typed leaflet, can then, in theory, be traced back to a particular keyboard. In Bucharest, as far as he knows, there are no underground publications. 'Unofficial' possession of duplicators is also forbidden, and the idea of a personally-owned photocopier is pure science fiction.

'It makes us mad', he says softly, but with sudden vehemence, 'that western socialist utopians, who are free to think and say what they want, still speak of the "achievements of socialism". Instead of giving us intellectual help and support [clasping his hands together], they give arguments only to Ceausescu.' He calls it 'our tragic drama' to have been 'abandoned in this situation'. 'And, what are these socialist achievements?' he asks me. He would have doubtless raised his voice if he had not been afraid of the neighbours. Nor did he wait for the answer.

'We have terrible feelings about the West, that we have been forgotten, as if no one has much interest in what is happening to us. We ourselves are not very informed about what is going on outside Romania. Being informed and not being forgotten', he says, the despair in his eyes reappearing, 'are important things for the individual.' He looked at me for a moment or two in silence. 'We need a mouth of fresh air,' he said, opening and shutting his jaws like a man drowning.

*

When I said to him that things were much worse here even than in Czechoslovakia, he replied: 'Ah, but that is a European country.'

*

The safe and officially sanctioned actor-playwright, fattened by the dictator's favour, is permitted to be (modestly) daring, and to commit his own kind of treason. A man of fashion, his accent turns slicker and almost American as the conversation progresses.

He is in a black leather jacket and jeans, his hair greying; recognized in the bleak street, the better-dressed women turn to watch him. 'There is no trouble here. Sure, we can speak to anyone we like, any time, any place.' But aren't you expected to make a report on your conversations with foreigners to the police? 'No.' But everybody else tells me they . . . 'I don't,' he says casually, shrugging.

Can you invite me home to talk? He lights a Marlboro to occupy the silence, and exhales slowly to prolong it. (What he is certainly not permitted to do is to put me up for the night. 'Lodging of foreign visitors in private houses is not practised', says the police regulation, 'with the exception of first-degree kinship relations, such as parents, children, brothers, sisters and their wives/husbands and children.') *'Comme ci, comme ça,'* he says at last, in answer to my question, tilting his hand from side to side to signify a precarious balance, but laughing.

'I'm all right, Jack', this Romanian laughter meant, roughly translated into English.

★

The Romanian police regulations relating to foreigners add that 'Private accommodation (let, sub-let) for foreign visitors is forbidden. To put at the disposal of foreign visitors a space for pitching a tent is also forbidden'.

★

Distinguished wife to the little *'Conducator'* – the Italian form was *Duce* – academician-engineer Elena Ceausescu is not only deputy prime minister of the Romanian People's Republic, but in 1979 was put in charge of the *nomenklatura*, or the personnel of the Ceausescu apparatus. She is also responsible for no less than the 'co-ordination of the scientific research activity, of the technological development, and the implementation of the technical progress'.

She also takes three different high-speed routes – randomly varied – from the Ceausescu residence to her palatial office, and back again; the Jianu district of Bucharest, where Romania's leaders live, is closed to ordinary citizens, who are not even allowed to walk its pavements.

'One of the most outstanding representatives of the scientific creation', according to an official publication, she travels in a Renault 21, accompanied fore and aft by a convoy of security officials; no citizen is permitted to come nearer than 20 metres from the flying column, sirens blazing; and all abutting roads, in a swiftly co-ordinated police action, are closed for her hurtling passage.

*

Three ducks, yellow-beaked and being carried in a rough canvas bag by a bent country woman in a shawl, are quacking brazenly in the cavernous gloom at 5.30 a.m. There are army officers, straight-backed and even swashbuckling, carrying briefcases; a militia patrol checking the papers of shabbily-dressed rustics (who are forbidden to come looking for food in the city); bulging sacks on stooping shoulders. There are dark men in black peasant trilbies, conical lambswool hats, and Chaplinesque bowlers; their women wear black skirts, stiffly brocaded.

The bare-lit, black-girdered nineteenth-century Gara de Nord in Bucharest, where you catch your train for Dracula's Transylvania and the border with Soviet Moldavia, is already thronged at dawn, freezing, and strangely silent.

Holding birch-brooms, swarthy, squat women and young girl railway-cleaners, who look like gipsies – or the *harijan* sweepers of India – stand in a huddle smoking, their teeth blackened. In one of the few pools of light, and neatly shod in polished boots, a fine lady in fur hat stands waiting; she would have a small dog in her arms, if this were de Maupassant or Chekhov.

Instead, it is like a scene from Dostoevsky; or Gustav Doré's London.

*

In the carriage to the north – with a moustachioed young army officer, bleary as if with a hangover, sitting in the corner – is an 'ethnic Hungarian' woman from a town on the Romanian-Hungarian border, who will turn out to speak passable English. She is pale, a factory worker in her mid-thirties; dressed neatly, demurely even, her eyes are red-rimmed from a night spent, she indicates, in the unheated station waiting-room. Now she seems lost in a reverie.

The officer soon dozes off, mouth open; he has gold braid, holes in his socks and red epaulettes. Approaching Brasov, looking out at the fields freezing into winter hardness, she says, 'Soon we will have snow. The land will be covered, and next year we will have what to eat.' At Feldioara, deeper into the Carpathians, and reassured – though not entirely – by the snoring, she says that 'it is a few years since I came to Bucharest', and that she is 'shocked' by it. Shocked by what? The officer is unstirring. 'It is becoming so poor,' she says quietly.

Before the officer wakes up, somewhere near Sighisoara, she tells me in a whisper, 'This is not a life. You see, I am Hungarian. In this country, I am a stranger.' After he had awakened, blearier than ever, she remained silent.

There is another man in the carriage, a rough lanky fellow in a leather jacket, with a couple of heavy suitcases. He has slept silently and heavily for two hours, as if exhausted. When he in turn wakes, he unexpectedly presses upon his fellow-passengers tins of Coca-Cola – unusually inscribed in Arabic. For a short while, he talks incomprehensibly to the lethargic, yawning officer about Libya, Tripoli and Athens. While he is speaking, in some ill-humour it seems, the pallid Hungarian woman, briefly shocked, looks intently at him, and looks away again quickly, catching my uncomprehending glance, but remaining silent. It is as if something in her were urging him on while he is speaking, but she says, and asks, nothing. Half an hour later, he is again curled up in his corner sleeping; the officer also, his mouth open.

Outside the window pass the wooden villages, the whipped-along pony carts – manes flying – the first snows on the unmade country roads and leafless orchards, the old church spires, and the synagogues of another, lost order. At Medias on the River Tirnava the synagogue, fleetingly visible, stands in the small market-square, its paintwork faded, its Star of David forgotten.

The infernal pollution of lead, zinc and carbon-black manufacture, set down in fields in the phase of forced industrialization in the 1950s and funnelling soot into a suddenly darkened sky, is another matter; these are exhalations of Avernus, and remind me of the satanic coalfields of Dhanbad in northern India. Around Copsa Mica, for example, amid mountains of slurry, trees, hedges, roofs, walls, sheep's fleeces and even the bare stubble in the fields are blackened for miles. Human hands and faces seem flamingo-pink in the grime of the local station.

'*Negru de fum*,' said the officer, stirring briefly. And then the villages returned, and the old, unchanging landscapes. The

Hungarian woman and I rose at this point and went to the restaurant car, where she shiveringly told me her story.

★

Warming her hands around a cup of grey coffee, she said that she had left her children at home in the care of a grandparent and come to Bucharest yesterday in order to greet her returning husband at the airport. He had been in Libya, working under a two-year contract, and had earned his first period of leave after a year's absence.

White-faced and dry-eyed, she described to me how the time had drawn slowly nearer to his arrival on the flight from Tripoli; how it had been announced that the plane had been delayed at Athens; how, in the next hours, the rumour had spread among the waiting relatives of a passenger jumping the aircraft there and seeking asylum; how, at midnight, she had watched the emerging passengers one by one being greeted and embraced by family members; and how her husband had not been among them.

The train racketed slowly north, climbing, carrying her homewards. She told me how she had made her way alone to the Gara de Nord in the small hours, and had spent the rest of the night among the sleeping bodies in the station's crowded waiting-room. Now, with her children waiting at home for their father, she was as if suddenly widowed. In the lurching, freezing carriage, she told me that if her husband had obtained asylum in Greece, she would never be allowed to join him. But if he were to be returned by the Greek authorities to Romania, 'our life will be over'.

In the dark provincial station of Blaj, the hissing train stopped and waited; many of the local passengers were sack-laden. She too waited in the silence, gazing blankly out of the window; the police, she said – once the clanking train had resumed its motion – might already have searched her house in the presence of her children. And the man in the carriage with the heavy suitcases and the tins of Arabic Coca-Cola?

He had been a passenger on her husband's flight from Tripoli, another Romanian contract-worker who had been in Libya. In a few tantalizing sentences to the army officer, he had described what had taken place during the Athens stopover; while she, sitting only a few feet from him, had had to listen in silence as he spoke, dismissively, of her husband's 'stupid action' in the airport. But he had mostly complained of his tiredness, because of the flight's delay and his late arrival. She had been too frightened to speak, or ask him questions, especially in the officer's presence, 'in case they became suspicious'.

Why did your husband do this? I asked her. She did not reply. Outside were grey skies and winter desertion. Did you know he might do it? She began to weep silently, looking out of the window. Eventually, I asked, 'Did he have . . . ? Was there . . . ?'

'We loved each other,' she answered, without expression.

When we returned to the carriage, the two men were talking to each other. But she sat silent, barely exchanging a glance for the next hours, until she got off the train: a receding figure who waved briefly, and, walking briskly, was quickly lost from sight on the platform.

★

As the winter closes in on Transylvania, Cluj-Napoca – with its eighteenth-century baroque town square, equestrian statues and soaring-gothic St Michael's – is short of food and bread is rationed. Some of the children you pass are warmly wrapped and sturdy enough; others, too many, are pale and thin-legged, their knees as bony as I remember from a Lancashire mill town in wartime.

At 2.15 on a Saturday afternoon outside Unit 207 – the bread shop in Petru Groza Street – there are 157 silent and orderly people, coupons in hand, queuing. I tramp the city's pavements, counting carefully. At 2.50 p.m. in Horia Street, opposite the old synagogue with its memorial plaque to Jewish wartime deportees, 141 people are queuing at the Rapid foodstore. Further down the same street, under a sky which is threatening snow, 290 people stand waiting at 3.0 p.m. in two converging queues outside Unit 262 bread shop. There is cake, though; Marie Antoinette would have been at home here.

Many people also seem to be wandering the streets carrying empty bags on the off-chance of finding something – the odd capsicum, a few wizened apples, a couple of greying carrots. There are children, too, with runny noses, trying to cadge hot chestnuts from a muffled street vendor. In the porch of the former Uniate Church, whose tower was built with a donation from the Empress Maria Teresa, an old woman wrapped in clouts is begging, as the day darkens; with a feathery snow falling, 93 people are queuing in Gheorgiu-Dej Street for packets of detergent – rationed to four per person – being sold from cartons stacked on the pavement; an itinerant street-hawker is crying his wooden coat-hangers, shaking and rattling them as he passes.

You could almost think yourself lost in some old photograph of the Warsaw Ghetto, among these staring faces and shuffling bodies – near to giving up the ghost, yet keeping going.

*

In Cluj-Napoca you are 150 miles from the Soviet Union, but a mere 100 miles east of the border with Hungary, and the turmoil of its liberalization. Once known as Kolozsvar, this is the capital of Romania's Hungarian province; after the collapse of Austro-Hungary in 1918, it was awarded to the new Romania, one of the victorious First World War powers. And in Cluj though every public sign and notice is in Romanian, the population is still predominantly ethnic Hungarian.

The Transylvanian city, its university and its Hungarians – so the scared local intellectuals, many of them Roman Catholics, will tell you – are feeling the pinch of 'Romanianization'. One of them, too frightened to give me his name, fastidiously calls it 'Ceausescu's proletarian racism'. But to Bucharest, with its own long history of foreign domination, including by Hungarians, it is a 'one-nation' policy of cultural assimilation and dispersal. 'Eat Romanian, speak Romanian' is one of its popular, or populist, slogans. Indeed, Ceausescu – now additionally alarmed by Hungary's reform process – has continuously manipulated Romanian national feeling to his own advantage by insinuating that Hungary still has territorial claims on Transylvania, and that therefore Hungarians in Romania are a potential, or even actual, fifth column.

In fact, the Hungarians of Transylvania, quite apart from differences with ethnic Romanians over language and religion (mainly Catholic on the one hand, mainly Orthodox on the other), have their own history of local political autonomy, economic prosperity and cultural achievement, with levels of literacy traditionally higher than elsewhere in Romania. Now they have their ears cocked, and minds open, to the transformations going on across the nearby border with Hungary proper.

Bucharest's squeeze on the Hungarian way of life in Romania has so far included closures of local educational institutions and publishing houses, discriminatory restrictions on Hungarian language broadcasting, and the organized migration of ethnic Romanians into

Transylvania. Such measures are seen in Cluj as culture destroying, even as the 'politics of extermination'; 'we have lived here for the past thousand years', say the Hungarians of Transylvania, 'and we do not wish to cease to exist as a nation.'

These are also acts of historic reprisal for what the Romanians regard as their own subjection, in Transylvania, to centuries of 'Magyarization' and enforced religious conversion, 'from the twelfth century to 1918'. When the elegant Banffy Palace in Cluj-Napoca was built in the eighteenth century it was the Hungarians who were the landlords, and the Romanians the peasants.

*

In the small second-hand bookshop in Cluj's Libertatii Square, a ruck of Hungarian-speaking students struggles in intense but word-less combat for a newly-dumped stock of Hungarian books: in heavy-breathing silence, they wrestle over the tattered poetry, broken-backed history and ragged science. One student, pulling his shirt-collar back into place, has got hold – seemingly at random – of zoology, politics and drama.

This is another kind of hunger. Not a stone's throw away – and stones will fly here – the university's deserted main bookshop has a 30-foot long display of the cobbler's writings in its window.

*

During the hours of daylight, cold as may be and with public buildings (including shops) unlit and unheated, some of the shadows and fears of the darkness nevertheless diminish; after all, there is beauty here still, with a fine town church, a women's choir, formal gardens, and – coming soon – a performance of 'Rigoletto'.

After nightfall the motionless silence is of a civil society in ruins; you can hear the sound of your own heart-beat, and every footfall. This is the silence of the grave. In most Cluj streets there is an entire blackness, broken occasionally only by the wan light from an uncurtained win-dow. On a moonless night, I could not see my own feet on the pavement; in the narrow back streets I walked with my arms extended. In such darkness a flaring cupped match is light, and the pinhead glow of an approaching cigarette, movement; it could be a red firefly, dancing. And even 'unauthorized writing on walls' is forbidden.

*

'Power supplies are cut off by day and by night'; the white tiles are grey in the 40-watt bulb light. 'I don't like the dark. I feel as if I am blind,' she says, sitting in her bleak kitchen where for some reason she feels safer from the 'microphones'. Her husband has spent years in prison; 'he is a brave man, he has suffered', she says of him.

Terrified by my presence she keeps me standing, offering me nothing – or with nothing to offer – and not wanting me to stay. 'There are only the stars in the sky and the moon to see with,' she says, standing up, but not coming to the door with me.

*

In the wilderness of Cluj, at 11.0 in the morning, an altercation is going on in the street between two citizens. A middle-aged man in a raincoat begins hectically to wave away a dozen curious passers-by who have gathered to listen; I take the man-in-the-raincoat to be a plainclothes security official, when I see him being briskly saluted by a uniformed militia officer, urgently getting out of a squad car. The man-in-the-raincoat, flailing his arms, angrily tells the curious to keep moving. 'What are you interested in?' he shouts. 'Is it your business?'

*

Before boarding the local flight to Bucharest, cowed passengers must empty all the contents of their pockets, or handbags, into plastic trays, for inspection by a taut security police major, and take their shoes off, in front of one another, for the metal detector.

*

Our three heads are almost touching. He turns up the radio as a precaution; paranoia rules here, not perestroika. 'We all live a double life,' she [Mariana Celac] says; she is one of Bucharest's most imposing and clear-minded intellectuals. 'We all speak two languages. One is the private language of our hopes and anxieties, of a real, true personal life. The second is the language of "normality" which we must use in public.' The result in public life is what she calls 'social apathy', and, more exactly, a 'rationing of feeling'.

'In our section', declares her other guest, who is an economic planner in a major government institute, 'everyone becomes more worried in winter. Every year we have thousands of deaths from hypothermia. All of us can see the children are pale, and poorly developed; in the institute we know that children and old people are suffering from bad diet. Everything is scarce. We are sending 4,000 tonnes of meat to the Soviet Union [per annum].' What he calls 'missing stuff' may suddenly appear in the shops, but quickly disappears again in panic buying; 'you have to be on the spot, it is a matter of luck, and you must be strong for such competition.' (This is Darwinian.) 'I myself have the other day seen children waiting to eat the scraps left on the plates in a self-service restaurant.'

What do people say to each other in your department when they discuss such matters? 'They say, "They eat badly, but at least they eat."' (This is not Bolshevik, but Bourbon.) 'But our top planners and Party leaders know that next year's production levels will be lower than this year's.' How? 'Because we have stopped the import of fertilizers, the quality of the land is deteriorating, and the energies of the people are falling. They know also that nobody knows what were this year's levels.' Why not? 'Because our production statistics in the agricultural and industrial sectors are false.' All of them? 'All,' he says, looking me firmly in the eye and without expression.

Instead, there is what she calls, whistling in the darkness, a 'compensatory private solidarity in the family' and in 'non-political friendships', which provides an 'escape from a divided and atomistic society, where social morality has been abolished'. (Oh, come back Karl Marx, all will be forgiven, if only you will lead the democratic counter-revolution against such 'socialism', and redeem the people!) 'Most of the intellectuals who tried to make an open stand have left the country. It soon becomes obvious to an intelligent person who has lost the right to teach, to exhibit, to publish, that he or she should leave.

'But, in general, taking a moral stance against power is not an historical trait of the Romanian people. This is a fatalist, peasant society in essence; the Orthodox Church is subservient; there are strong traditions of bribery and corruption. There is also no way for us to bring news to the public. Therefore, nearly everyone feels it is simply more *intelligent* to agree with the authorities, if you want to preserve the inner part of your existence.

'In private, you could say in secret, there is very much derision against Ceausescu. They say he should have stayed with shoemaking instead of ruining Romania, and so on. But it is impossible to persuade people to sign a letter, or to arrive at a common position. There is so much suspicion because of the penetration of the Securitate in absolutely every institution; everybody thinks everybody else is spying on them.' Bucharest paranoia picks out trade union representatives, bus conductors and waiters as particularly suspect. 'In my department there are five of us, and it is certain that one of them is reporting on me. But I refuse to ruin my life wondering which is the one.'

They tell me that they hear 'rumours' of strikes and reprisals for strikes, and pick up what they can on foreign radio. Neither of them (taking a great risk with each other in talking to me together) believes in the existence of underground groups of dissenters, though such groups are occasionally referred to in foreign broadcasts. The names of individuals and organizations I mention – such as Dumitru Iuga, an Amnesty prisoner of conscience apparently sentenced to ten years for 'propaganda against the socialist state', or the 'Romanian Association for the Defence of Human Rights', or the 'Free Trade Union of Romanian Workers', or an organization of young Orthodox priests calling for a halt to the demolition of churches – are all unknown to them.

They believe, rather, that isolated dissenters from time to time raise their heads in protest, or succeed in smuggling out to the West a grandiose declaration. But political 'show trials' of such dissenters are not held, the regime preferring not to make a public example of them. Instead, they say that the 'awkward' are sometimes set upon in the streets by plainclothesmen as an informal warning, or subjected to brutal interrogations; that if they persist – or, in the case of certain intellectuals, fail to take the hint to leave the country – they disappear into long years of imprisonment or internal exile; and that hard cases are done away with, as if they had never existed. (There have been unexplained assassinations of priests, writers and strike-leaders.) All of them have one thing in common: they commit their crimes of dissent in a deafening silence, and are dispatched without public notice. It is a fine old reign of terror.

Twenty-two years of the '*epoca Ceausescu*', as the party eulogists like to call it, have truly left their mark: the mark of a political beast, unknown even to *Animal Farm*, which seems to have reduced a whole nation to a state of shared depression.

'This system', they told me together, for some reason beginning to laugh and tolling off the words on their fingers, 'is morally, culturally, economically, politically and socially worthless.' Comrade Ceausescu, cobbler at your last – I hope – did you hear that?

*

These days had brought my first direct experience of fascism; a 'workers' democracy', Ceausescu calls it. 'We trust that one day we will meet again in more normal circumstances,' they said to me at our parting; and, like a thief in the night, I stole away into the embracing darkness.

4

Czechoslovakia, February 1988: The ground shifts

The restoration of Prague's Old Town is proceeding apace, and the Czech Communist Party has a new first secretary, Milos Jakes (pronounced 'Yakesh'); Husak's successor is promising perestroika, or (in Czech) *prestavba*. Under wintry skies, the crumbling plaster of the Italianate palazzi – once all dirty beige and grey ochre – is being refurbished in chocolate, pastel grey and terracotta. Now you can see how finely carved are the keystones of arches and portals, with their heads of satyrs, cherubs and heroes, and how richly rococo are the plaster mouldings of garlands, rosettes and overflowing grape clusters. Early last year, on a similar February day, I was told in Prague that 1987 would be a crossroads. It wasn't.

This February it is forty years to the month since the 'definitive defeat of the Czech bourgeoisie and the victory of the Czech proletariat', as the official history puts it. That victory in 1948 brought the Czech Communist Party to power and, in the name of socialism, swept the great cultural metropolis of Prague into the eastern bloc and out of central Europe. Now I have come to understand what was involved in this political 'liberation' of the Czech working class: the arrests of the leaders of the democratic parties, the systematic wrecking of their headquarters, the flight of tens of thousands from the country, the selective political assassinations. Nor, as I now know, was foreign minister Jan Masaryk merely 'found dead' in the courtyard below his window in the Czernin Palace; he was barefoot and almost naked.

Or, if I were to prefer the Party historians whom I have been re-reading, 'all attempts by reactionaries in 1948 to reverse the democratic developments were definitely thwarted, and working people assumed full power under the leadership of Clement

Gottwald'. There then followed the long and fearsome process of Stalinization in the 1950s under the drunken Gottwald's successor Antonin Novotny. The son of a village bricklayer, Novotny in his speeches used to warn Czech workers to be on their guard against a 'dictatorship of intellectuals'.

Mid-to-late Sixties de-Stalinization was no more than an interregnum. Soviet armour put paid to Alexander Dubcek, and re-Stalinization – or 'normalization', to use the chilling official term explored in the work of the Czech writer Milan Simecka – resumed the task, under Gustav Husak, of crushing Czech spirits. The wide-ranging crackdown on human rights activists after their promulgation of a Charter of demands in 1977 was merely part of this schema. Indeed, Stalinization, de-Stalinization and re-Stalinization represent the three stages of a Czech dialectic, but one unknown to Marxism.

In the 1969-70 purges of the supporters of the Prague Spring, which forced 500,000 people, Dubcek included, out of the Party, and in which 280,000 people (including some 900 academics) lost their jobs, an energetic part was played by the new first secretary of the Czech Communist Party, Milos Jakes.

★

It is not merely that, as a result of these sackings and victimizations, an evangelical Protestant theologian and master of Hebrew now mops the floor of the Slovanski Dom café. For now I have seen how the sins of the fathers were visited on their children; how systematically they too have been hounded, among other things by being denied access to further education. Some of them are caretakers and stokers like their fathers, unto the second generation.

It was a brave new world which was created throughout eastern Europe, of Party élites and proletarian hard labour, a world where the victimization of dissenters has been continuous. It has given Czechoslovakia a most cultivated sub-proletariat: mopping floors, or stoking boilers, with eternity or liberty in their heads, and a Bible or *samizdat* Orwell in their pockets.

★

On the study table of the acerbic Pavel Bratinka – former member of the Czech Academy of Sciences, leading Catholic layman, and (latterly) central heating stoker, whom I first met a year ago – are copies of the *Spectator*, as well as of *Rude Pravo*, the Czech Communist

Party daily. He waves dismissively at the latter; today's issue contains what he calls 'sepulchral odours' and 'the usual Bolshevik reflexes'. On his bookshelves I can see poetry, Catholic exegesis, physics and Hayek in *samizdat* translation.

'Before, the gang-in-power here [the 'living dead on the central committee', he calls them] always had the reassurance of the iceberg in the East and the blast of cold wind from the Soviet Union, if things began to warm up in Czechoslovakia. Now you can imagine their dilemmas. Every day', he says mordantly of Czechoslovakia's *prestavba*, 'something unheard of happens here, but nothing changes. '

Yet more than 300,000 people have signed a new 31-point Catholic petition to the authorities. And the Vatican has been locked in intense and largely secret combat with the Czech regime over a new Church-State concordat since last December. 'Dialogue is not the word,' says Bratinka. 'The Vatican is unmoving.'

Equally notable has been the stubborn refusal by the aged Cardinal Frantisek Tomasek of Prague – 'a man of rather timid nature' – to back down on the Church's demands for greater religious freedom, or to give way on the Church's nominations to vacant bishoprics. 'In the past', Bratinka declares, 'he would have had difficulties standing up to a district official.'

The issue of *Rude Pravo* to which Bratinka takes exception lies between us on the table. It carries a long, four-column attack by Andrej Dobry on what it calls 'Clerical-Fascism', under the banner headline SECRET CHURCH IN THE SERVICE OF ANTI-COMMUNISM, and singles out for abuse a prominent Slovak Catholic family, the Carnogurskys of Bratislava; Jan Carnogursky, a lawyer, is active in the human rights movement. The article accuses his father of having collaborated with the Nazis in the wartime deportation of Slovak Jews, and is illustrated with blurred archive photographs of German panzers and rows of exhumed corpses.

The grey columns of official prose are close written. 'You see how they bare their fangs. This is the kind of Orwellian performance', Bratinka continues – reading aloud of secret Church circles working in the service of anti-socialism and world reaction – 'which was common in the 1950s.' He puts the paper down with fastidious distaste. 'Its purpose is to arouse anti-Catholic hatreds by linking Catholic activism with Nazism. It is a scurrilous reprisal, in typical Stalinist fashion, for the awakening of Catholic feeling in Czechoslovakia. It is also an indirect attack on Cardinal Tomasek. Our petition is a demand for religious freedom, and they shout "Fascism!" The method never changes, the language never changes. The miasmal odour of it is also constant. But there is one important difference from the 1950s,' he adds, hands folded and resting on the edge of the table. 'Now, after such articles, they do not shoot anybody.'

At this point he exploded with laughter; laughing so infectiously that for some time we laughed together. He wiped his eyes. 'Systems like ours', he says as he recovers, but still laughing, 'are ruled by these Bolshevik spells and incantations. If 300,000 people show that they are not bewitched by Bolshevism, to the Party it seems like an attack by twenty armoured divisions.'

The 31-point petition is the brain child of a railway worker from Moravia, Augustin Navratil, and his friend Josef Adamek, a typographer from Brno, and has been circulating in the country since last November. Calling, *inter alia*, for the separation of Church from State, for the urgent appointment of new bishops, and for rights of Catholic religious publication, it has been signed not only by the Catholic faithful in their tens of thousands, but by atheists and evangelical Christians, by Jews and by human rights supporters of Charter 77.

Its significance is two-fold. First, it can be regarded as a kind of plebiscite in a nation suffocated by neo-Stalinism. Second, it has brought together Catholics and non-Catholics in a human rights action led for the first time by the Church, and explicitly endorsed by the venerable Cardinal Tomasck. As the Pope's divisions stand up to be counted, so the old man's moral authority has grown also.

'Between Catholics and Bolsheviks, what moral understanding can there be?' asks the erudite furnace-keeper, tapping the spread-out pages of *Rude Pravo* with his finger and smiling with anger. 'When we die, our hopes are of life everlasting, but theirs are of posthumous rehabilitation.'

*

'Do you think that Communist bureaucrats can become genuinely market-orientated, or that committed totalitarians can bestow individual freedoms upon us?' Bratinka had asked me in passing.

*

After what was described to me as a 'long struggle within the Party', Prague cinemas are currently showing to packed houses the anti-Stalinist satire from Soviet Georgia, Abuladze's *Repentance*.

'When the lights come up', I was told, 'you can tell who are the apparatchiks and the secret policemen. They are looking at their shoes. Normal people are standing up and applauding.'

To add to the cultural confusion, you pass along the fiction shelves in the bookshops straight from Juliusz Kaden to Alexander Kanevskij: Franz Kafka is still missing. But it is naive to ask why Kafka's work continues to be prohibited by the Czech regime, and why Kafka is still treated as a non-person. (Rehabilitated in 1963, Kafka was banished again in the early 1970s.) For who could not see today's regime in his prophetic and terrifying fictions, *The Trial* and *The Castle*?

Since in Prague everyone knows that this is the explanation, the continuing ban merely provides proof to everyone – if proof were needed – of the regime's continuing recognition of its own real nature. Only Kafka himself could have done justice to such a Kafkaesque folly.

*

I have counted nine closed-circuit cameras in the lobby and lounge of the Alcron hotel, where I (in common with many foreigners) am staying. I am told that in the apartment building next to the hotel there is a police listening-post, on continuous duty recording the hotel's bugged conversations. Tonight, *prestavba* notwithstanding, two plainclothesmen – callow young thugs in jeans, trainers and padded ski-jackets – get out of their parked car and follow me up the dimly-lit stairs of a block of flats, in order to find out exactly where I am going.

It is to meet Vaclav Slavik again, the former (Stalinist) head of the ideological section of the central committee's secretariat from 1953 to 1961, who had made a sufficient somersault by 1968 to have joined Dubcek's inner circle of reformists, was subsequently expelled from the Party in 1970 – becoming a bulldozer driver – and has since remained close to Dubcek.

Now, if you part the curtains, you'll see them waiting too, on the other side of the dark street. In a wan pool of light, collars turned up, they stand talking together. There is no effort at concealment.

*

'Today, in his conversation', Slavik declares, 'Alexander refuses the terminology East and West. He insists that Czechoslovakia is part of a common culture in Europe, not only artistic but political, a culture of basic political rights. We are part of a unique European heritage.

'That is why we think our deplorable cultural life in Czechoslovakia must be freed from domination by cliques and gangs of mediocre, sub-standard intellectuals. That is why the Czech people will not accept the hypocrisy of those who merely talk about perestroika; they will not accept rule by the sub-average while millions dream of emigration. As Machiavelli wrote, those who have once tasted freedom never forget it. They demand real changes.' (He clenches his fists in desperation.) 'They must get back their basic rights.'

How? Slavik sidesteps the question. 'People in this country, and in the rest of central Europe, know what European values represent. Both the United States and the USSR under Gorbachev have begun to realize that we possess this knowledge. Moreover, unity against a common enemy', he continues, 'is one of the great characteristics of the European heritage.' (Well yes, and no.) 'I am paraphrasing De Gaulle' – the former central committee apparatchik later quoted Churchill also – 'but what does it matter?'

What are you driving at? 'As Jan Masaryk used to say, the Czech lands are something in-between. But we must not exclude the Soviet Union from central Europe. We cannot say to them that central Europe is not their business. If we want the Soviet Union to become part of our European political culture – and for us Europe starts at the Atlantic coast and ends at the Urals – then it must be on the basis of co-operation with central Europe, not domination. After all, we in Czechoslovakia have dreamed for a long time, for centuries even, of an independent federation of central European countries.'

The commissar of the 1950s has come a long way in his ideological journey; even if his dreams are those of a bulldozer-driver who helped to build the Prague Metro, and who, in his late sixties, seems as far from rehabilitation as ever. 'How would you describe yourself now, politically?' I enquire. 'I would describe myself as a follower of Antonio Gramsci,' he answers.

*

What is the attitude to Dubcek today of the apparatus you once belonged to? I ask Slavik. 'The editor of *Rude Pravo* has recently described Alexander as a "political corpse",' he replies coldly. 'The Party press has also called him an "unprincipled opportunist" and a "counter-revolutionary defeatist". Imagine', Slavik declares with sudden ferocity, 'a fucking Fojtik [the Party's ideology chief] saying that Alexander lacked the qualities of a leader! I tell you frankly we are tired of such habits of demonization, the demonization of our history, the demonization of individuals.' So aren't you disappointed, I ask him, that Gorbachev has still done nothing to secure Dubcek's rehabilitation?

After a silence Slavik replies cautiously, weighing his words; these have been long years of waiting for a restoration of truth and reason. 'We have to respect realities, and we have to handle it discreetly, since we don't know who could be listening. When our friend Gorbachev was here last year, officially he did not mention 1968. But informally' – here Slavik hesitates – 'he inclined to say, "You and we have passed through difficult times together."' (Later I heard, from another equally discreet source, that during Gorbachev's visit to Prague members of Gorbachev's party had talked informally with '1968 people'. Did any of you try to see Gorbachev himself? I had asked my informant. 'We wrote to him beforehand in Moscow, asking for such a meeting, but it was impossible,' he had answered.)

'It is easy for us to appreciate', Slavik continues, 'why Gorbachev had to pretend to see things here in a better light than they are. In this way he avoided many problems. Self-criticism for the Soviet invasion would be a very big step for Moscow. In some respects, it is enough for us that a Brezhnev cannot come to Prague now and tell us, as Brezhnev told our politburo in 1968, "Keep firm, and smash your troublemakers!"' He used those words? 'Those words. I heard them. But I say to you openly that if Gorbachev himself wants to succeed he will have to solve the Czech problem.' How? 'The Soviet Union will have to admit that the 1968 invasion was an error.' (And, at a stroke, the present Czech leadership – placemen of the Brezhnev era – would not have a leg to stand on between them.)

Later, when we left to catch the metro together, hurrying along the near-deserted midnight streets, we were followed by the two young men in jeans, trainers and padded ski-jackets.

*

'During the night of the Soviet invasion, a Russian officer burst in on us while we were all together talking. It was the early hours of 21 August 1968, about four in the morning. There were other Soviet soldiers armed with submachine-guns. I addressed the officer in

French; I was not prepared to speak Russian. On the wall of the room there was a painting of Prague Castle. Strangely, the officer asked me what the painting represented; I informed him, in French. He then exclaimed, in a banal way, that Prague was a beautiful city. "It would be beautiful", I answered, "if it were not occupied by an invading army." He seemed surprised by the tone of my voice, but understood very well what I was saying. During these exchanges, Alexander sat in silence. Then the Russian officer asked uneasily, "What is that statue?" It was a statue called *Fraternity*, a symbol for us of the end of the war in 1945, showing a Czech soldier and a Soviet soldier embracing. I told him what it was, adding, as Alexander continued to sit quietly, "You have destroyed those feelings for ever." "It is impossible to talk to you," the Russian officer said angrily, as the room filled with soldiers. "What have you come here for?" I said to him, still in French. "You were planning a special Party meeting in September," he shouted at us in Russian. "So your tanks are supposed to contribute to the solution of our inner Party problems?! We thought you had come because of the counter-revolution!" I shouted back at him in French.

'He was enraged. Alexander, who was on the point of arrest, got up in silence and went towards the window. "I forbid you", the Russian officer declared, "to look out of the window." They then arrested him. My friend', Slavik said to me, smiling, 'we know about the Soviet Union.'

*

Even Slavik's degree of revisionism, startling as it is, is not enough for the new generation of Czech radicals. For them, an ultimate term of abuse is 'Bolshevik'; 'Communist' means 'villain'; and ex-Communists like Slavik – and Dubcek, too – are regarded as out-of-date, amateurish or 'primitive socialists'.

'They are nearly all very orthodox in their thinking by our standards,' said Jan Urban, the former schoolteacher and Charter activist whom I first met last year. 'They are always talking among themselves in their old Party way, speaking in their dead collective language. They still use the term "comrade" for today's leaders; I have even heard them refer to "Comrade Ceausescu". Most of them have forgotten nothing and learned nothing. Everybody else knows that we cannot go on in the old style much longer.'

He is particularly exercised by Dubcek's recent interview with the

Italian Communist Party daily *l'Unità*, in which the hero of 1968 has, for the first time in two decades, shown his hand, discussed the past and restated his positions. 'Why', Urban asks angrily, 'did he wait twenty years before speaking up? Why did he say nothing for twenty years about our political prisoners, or the shooting on the borders of people trying to leave Czechoslovakia? For eleven years, Charter has been speaking about such subjects, and he has kept silent. Now he weeps that he and his family have been under close surveillance [one of Dubcek's recent disclosures] but there were so many who were in a worse position, and tens of thousands who had to leave the country.

'He had the opportunity to use his moral authority throughout this period. Can you imagine that he never sent messages even to the families of his former colleagues who had been arrested? He spent twenty years working peacefully in Bratislava, without a word to anybody. Today, his sentimental feelings about himself and Czechoslovakia are not enough to change the country. He has jumped on the bandwagon only when conditions have become a little freer. Perhaps he is looking for a job, but many of us feel that he has disqualified himself morally. He has waited too long before speaking. He is still a symbol of the epoch but he has behaved like a coward.'

Don't you think Gorbachev could have done more for him? 'Why should Gorbachev help Dubcek? Why should he honour him? It would only bring Gorbachev more problems, and the Russians don't support losers. In any case, they would back the Devil here, if he was keeping Czechoslovakia quiet,' said Urban.

★

Jan Urban has recently become known in Prague as 'The Moscow Connection'. Although yet another non-person in Czechoslovakia, with no right to leave the country, he has just made a daring journey, under the noses of the authorities, to and from Moscow – an escape from Prague to Moscow! – where he spoke at length to Andrei Sakharov. 'I thought that if I could meet and talk to him, it would help in my own struggle for survival.'

To Urban, a proud man who has made the best of his enforced years as a building worker, the atmosphere in Moscow was surprising, with its new, independent political discussion clubs and 'so many brilliant young people thinking and speaking openly about the possibilities of the future. It was tremendous,' he exclaims. 'We have heard for so long from Kremlinologists that the Soviet system is immoveable, that its intelligentsia is corrupted and so on. But where did all these young people come from who feel they are citizens in a European sense, and who think that formal apologies should be given to Czechoslovakia for the 1968 invasion?'

'They felt guilty about me,' Urban added.

'But Sakharov told me that no political system had ever wilfully committed suicide. Therefore Soviet reforms, he said, would reach their own limits sooner or later, but no one can say where and when. But they would stop eventually, and ossify. He believes that in the meantime citizens' movements must work without cease to "widen every independent space" in each of our countries. "It's a case of activity now," he told me.'

Urban was arrested on his return to Prague, released after twelve hours, and two weeks ago was taken in again by the secret police for interrogation. 'Their first question was very unusual. They asked me, "What religion do you believe in?" I said I was an atheist. They said, "Strange, you look like a man who has faith in something." They kept asking me about Sakharov; "your Academician", they sarcastically called him. I told them nothing. They were very polite, even though I refused to answer any more of their questions. One of them even asked me meekly, "Don't you think things might be different from the way you see them?" I read the newspapers, and spoke about football and Ivan Lendl. There was a different atmosphere from a year ago; they now have orders, I am sure, not to beat us.

'Only once, when I made some light remark, a plainclothesman suddenly said, just like the old times, "Don't joke with us, Mr Urban." But eighteen months ago I would have got five years, under Paragraph 112 of the Criminal Code, for harming the name and interests of the Czech Republic abroad. They released me after only seven hours.'

So what are you saying? 'I am not saying that the secret police are thinking anything new, or that they have any respect for dissidents. But people are losing some of their fears, and the police are no longer sure what they are doing, or where everything is going. They don't know what to do with people like me, while I sleep like a lumberjack and am no longer afraid of their interrogations. The situation is pregnant with change, but they are not getting a clear direction.'

The room is almost bare, and his voice sounds hollow. High above us, up the steep cobbled street, is the Presidential Palace with its blank staring windows – Kafka's own Castle. In the silence, as he waits for my scribbling to catch up with him, I can hear the distant trams passing. 'If nothing is changing', Urban suddenly says with irritation, 'how does it happen that I am talking to you, instead of sitting in prison?'

*

At every turn in Prague, exquisite capital of that 'faraway country of which we know nothing', is the tantalizing mirage of a lost culture, its life energies drained away in the name of the dictatorship of the proletariat, its imperial Habsburg presence faded to the grey provincialism of a backwater somewhere in eastern Europe. Yet Czechoslovakia, having borders with East and West Germany, Austria and Hungary, the USSR and Poland, is in a key position in central Europe; Prague, in the north-west, is a mere 120 miles from Dresden, while, in the south, Bratislava faces Vienna across the border.

You can hear your own footfalls in these arcaded medieval alleys and cobbled courtyards, the baroque church-bells chiming in distant recall of the times before socialism rolled up its sleeves, and got to work on Czechoslovakia. For this is also the city which boasted the largest Stalin statue in the world – 18,000 tons of it – until it was brought down by Dubcek. All that remains of the statue now is its concrete base, which was turned into a potato cold-store, and its long dark shadow.

*

There is a new alternative Prague monthly, *Lidove Noviny*, unlicensed but so far uncensored. Its first home-made issue, which came out in January, contained articles on 'Avoiding Illusion', on Boris Yeltsin, on ecology, on Charter 77, on Sakharov and the 'risks of truth', on the Hungarian Parliament, and on a Prague human rights demonstration. It also contained a short piece by Milan Simecka, whose book *The Restoration of Order* is a political masterwork in a near-ruined intellectual landscape. Its account of the condition of Czechoslovakia between 1969 and 1976 might serve as an epitaph to the failures of 'real socialism' the world over.

'*Lidove Noviny*', says Petr Pithart, an ex-Communist and one of its editors, 'is the first real paper we have had for twenty years in Czechoslovakia. It is an attempt to get out of the walls of our ghetto and address a wider audience.' What ghetto? 'The ghetto of dissidence. We have all been isolated in it, but we helped to build up those walls ourselves,' he adds surprisingly, 'not just the secret police. It has been even more difficult for us than we expected to speak to people who have not had our experience.'

What do you mean? 'We have the mentality of a sect, a sect in opposition to the sect in power. It is difficult for us now *not* to write about police repression, when for twenty years it has been the main topic of conversation between us. We are obsessed by police actions, and we are handicapped by our own cheap and easy criticisms of the regime, our black-and-white perceptions. And as ex-Communists we are fascinated by 1968, as if in that year life ended.'

Pithart's is also the representative voice of yet another group of the walking wounded in a moribund social order. 'In many ways, life was easier inside the walls,' he added.

★

Dressed in jeans and pullover, young Father Vaclav Maly is the most turbulent priest in Czechoslovakia; an elusive figure, he seems earmarked for martyrdom – a Czech Popieluszko – were the covert struggle between Church and State to descend into a Polish maelstrom. Ordained in 1976, he signed the Charter in 1977 (contrary to Church instructions), lost his State licence to work as a priest, and spent months in prison. He comes from a rebellious family; his father, formerly a teacher, was turned into a stoker in the 1960s.

'The government and Communist Party', he says dangerously, 'want priests and bishops who are basically secret policemen. In the talks with the Vatican they are insisting on Frantisek Vymetal as Bishop of Olomouc. The Vatican will not accept him. The State began to create Vymetal fifteen years ago. They made him a leader of *Pacem-in-Terris* [the State's front organization for pro-regime clergy, proscribed by Rome in 1982], the dean of a theological faculty, and administrator of the Olomouc diocese. He is a compromised man, a man without abilities. He is the secret police candidate for Bishop of Olomouc.'

What about Cardinal Tomasek? Wasn't he too regarded for thirty years as the regime's creature? 'It is true that the State authorities are shocked and disappointed by Tomasek. They knew him too as a compromiser; in 1968 he was not courageous. Catholics used to consider him as a collaborator, whose rise in the Church from parish priest to archbishop was always approved by the Party. In the Stalinist purges of the 1950s, 13,000 nuns and priests, including Tomasek, were imprisoned. Those who refused to co-operate were harshly treated. They were sent to uranium mines and labour camps. Many were accused of being spies and given life sentences; and many died in prisons, such as the military fortress of Leopoldova. Tomasek was released after three years of hard labour.' (The pliable, Pavel Bratinka had told me, were released early.)

So why is he now standing up to the regime? What has changed him? 'He has been changing gradually since around 1980. [By then Tomasek was already an old man in his eighties.] He has been influenced above all by Pope Wojtyla. Tomasek obeys and respects the Polish Pope. We can say that the Pope has clear ideas about the Communist system.' Father Maly talks rapidly; he is almost hectic in his desire to register his opinions. 'The Pope has inspired him to feel a sense of his own dignity and responsibility to the Czech people.'

Have you spoken often to Tomasek yourself? 'I have argued and argued with him for many long hours that it is the Christian's task to defend all those who are unjustly persecuted. He used to say to me that Charter 77 was in the hands of ex-Communists, and that it was not possible for a Christian to co-operate with them. He would say, "They are trying to manipulate us." [I have also heard it said in Prague that when the Catholic Petition itself was first shown to him, Tomasek had not wanted to support it.] But at the end of his life he now sees that religious rights are a part of human rights, he sees that a life of compromise is unfitting for a Christian.'

Father Maly is pale and perspiring. The retelling of this struggle with a cardinal's conscience, and the part-conquest of it by radical Catholic opinion in the Charter movement, is itself an arduous business. He mops his brow; an ordained priest in jeans and pullover, forbidden to follow his vocation, who after his release from prison found work as a lavatory cleaner.

*

Despite the new profession of commitment to reform – which includes the regime's claim to be weeding out of the apparatus those 'unable to think critically' – the Czech authorities censored the very message of congratulations sent by Gorbachev to the incoming First Secretary Jakes.

In Russian, and as published in *Pravda* (in December 1987), the

Soviet leader wrote: 'I wish you health and vigour in carrying out the tasks of the renewal of socialism in Czechoslovakia.' But in Czech, and as published in *Rude Pravo*, the Soviet leader declared: 'I wish you health and vigour in carrying out the tasks of the strengthening of socialism in Czechoslovakia.'

What's in a word? Everything. 'Renewal' is a word associated in Czechoslovakia with 1968, and the speeches of Alexander Dubcek.

*

'What happened', he bellows in Czech into the mid-day restaurant hubbub, his interpreter shouting also, 'when they burned Giordano Bruno and forced Galileo to deny the circulation of the globe?' Vanek Silhan leans forward in his chair, plates clattering around us, heads at the neighbouring tables turning.

A former professor of economics in his early sixties, hands rough from labour as a building worker, he is the man who on 22 August 1968 was authorized by the secret Vysocany Congress – which Brezhnev called the 'Vysocany Riot' – to take over temporarily from Alexander Dubcek after the latter's abduction to Moscow. (Dubcek spent most of his time there semi-conscious in a bed in the Kremlin, after 'slipping on the floor and striking his head on a table'.)

'Scientific progress', Silhan continues, his voice raw and clutching an unopened pack of cigarettes, 'moved from Italy to northern Europe. That is our problem also, here in Czechoslovakia. Only in small enclaves can we speak freely,' he shouts. Heads at more distant tables turn. 'But without dialogue between the citizens and the free circulation of knowledge, what progress can there be in Czechoslovakia?'

He taps out a cigarette, fingers thickened, almost courting the uneasy glances of other customers. 'The people here are thinking deeply', he declares noisily, 'but they are also deeply pessimistic. There are no political expectations among ordinary people. They think things must be changed, but can't be changed. They hear of reforms in other countries, but most of them believe Gorbachev will not make it. The last twenty years have scarred them, deformed their existence! They believe [shouting] that political power is still playing a game with them, and that they can do nothing to stop it!'

What about perestroika? 'Ah, perestroika, perestroika,' he exclaims raucously, his voice like gravel and inhaling deeply, neighbouring ears pricking almost visibly. 'Here in Czechoslovakia the old rules do not work, but the new rules are not in existence.' He laughs, coughing, his face reddening. Why not? 'Because those in power are in the mud up to here,' he answers, still coughing, and putting both his hands above his eyebrows. 'It is they who created the hatreds in our society, with their primitive slogans for twenty years, their inner Party apartheid, their crude class language. The workers are fed up with such things [voice rising], it is at the base of all our problems, I have been a manual worker [shouting], they are fed up with such things!'

There is alarm at the next table. Do you want me to write all this down? 'Everything,' he says, stubbing out his cigarette as if he were screwing it into the ashtray. 'Now in *Rude Pravo*, Jan Fojtik [an active supporter of the post-1968 "normalization"] tells us that Alexander Dubcek was banned by right from public life. They portray us as enemies, as foreign spies and adventurers, as pedlars of lies and half-truths. But for forty years I have known Fojtik,' Silhan says, speaking the name with loathing, and briefly eyeing the people at the next table. 'Such men', he continues, dropping his voice a little, 'are like Japanese *bonzes* [traditional clergy]. For the last twenty years they have paralysed Czechoslovakia. [Less loudly] They got their positions by the aid of Soviet guns, but it is their own spinal cords which were broken.

'Now, as in 1968, it is we who once more have the right to say, "Gentlemen, for twenty years you have been in charge, and we are still in trouble."' And what about Jakes? Here, the back of the nearest diner, only three feet away, seems to stiffen. 'He knows nothing,' answers Silhan, lighting another cigarette. 'He even does not know what he wants. He is a clerk without conceptions, who speaks only in Party phrases.' (Jan Urban had described him as 'a hardliner, waiting'.) Silhan looks at me for a few seconds, his cropped grey beard yellowed at the mouth, a sturdy and aggressive figure.

'There is an iceberg here. Nine-tenths is below the surface; no foreigner can see it. Even the children were punished. They took them hostage. For twenty years they have imprisoned our nation, our moral qualities, our culture, our younger generation.' This is the coldest of furies. 'It would take a great literary figure to do justice to the crimes they have committed. Only art could do it.'

★

Silhan is yet another ex-Communist, stripped of his job and Party card, whose positions combine free thought – and the 'heresies' which free thought produces – with formal socialist commitment expressed in the grimmest kind of Party language; the kind used by Jakes. It is a bewildering and often incoherent mixture.

'On the one hand, the world of socialist production is a world of nonsense production,' says Silhan. 'In such a world, State ownership robs the worker of his sense of purpose and belonging, blocks private initiative, but at the same time misuses public resources. All the wastefulness of the State, all its errors, fall on the backs of the workers; the harder they work, the more that is wasted. They ask themselves, "For whom do I labour?" and "Why should I work harder?"'

On the other hand, and only a few minutes later, Silhan's list of socialism's achievements includes the 'liquidation of parasitism', 'social justice', 'the directing of capital towards the national interest' and the 'creation of social organizations in which men and women can realize themselves'. Then, in another turn of mind which characterizes the (insoluble) dilemma of the 'socialist project', he tells me that the biggest problem in Czechoslovakia is caused by the monopoly of power in one Party. 'Some of the 1968 comrades have changed their views entirely.' How? 'They do not believe in the possibility of any kind of reform of the system.'

And what do you believe? I ask him. 'It is impossible that a society, any society, could become incapable or producing new kinds of social and political institutions.' Such as? 'There are other methods of establishing public ownership than through State nationalization. We cannot un-think the system which exists here, but we have to find other means of co-operation, another relationship, between the producers and the means of production.'

Obviously, the socialist agony is universal; you could feed this straight into the British Labour Party's review process. 'I am not recommending English pragmatism', he continues, pre-empting my next question, 'but you cannot pressure a whole people with dogmas. Even our reform Communism in 1968 had too little realism in it. I have had many years of manual labour; real life is more complex than theories.'

Why then bother with socialism at all, since in seventy years no society has abolished wage-labour or commodity relations, and never will? Does it have a point any longer? 'I criticize what socialism has done, not what it is,' he answered, Jesuitically. 'Socialism cannot be expunged from society, neither ours nor yours, and neither by words nor actions. Or do you think that the lot of producers would have been easier if there had been no socialism in the world?' he asked with asperity. But wouldn't Czechoslovakia have done better since 1948 without it?

He eyed me, hesitating for a moment, and then cast taboo aside. 'In Czechoslovakia we have no hungry or homeless people. Our houses are warm, and all children go to school. But we lost much more than we gained, this I tell you very frankly, by growing up after 1948 in the shadow of theories of class, and the legitimacy we gave to class hatred. By dictating who was acceptable and who was not, we lost the co-operation of millions of our population.

'Real human virtues and interests were sacrificed. It was barely possible to live through the struggles for survival and power which were unleashed in our society, when people who had lived side by side for decades were set against each other. People of a low cultural level came to feel hatred on the basis of a psychosis, which the Party encouraged, about property ownership and cultural achievement. How could you ask for humane responses from people who were trained in such attitudes?

'But your societies were also to blame for the disasters which we suffered. The negative example of what capitalism does to its peoples, its present and historic excesses, forced upon socialists – and still forces upon them – a black-and-white attitude to the world, which deformed our development. It has prevented us for forty years from getting to the rationality of things. It gave us our totalitarian attitude to power. It even destroyed knowledge itself. Now we are searching for a way out for ourselves, but with no new theories and no new leaders. It is not so simple.'

*

It is a milder winter than last year. The swans bob serenely on the shining Vltava, and the cut-glassware – some of it said to be made in Czech labour camps – glitters in the shop-windows. There is also gallows humour, à la Schweik, in plenty. 'At least there was snow when we had Husak,' I heard someone saying.

*

A senior member of the bureaucratic apparatus, father of a dissenter, does not want to be named nor otherwise identified; neither would he let me take a note verbatim. (This was written down from memory, immediately after our conversation.) 'Here', he had said, 'stability does not rest so much on repression, despite what Charter and the other groups keep saying. It rests on the people's resignation.' ('I really don't know why I am here', said the stoical Schweik in his detention cell, 'nor why I don't complain about it.') 'When this starts to change, the system could simply melt away. Since it may be unreformable, this might even be the best solution.

'However, for the time being, reform is the new propaganda, although here we can only pretend to make changes. In the leadership there are people who see very well that change is desperately needed. Yet they lack the skills to supervise a serious attempt at transformation. They have only their radar, not actual knowledge. We ourselves have no Gorbachev. There is no one. He would have to be a cultural liberal, a technocrat, charismatic, still in his fifties, and a Communist. There is no such person in Czechoslovakia.'

Why not? He had paused for a second. 'Because there are no Communists in Czechoslovakia,' he answered, laughing loudly.

*

Vaclav Havel, Czechoslovakia's leading playwright and one of the founders of Charter, holds daily court in his spacious apartment overlooking the River Vltava. Born in 1936, the son of a rich entrepreneur who made his money from a popular theatre and dance-hall, Havel was denied higher education in the 1950s because of a 'bad class background'. Himself a former Party member, he has also suffered a nineteen-year ban on the performance and publication of his works, nineteen years without a passport, and nearly five years in prison, from 1979 to 1983. ('The head of our prison camp was fascist. He would say to me "I would like to kill you." Such people are atypical,' Havel added briskly.)

But in his own political kingdom of foreign visitors, he is sovereign; a man with a small greying moustache and baggy trousers, who continues to believe in civil liberty and truth-telling, in a nation whose citizens have been humiliated by four decades of lies and violence. He scuttles about at the double like an overworked clerk, doorbell and telephone constantly ringing.

For Havel, the only antidote to such humiliation for men and women who have hitherto 'feigned outward loyalty, while inwardly ceasing to believe in anything' is to 'straighten up as human beings once more', to act as if they were free citizens of a free country, and to keep alive the habit of thinking freely, so that such habits might survive even under totalitarian conditions.

He says to me, between phone-calls, that he thinks the situation in Czechoslovakia is changing, though the present leader (Jakes) is 'worse than the one before'; he calls him a 'functionary without a face, who cannot utter one sensible sentence'. But 'there are signs, like the Catholic petition, that society is gaining courage. The Church's role here is not comparable with that of the Polish Church, but it is gaining more believers. It is another reason for hope, another pressure from society on the country's leaders. People are starting to watch TV, listen to the radio and read the newspapers more carefully, as if they were expecting something. However, the change is in the atmosphere of life, not in official policy or in the institutions.'

He is also aware of a 'drift to the right' among some Czech dissenters; 'new moods', he calls them. 'It is due to the world-wide wave of neo-conservatism, which has reached here also. Such moods have mainly affected Catholics of the younger generation; it is relatively understandable in our circumstances. But I am irritated with Roger Scruton, who has said in the *Salisbury Review* that I am myself a typical neo-conservative. It is not true, and everyone who knows me knows this.'

As for his own situation, 'after nineteen years, I have again asked for a passport, although I don't think they will give it to me. Even with a passport it would be dangerous for me to travel in western Europe; I would probably lose my citizenship and be unable to return to Czechoslovakia. So I must try to travel in eastern Europe. But the authorities hate it even more if we make contact with other independent people.

'Yet for the first time in nineteen years, I am being asked to submit texts of my plays for consideration. Later today, I have an appointment with the *dramaturg* of a Prague theatre. I do not think my work will be performed. This year may be even more repressive than the last one. I have no illusions. But the fact that some people have courage to ask to see my work is a sign that something is changing. Before, they were afraid to meet me.'

The doorbell carries Havel away again, his dog barking savagely at the next newcomer. It is Dubcek's foreign minister, Jiri Hayek, now in his stooping mid-seventies. He stands talking with Havel in an undertone in the dark hallway; moral exiles both, in their own country.

★

Vaclav Havel has written on Charter 77 as follows: 'It does not go out looking for new signatories. Anyone can sign it at any time, of course, but no campaigning for signatures is ever undertaken, anywhere. The Charter does not compel anyone to do anything. It does not seek to win citizens over or issue appeals to them. It makes no attempt to teach people lessons. It does not seek to represent anyone else. And it bears no grudge against those who do not support it.

'The only sense in which it constitutes an appeal to others is as an indirect challenge . . . At most, its example serves to show what is possible, i.e. that even in the most difficult of conditions people can behave as citizens, claim their rights, and try to exercise them. It demonstrates that even where the institutionalized lie holds sway it is possible for citizens to speak the truth, and that everyone may assume their responsibility for the whole without instructions from on high. In short, it shows that each of us can start with ourselves, and right away.'

★

The sound of light music seems unusual in this setting. In the stately ante-room – with its polished parquet, red plush and high casement windows – an old clock stands unmoving on an ornately carved table. There are crisp daffodils in a vase, white cyclamens and a dark *Assumption*. A side-door leads to a private chapel; and in the silence, the light music and low voices.

The music stops and there is a sound of creaking footsteps; the rococo double-doors, with their delicate ormolu brasswork, open before me for a respectful figure who bows out, more or less backwards, closes the doors, and scurries away down the red carpet.

A moment later, the doors re-open. Cardinal Tomasek, genial and ruddy as any Moravian farmer, but Rome-educated and Italian-speaking, beckons me into his study. His pectoral cross is inscribed with the words 'Synodus Episcopi'; on his head a crimson skull-cap, his black cassock bound at the waist by a crimson cincture.

'The people', he says, speaking in Czech-inflected Italian and setting to matters quickly, 'are coming with us in increasing numbers.

The life of the people is with us. Hundreds of thousands have signed the Petition. For the Party and the government, it is causing an increasing problem. They ask themselves, *Come mai*, how come?' He chuckles briefly at the thought of it.

On his table is a bowl of pink carnations, and a small pocket transistor. 'For the Church in other countries, where there is *la dolce vita*, there are different problems. Here, there is a Church without bishops.' [10 of the 13 Czech bishoprics are vacant.] 'It is like a body without a head,' Cardinal Tomasek continues. 'The government is creating grave obstacles, *grandi ostacoli*, in their appointment.' Is it true, I ask him, that the government is insisting there should be members of its own 'peace organization' for clergy, *Pacem-in-Terris*, among the new bishops? 'What is this organization?' he says obliquely, but giving me the answer. 'It is like a department, an agency of the State. The government wants to do everything – *tutto, tutto* – to support it.'

Why? 'To divide the Church in Czechoslovakia,' the Cardinal answered. In Prague, *Pacem-in-Terris* is more brutally described as the State's fifth column among the clergy; 'even an innocent person', Pavel Bratinka had said, 'can see that it is fishy.' 'But how many of the priests belong to this organization of theirs?' Tomasek continued. '*Pochi, pochi*. In Slovakia five per cent, in Bohemia seven per cent, and ten per cent in Moravia. It is few, very few.'

He falls silent, an old man ruminating, staring at the surface of the table; his cassock has small crimson silk-covered buttons, and is edged with fine crimson piping. 'It is for the purpose of the State supervision of the Church in Czechoslovakia,' he declares suddenly. 'We will not accept that. We do not accept State supervision. We do not accept that the Church is part of the State. We do not accept that the Party and the government can impose themselves upon us. Seventy per cent of the people are Catholics. It is very strange,' he adds vaguely; then again falls silent.

'Since 1949' – passing an aged hand across his forehead – 'our religious life has been obstructed. Now I am eighty-nine. I myself suffered three years of forced labour. Many of our priests are not permitted to work as priests but must remain as workers, our religious literature cannot be published. *È un grande problema, un grande problema*. Even if they allow priests, they do not want bishops. Why are they making these difficulties?' he asked. 'It is hard to understand it.' Again he is silent, or tiring. '*Non è normale*,' he added quietly.

But you, I ventured, were seen as a man of compromise, even a weak man, for so many years. (Here he looked at me attentively.) Why have you changed your position? Why have you now declared so boldly, after years of silence, that 'cowardice and fear are unworthy of a true Christian?' He does not hesitate. 'It is necessary to act in this way, *bisogna fare così*,' he answered simply, looking straight at me.

What is the result of making this stand? 'Small steps, but steps forward. They are ready, the government and the Party, to give a little more than before. Not everything at once, *ma sempre avanti*. We have made our choices for the bishops of Trnava and Olomouc, and for the auxiliary Bishop of Prague. We are expecting [this said very firmly] to have these bishops appointed. We expect something concrete. *È molto, molto urgente*,' he said, almost in a whisper.

Once more he fell silent, absently twisting at the bracelet of his gold wrist-watch. 'We are always driven to clandestinity,' he says unexpectedly. 'I also had to be consecrated in secret as a bishop. The conditions which the State imposes on us are truly primitive. In Romania, it is – aaah! [clasping his head] – *orribile, orribile!* This is what the Communists call the earthly paradise. But it is harder for us here than in East Germany, Hungary or Poland. Now the expectations of the people are turning to us,' he says, sighing, as if burdened by the prospect. 'It is a new hope for the future,' he added, without expression.

Cardinal Tomasek's official residence, in the old cobbled square of Hradcany, stands in the very shadow of the Presidential Palace. Its guards have a grandstand view of the clerical comings and goings, and even the Primate of Czechoslovakia, when he is speaking to visitors in Czech, plays light music on his transistor.

★

In animated conversation, at Bratinka's table: 'More and more people in the bureaucracy and Party are looking for Jews to save.' I don't follow, I said to him. 'They feel the ground shifting, so they are beginning to develop a conscience.' I still don't get you. 'They are starting to lend a hand secretly to dissenters, passing out information and so on.' [The same thing was going on in Hungary in the mid-1980s.] 'Soon, everybody will have his own Jew,' Bratinka repeated.

★

'My guards have been removed from outside the house,' he says. In the early 1970s, when he used to go jogging around the neighbourhood accompanied by his dog, the police would follow slowly in a car. Eventually they found a secret policeman to run after him, since the car was unable to keep on his tail when he left the pavement to cross open ground. 'Sometimes', he continues, 'this man used to run alongside me in his tracksuit, and we would have a conversation.' In the glass-fronted bookcase behind him, propped against the books, are postcard reproductions of Michelangelo's *David* and Botticelli's 'Three Graces' from the *Primavera*.

Jiri Hajek, once Dubcek's foreign minister and yet another ex-Communist purged during the 'normalization', is seventy-five now. ('It was a crime', he says; 'we were humiliated.') A wizened, bird-like man with grey-sandy hair and pebble glasses – a slippered pantaloon, almost – he lives out his days in a distant Prague suburb. Unlike Dubcek, he signed the Charter in 1977, and was one of its first spokesmen. But then Hajek's earliest political allegiance was social democratic; his party was 'merged' in 1948 with the Czech Communist Party. He was also Czech ambassador in London from 1955 to 1958, and recalls, among the dusty rubber-plants in his sitting-room, the close contacts he had with the CPGB's John Gollan in that period.

'The present Czech leadership', he declares in his studious English, 'cannot get out of its own shadow. They were put in power by the same Brezhnevite group which, until Gorbachev, was blocking reform in the Soviet Union. They are trying to muddle through here, but with a certain hope' – as he delicately puts it – 'that Gorbachev is a mere episode in the Soviet Union. The result is simple Don Quixotism. The only changes they are preparing are administrative. The rest is just talk.' On the bookshelves behind him are volumes of Apollinaire, Paul Valéry and Gotthold Lessing; even (can it be his?) a book of City Lights beat poetry from San Francisco.

'All these people in the apparatus who are against reform have gained great material advantages from power – villas, and such things. For them the main problem of perestroika is how to keep their possessions,' he added, laughing and wheezing. But what about Soviet pressure for reform in Czechoslovakia? 'Direct conflict with the Czech leadership would be too risky. In any case, what advantage would it bring to the Soviet Union? They would like our economy to be more flexible and efficient, but they don't want troubles here. They have enough troubles in Poland and inside the Soviet Union.'

Aren't there any reformists in the Czech politburo? I asked him. 'There are fake reformists. "Democratization" is the word these fake reformists have begun using a great deal recently. But what does it mean? For them it means only a more spontaneous execution by the people of duties and orders. They only want people to work harder, but under the same bureaucratic leadership of the Party. It is their limited conception of democracy which is the heart of the matter. They know', he continues, 'that they need the active support of the Czech people, but if they were to get it, this support would carry them beyond the limits they have set themselves for their changes.

'The result is that they can do very little, not least because reform for the Czechs means a return to 1968, or nothing. The leadership also knows that if a genuinely popular democratic movement was aroused here, it would not respect the Party.' Why not? 'Because it is not respectable,' he replied swiftly.. 'This is also the problem in the Soviet Union. That is why Gorbachev is trying to bring about democratization under the control of the Party, even if that is itself a contradiction.'

Why is it a contradiction? 'Because democracy is a matter of the sovereignty of the people, not the sovereignty of the Party.' [He too is throwing political caution to the winds.] 'That was our problem in 1968 also. But then the tanks came, so that the question of how democratization was to be carried out in Czechoslovakia disappeared, so to say, without being answered. In 1968, my Stalinist colleagues were shocked by everything that we were doing. I used to tell them', he says, chuckling and beginning to speak very freely, "Not even the Paris violence in May ['68] has so far overthrown De Gaulle, so what are you so frightened of?" I also used to say in the politburo that the only role of a Communist Party was to fulfil certain political duties to the people. I would tell them that it was quite forseeable that, one day, some other Party could equally carry out these duties.

'For them, this was the worst heresy: this understanding I had that a Communist Party should be considered as having a transitional role only. They were afraid of it. The problem will arise for Gorbachev also, if he succeeds. If he fails, those who follow him will nevertheless have to face it also. In 1968, because of its conservative and backward position, the Soviet Union unfortunately failed to see that developments here might have been a pattern for them. Our efforts were crushed. But with their tanks they merely postponed their own crisis. Now it has ripened and fallen on them also.'

Do you still have a political role to play? I asked him. He is wearing a grey-buttoned cardigan, faded trousers and brown slippers. 'We are old people,' he answered. '1968 is just a memory.' There was a silence. 'In my youth, I was social democratic,' he added, as if answering an unspoken question. 'That is my background.'

*

How many turbulent political voices – of fear and anger, of pessimism, of impatient and patient waiting for salvation – fill the air, yet how silent is this early Sunday morning!

It seems, too, that the spring is a long time coming, mild though the weather; with no signs of life (and not much inspiration) to be found in all these blackened Prague statues of old Bohemian kings, bishops and heroes; stone-deaf, the lot of them, to Czechoslovakia's present Passion.

In Maislova Street, where the obliterated Jewish Kafka was born and which leads to the ghetto of the Eternal Martyr, you will see a café waitress mopping the floor: bending forward, straightening up, bending forward. Look more closely, and you will see that a small gold crucifix hangs from her neck; swinging back and forth on its fine gold chain, as she bends and straightens on this silent, silent morning.

*

Between Zohor and Bratislava, the train – on its way from East Berlin to Sofia – runs directly along the Czech-Austrian border. At one point, the barbed-wire is a stone's throw away. There is a vivacious young actress (in black boots, black leather skirt and glossy lipstick) opposite me, who is going to Bratislava for rehearsals. She speaks fluent English, American-accented.

Does anyone ever mention Vaclav Havel's name in the theatre? I asked her. 'No,' she answered. Have you heard of him? 'Oh yes, he is famous.' There was a brief pause. One can imagine, I continued, how hard it must be for a dramatist whose work is forbidden in his own country. She shrugged her shoulders and looked out of the window, at the passing barbed-wire and the watch-towers, in the brown ploughland.

*

'These are ugly things, lies and half-truths,' declared the Slovak Catholic activist Jan Carnogursky hotly, referring to Andrej Dobry's onslaught on him and his father as 'clerical-fascists' in *Rude Pravo*. I am in a rainswept tower block of weeping concrete in a Bratislava suburb. Here there are walls inscribed with 'Deep Purple', and 'Chelsea'.

He has strangely blazing dark eyes, and launches into a monologue defence of his family history with barely a preamble. Tossed aside on the sofa is a subscription copy of the Austrian TV guide *Telexy*, with a lurid Aretha Franklin cover. Television transmissions from nearby Vienna are eagerly watched in these Bratislava bunkers. 'Five years ago there was a similar attack on Milan Simecka', says Carnogursky – a lawyer by profession, whose doctoral dissertation was on the wartime Slovak State's racial legislation – 'but they accused him of other ugly things, not a connection with the Nazis.'

He says, sitting tensely in his chair, that since last spring the secret police have been searching the archives for documents to prove the collaborationist activities of his father, a former member of the Slovak People's Party. A conservative-nationalist Party which held power throughout the war under Nazi protection, it had its own armed militia. His father served briefly in it as a staff commander in 1939 before, Carnogursky insists, being 'removed for anti-German actions'. (Eventually, the militia fought alongside the Nazis.) Nevertheless, 'out of economic necessity' his father continued as a deputy in the Slovak Parliament at the time of the Jewish deportations to Auschwitz in 1942.

'My father had no governmental position', says his son, barely pausing for breath, 'he was not in the pro-Nazi faction of the Party, he had nothing to do with deportations – he abstained during the votes on racial legislation – he was never an anti-semite, and he was not tried for his activities when the war ended.' (Father Tiso, the Catholic priest who was head of State in wartime Slovakia, and Bela Tuka, the prime minister, were both hanged; the minister of the interior, Alexander Mach, received a life sentence, emerging from jail in 1968.)

Carnogursky cites, in forensic detail, chapter and verse of the evidence against *Rude Pravo*'s allegations. For example: 'In 1940, my father bought a house in Bratislava from a Jewish doctor, after the anti-Jewish law of expropriation had been passed by the Slovak Parliament. The doctor was a family friend, and he continued to live and practise in the house, and we took an apartment in it. He wanted to sell the house rather than abandon it. It was done to help him, to protect him,' he insists, perspiring. 'This my father could do, because he was a prominent Slovak politician. As long as my father was there, the doctor survived the deportations. But in 1944 my father returned to his native village.'

And what happened to the doctor? 'The doctor was taken to Auschwitz,' he replies, barely checking his stride. 'Now *Rude Pravo* accuses our family of "taking advantage of anti-Jewish measures". My father was always a conservative Slovak nationalist and a Catholic, who wanted an independent Slovakia. The Germans encouraged this in 1939 because it suited their own aims of breaking up Czechoslovakia. But that does not mean that he was a fascist. He committed crimes against no one. He was a typical central European nationalist of that period, a kind of Christian Democrat, not a Nazi.'

It is a son's passionate apologia for his father, and he is exhausted with the uninvited effort of it. What are *you* accused of? I ask him. 'I am accused of being the son of my father,' he answers, his forehead shining.

*

Carnogursky has his own (unsolicited) views on the Jews. 'In the Slovak villages before the war many of them were tavern-keepers. They gave credit, so that in order to pay their debts the peasants often had to sell their fields and houses to the Jews, and emigrate to other countries. My father's opinion today is still that something had to be done, so that Jewish creditors could not claim the houses of their Slovak debtors.' Annihilation? 'Not annihilation', says Carnogursky without a pause, 'legislation. Today anti-semitism is less in Czechoslovakia. In the 1950s, during the Stalinist trials in Prague, you could read each time the phrase "of Jewish origin, with no Czech or national roots". In the past, it was much stronger and more open. Now, they have turned it into criticisms of Zionism, but they are the same kinds of people with the same kinds of opinion as we had here in the war period.

'In the Prague government even today they allow no Jews, and the secret police are very anti-semitic.' How do you know? 'I have heard it when I have been interrogated. When they want to know about someone I have met with an unfamiliar name, they ask me, "Is he a Jew?" But in all nations at certain periods, this I can tell you, the Jews are a problem,' he added unexpectedly.

This is a miasma, from which I retreat into my own silence.

*

'Yes', the writer Milan Simecka declares, standing in his kitchen, 'it is an absolute rule that there can be no Jew in the government or in the central committee. We have had anti-semitism here for hundreds of years. It is a tradition. For instance, these old arguments about Jewish innkeepers are typical. It was the world that Chagall painted. It was not evil. You know, they even asserted on Czech television that the "77" in Charter 77 [founded in 1977 to defend the principles of the Helsinki Accords] was "taken from the Jewish Kabbala".'

I hear that anti-semitism is not as overt, I say to Simecka. 'It is true that it is not as overt. But only a week ago Moscow *Pravda* carried an article attacking the "Pamyat" nationalist movement in the Soviet Union for a number of things, including its anti-semitism. The reference to anti-semitism did not appear in the *Rude Pravo* translation. It was the only change from the original; I compared them closely. To me, this kind of thing is highly significant.'

He suffers from glaucoma – 'since my time in prison', he says briefly, pausing in his conversation. 'When you read official histories of the Second World War here', he resumes, 'the fate of the Jews is marginalized, or even excluded. They write above all of the tragedy of Party members and the working-class movement. But the holocaust was a great tragedy for our nation: we lost more than 150,000 Jewish people, some of the best of our Czech and Slovak intelligentsia. In 1948, after the Communist takeover, there were 200,000 emigrés, mostly educated people. After 1968, we lost maybe another 200,000, including some of our leading scholars, social scientists, economists, writers. This is a small country of 16 million', he says, 'a small country which is now under the domination of plebeians.'

'They could even send me back to prison,' he added. 'My case is still open.'

★

Simecka lives in a grey, spartan flat beside Bratislava railway station. 'Dubcek's house', he says, going to the window, 'is over there, 300 metres away. Sometimes he sits at this kitchen table talking to me, where you are sitting.'

There is not much enthusiasm in his voice. 'We were in prison, but he spoke up for no one. He tells me that all this is a great moral problem, but he kept silent for twenty years, and his three sons were educated. They all studied at university. One of them is a doctor, another is an engineer, a third is I don't know what. My son is a stoker; he was not allowed to go to the high school and continue his studies. It was a terrible experience for us to hear him weeping. We paid a high price, we were all damaged.' ('I inhabit another world,' his son said to me next morning.)

'Today Dubcek is completely preoccupied with the smallest details of what happened to him. He constantly asks everybody, "What did I do wrong in 1968?"' The whole subject seems to be tiresome to Simecka. 'He wants rehabilitation. This is his constant topic. He even wants to get back his Party card which they took from him; he says that his expulsion is a "blow which bleeds and refuses to heal". He keeps writing to the central committee, but he says "They have been filing my letters. I have not had a single reply from them."' (Shades of Kafka's *Castle*!) 'For him, there is only one question: who was right in 1968? But if the Soviet Union says "Dubcek", there would be an absolute explosion in Czechoslovakia.'

From 1954, when he was twenty-five, Simecka – then a Party member – taught political science at Bratislava's Comenius University. In March 1970 he was expelled from the university and the Party, becoming a van-driver and later a building worker. Detained without trial in 1981-2, he is fifty-eight now, prematurely retired, his sight fading.

'The future seemed fantastic when I was sixteen, just after the war was over. What dreams ["terrible dreams", he called them later in our conversation] we all had for our country. There were so many of us who joined the Party, pioneers of the left movement! We were becoming members of the power élite, but how could we know it? Who of us imagined in those days that our liberation would turn into this dictatorship, or that in building socialism such a community of fear would be created? We thought that Communism was the right thing, that it had a relevance to us. We were all friends, we were all poor, we were all students.'

Did you really believe in this Communist future? 'I don't know now if I exactly believed in it. Let us say that I half-believed that the socialist countries would be the models of a new society. After the death of Stalin, when I was twenty-six or twenty-seven, things became gradually clearer to me. I was reading Orwell. From him I was beginning to know that the most important thing in the world is the right to say, "Two plus two equals four", that the basis of everything is intellectual freedom.

'From the moral point of view, I could already see then, even though I was a Party member, that it *might* be better for us all to get out of Communism entirely. But in the late 1950s and early 1960s, I continued to urge my students to join the Party. Even though I myself was gradually finding in the Party people of every political line – Christians, anti-Communists, partisans of capitalism, anti-semites and so on – I persuaded the best of my students to be active in the Party.' Why? 'Because with part of myself I still thought that it was the only way to reform society. I also had a secret dream that the Communist Party could be reformed also.

'After the Soviet invasion of Czechoslovakia, it became obvious that this was not the way. And after the "normalization" in 1969 and 1970 there were no reformers left in the Party. The Party got rid of its most idealistic and independent-thinking members, and it was clear that the only alternative was open dissent and opposition. If I had remained silent, I could have remained in the faculty even in 1970 during the purges, but I simply could not do it.' ('The dictatorship of the proletariat', Simecka was eventually to write, 'actually means a kick in the guts to anyone who holds other than officially approved ideas'; and, worse, 'existing socialism has stolen from socialism any future it might have had'.)

'It was very hard. I had been a professor here at Comenius University, and I found myself a van-driver, living in this ghetto as a simple worker; later I was a building labourer, digging sewer trenches with an excavator. My wife, who was a teacher, had lost her job also. One day, not long after I had started my new work, my boss said to me, "Simecka, go to the laundry and get me my suit." I said to myself, What has happened to me? Yesterday I was a professor, and today I am driving this dirty van to the laundry.

'I was terribly depressed, and lived without hope from 1971 to 1977, until I began to write my book *The Restoration of Order* in this kitchen late at night, after the day's work was over. While I was writing, I had for the first time a sense of freedom. I felt that the space I had at last found could not be taken from me. In my circumstances, Havel's idea that we must "live in truth" was very important to me; the poverty of what I call my second life became preferable to the self-censorship of the 1960s. I could even imagine during those hours of silence at the kitchen table, when nothing was stirring, that my life was normal.

'Yet I learned a great deal in those years of manual labour.'

['According to my wife, the sound of my voice and even the way I sit became different,' he said later.] 'Most of my fellow-workers hated what they regarded as the "typical attitudes of all these intellectuals"; now, for me too, some of the values of intellectual life have been reduced in my eyes, especially when I read the artificially sophisticated writings of academics. For many years I also reconsidered the foolishness which is responsible for much of what has befallen us, this middle-class anxiety of ours in the face of the working class, our guilt, our uneasy feelings.

'They have desires for freedom too, but I learned how purely materialistic are the aspirations of most working people. I also discovered how many of them, and not only the dissident intellectuals, hated the regime and the Party. Some of my fellow-workers would say to me, "We have our jobs, we have our apartments, we have our families, and we shit on them and their Party." A few of them even believe they are independent, and, apart from the right to travel, they think they have freedom also.

'Other workers had a different attitude. They would say to me, "You must be a lunatic, to have lost your job as a professor. You had the best life of anybody, with your books and your writing. It is not you, but we, who are in prison." It was also a kind of jealousy; a couple of years after my book was published in Paris, a special TV programme in the plebeian style was made against me, showing hands counting western dollars.

'Generally speaking, non-proletarians of my generation have their own perspectives and emotions. For them, what has happened to our country is also a moral issue. Many of them have feelings of devastation. They feel that they have lived cowardly lives, lives of hypocrisy, despite what has been done to them and their children. Some of these people hate the regime with utter loathing; when I think of them, I can see hangings in Wenceslas Square, revenge-seeking.

'The new generation is quite different. Many of these young people, in the Soviet Union also, are more dangerous to the system than we have been.' Why? 'Because they are normal.' What do you mean? 'We were deformed by our experiences,' Simecka answers. 'We were deformed by our education. We were deformed by our reading. We were deformed by what we believed. But for them Marxism, all this ideology, is absolute nonsense. Things for them are much clearer. And this is not the thousand-year Reich. It has devastated Czechoslovakia, but it will not last for ever. Some say that it is nearly over. One year more, two years, three years? Let us see.'

★

Simecka told me that during his intellectual travails he had once met and had a long conversation with the distinguished British Marxist historian, the late A. L. Morton, who was on a visit to Bratislava. 'I was surprised by one thing in particular, which I have never forgotten. Morton said to me in our conversation that he himself had lost his faith in socialism. Have you said this openly in Britain? I asked him. Do you know how he replied? "It is too late now to admit it"!' Simecka still seems incredulous.

But I don't understand your surprise, I say to Simecka; I thought you were an expert on the subject of intellectual treason.

★

At a dawn brew-up in a cosy workmen's hut on a muddy building-site outside Prague, there is a clumping of hob-nailed boots and the smell of coffee. The hut has a rough bed for the nightwatchman.

The big fellow in blue overalls ('he could eat a Communist for breakfast,' someone says of him), with blackened hands and holes in his tattered pullover, stands at the small store, cursing sourly; I have also been told that the thin and taciturn chap taking off his muddy gumboots in the corner of the hut thinks that the Soviet Union should be destroyed, and frequently says so.

'Here, everything is violence,' says the big man loudly, eyeing me writing and in the hearing of all the others. What do you mean? I ask him through a go-between. He turns full-face, steaming pan in hand. 'If somebody believes in God, why should he not believe? Why do they bother to put it in their notebooks that a man goes to church? It is not freedom, it is terror,' he adds, turning back to the stove, his voice near lost in the clatter.

Is anything changing with Milos Jakes? The whole hut treats the question as plain foolish. At first no one even bothers to answer. 'If Dubcek came back', says the big fellow eventually, 'maybe it could be better.' (In here, he is of the moderate Party; the others don't even believe that.) 'He wanted us to be better off than the Russians but the Russians pushed us down again,' he says, stooping to a small fridge for a milk bottle.

So what do you think is going on now at the top? He takes his time, pouring mugs of coffee. 'The masters' [*pani* in Czech means 'lords' or 'masters', and has an almost feudal ring to it] 'are fighting among themselves around the pig trough.' No one demurs, or comments. The sound is of spoons stirring, and slurping; and his the archetypal voice of the downtrodden proletarian. Here it is the dismal world created in their name, the name of labour, which, forty years on, the men in this hut seem to have utterly rejected. There is not even any point in asking them further questions.

5

Yugoslavia, October 1988: 'A feeling of pressure'

Autumn nightfall, becoming quickly dark in a stink of diesel. There are no red flags to celebrate socialism in these parts, and no wonder; not a single heroic exhortation. This is a cafe, its television set blaring, somewhere on the axle-shattering road in the Socialist Republic of Serbia. It is the largest of the six constituent republics – Serbia, Slovenia, Croatia, Bosnia, Montenegro and Macedonia; each with its own flag, government, Communist Party and Party line – which make up the ramshackle federation of Yugoslavia.

The thundering juggernauts head south to Belgrade, and on to Bulgaria, Greece and Turkey. In front of the cafe, the beat-up second-hand Mercedes of swarthy Yugoslav guest-workers, heading back north to Munich and the car-plants, stand in water-filled pot-holes. The cafe manager, melancholy and indifferent, sits in a poor light and a leather jacket beneath a framed portrait of Tito, taking in the limp wads of sour-smelling grey banknotes, at 4,000 dinars (70p) for a sandwich. After a sale, the tired waitress checks the whisky level in the bottle with a wooden ruler, entering the measurement in a ledger.

Inflation is 200 per cent per annum and rising rapidly. The weak (Bosnian) prime minister, Branko Mikulic – a hostage of the separate statelets' Byzantine interests – has just seen his eighteen-month-old 'austerity programme' collapse in ruins. Politically and economically Yugoslavia is under internal siege, with a huge foreign debt of $20 billion, over 1,000 strikes this year, pay rises of 40 to 100 per cent, trials for fraud in the State-owned enterprises, incoherent market-orientated reforms and mounting pressures for a further bout of constitutional changes.

At the heart of the matter is the impotence of a federal government

which has been unable, since the death of Tito in May 1980, to impose its will on a country of fractious republics divided by history, by language, by ethnicity and by religion. In microcosm, it may point ahead to the future condition of the Soviet Union.

*

Over 35 per cent of the Yugoslav population is Serbian. Belgrade, the capital of Serbia, is also Yugoslavia's capital. Most of the Yugoslav army's top-brass are Serbs. Serbia contributes around 40 per cent to Yugoslavia's national income. And a third of Yugoslavia's territory is in the sprawling republic of Serbia, which has borders to the east with Hungary, Romania and Bulgaria, and in the south west with Albania.

Historically Orthodox Christian, autonomous from 1830 and an independent kingdom after 1882, it dominated the States of Croatia and Slovenia between the wars as 'Greater Serbia'. To cut it down to size in the new 'balanced' Yugoslavia fashioned by Tito – who was himself half Croat, half Slovene – Serbia was deprived of control over two of its old regions: Vojvodina to the north, and mainly Albanian Kosovo to the far south. They became 'autonomous provinces within the Republic of Serbia', each again with its own government, flag and Communist Party, making a total of eight such entities in Yugoslavia. 'This is not a one-Party State, it is eight one-Party States,' Belgrade wits will tell you, without laughing.

*

Outside the cafe, in the darkness, there is a stench of urine from the broken-down latrines; you could be beside the Grand Trunk Road in northern India. Inside, a thin film of capitalist crud – soft pubic porn at 2,000 dinars a mag, a rack of rock videos, Rambo postcards – is smeared on the fly-blown surface of socialist failure. (Is this what the partisans fought for?) On the TV screen, orating Serbian politicians, their hair limp and their faces pallid with effort or excitement, declare that Serbia 'will no longer be pushed around', and denounce the (Muslim) Albanian leaders of Kosovo for organizing a 'reign of terror' against the 200,000 minority Serbs – outnumbered eight to one by the Albanians – who live in the province.

In June 1389, when Ancient Serbia was the most powerful State in the Balkans, Serbian warriors were vanquished in Kosovo, heartland of its medieval Christian tradition, at the hands of Muslim Turkish invaders; it took until 1912 to liberate Kosovo from the Ottoman Empire. Today the Muslims of Yugoslavia have inherited a reviving Serbian odium as 'occupiers'; it is as if their very presence reminds the Serbs of defeat, 600 years ago, on an historic battlefield.

'Serbia', the TV set declaims hotly, 'is awakening'; the fulminating rhetoric is crowing on the dunghill of Yugoslav socialism, as its collapse deepens. The non-Serbs in the cafe shift uneasily at their plastic-topped tables in the roar of traffic, as the Serbs applaud every mention of the forty-seven-year-old Serbian Communist Party leader, Slobodan Milosevic, who came to power two years ago. 'They are killing our people down there, they want to make a big Albanian republic, they are fucking us over,' shouts a Serbian youth in jeans with an Americanized accent, cupping his mouth in the bedlam. In 1914, another Serbian nationalist assassinated the Austrian Crown Prince in Sarajevo, giving Austro-Hungary the pretext for declaring war on Serbia, with consequences which engulfed Europe.

The shadows flicker: gaunt ghosts of the world-before-Versailles, freed from their graves by perestroika and economic chaos, and setting out once more to stalk the Balkans.

*

'There is going to be civil war here,' the Serbian youth had said, leaning, as if drunkenly, over my table. Why? 'The political system is shit anyway,' he had added, ignoring the question.

*

The red Coca-Cola truck, its bottles jangling, leads the way across the Danube bridge and down the long deserted road – each roadside field numbered – towards Novi Sad, capital of the north Serbian 'autonomous' province of Vojvodina. Its fertile plains have been variously conquered by Celts, Romans, Huns, Avars and Turks, and in the Second World War it was divided up between fascist Hungary and the quisling State of Croatia. Today, Vojvodina's population of 2 million is 55 per cent Serbian, with a large minority Hungarian population of 400,000. (Are there 18 or 20 separate nationalities in Yugoslavia?)

On a warm day in October, there is a shimmering heat-haze over the endless rolling flatlands, deep in maize, which stretch from here to the Hungarian and Romanian borders. In Novi Sad, a quiet university town where a Monti Pajton film, directed by Teri Džons, has just been showing at the local cinema, you would not know that the Serbian whirlwind had just passed across the dozing landscape, knocking down the local leadership like skittles.

'Serbia is One', 'Give us Arms!' and 'Kosovo is Ours', the 100,000 Serbian protesters in Novi Sad's main square had shouted only a few days before. Some say that a 'hardcore' of 'around 500' itinerant demonstrators had been bussed in at the behest of the Serbian leader Milosevic. (*'Vozd'* or 'Leader' his followers call him. *'Slobo-Duce'* is the spray-painters' name for him further north in hostile Slovenia, which is prosperous, increasingly liberal and almost Austrian in its culture.)

Attacked by the huge crowd for economic mismanagement, for being Stalinists, for being Serbian 'traitors' to the Serbian cause, and above all for being soft on the oppression of fellow-Serbs in far away Kosovo, the scared Vojvodina leadership quickly went under in a welter of resignations and a hail of missiles. Buried with them were their earlier, fatally defiant objections to Milosevic's 'hegemonistic ambitions', to his 'Serbian nationalism', to his increasingly close involvement with the hierarchy of Serbian Orthodoxy, and his desire to centralize all power in Belgrade, his own fiefdom.

Today, there is no sign of the agitation. At mid-morning in Novi

Sad's trendy Ruzica Street, behind the Catholic cathedral, Jonathan's and La Vista Boutique – thudding with rock music – are selling their jewellery and stone-washed jeans to youth at its most lissom. In a dim pin-ball saloon at the street corner, a group of lanky teenagers is playing the machines, lights flashing, beneath another framed gaze of Tito. 'Punk Anarchy' reads the graffitto; there is not a sign of Milosevic's 'Greater Serbia'. A few streets away, the motherly cook in the restaurant, sitting down to an early lunch, covers her face with her hands in prayer, before eating.

★

'We are with Milosevic, we wanted a strong leader,' declares Dragan Lakicevic, a freethinker who teaches philosophy at the University of Novi Sad, and who did his doctoral thesis on the writings of Friedrich Hayek; a Serbian, Lakicevic too is going under to the wave of anti-Albanian feeling. 'In the past', he adds, 'Tito's Serbian protégés were lackeys, without strength or faith in anything.'

Is Milosevic a fascist? 'Who knows?' he answers. 'No one knows. We have never had real representative democracy in Serbia. He could turn out to be a fascist or he could be a democrat, or he could be a Stalinist. But if he is using the people's grievances against the bureaucrats like a Mussolini, does it mean that he is a fascist? He does not know himself what he is. But for the first time politics in Yugoslavia has become more than slogans.'

Yes, but what is he achieving? 'It is a strange kind of Gorbachevism, which has touched the emotions of the Serbian people. He is doing great things for Serbian national pride. We are one third of Yugoslavia, but we have only one sixth of the power. Now we want to feel secure in our own country under the rule of law. I too would like to see an independent Greater Serbia which is strong enough to impose itself on this part of the Balkans. The Serbs are not safe in Kosovo, because the Balkan problem has never been settled. I feel under pressure in other parts of Yugoslavia also.'

What kind of pressure? 'Every Serbian has begun to feel it. It is a really unpleasant feeling.' I don't understand, nor could any outsider. I tell him that it sounds more like paranoia. 'It may be paranoia, but we are being forced to move, including leading intellectuals, and not only out of Kosovo. We Serbs are looked upon as "national enemies" in Catholic Croatia also. I would never be able to live there. For instance, if a Serb asks the direction in the street in Zagreb, he might not be told when they hear his accent. I feel safer in West Germany or Austria. Now Serbians are moving from Bosnia too. There are thousands of Serbian refugees in Belgrade living in poor conditions.'

But what sort of pressure is this? 'It is a feeling of pressure,' he repeats bleakly; and, hesitating a moment, adds 'including the pressure of Muslims.' You mean the Islamic revival? 'That is a factor. We have at least 2 million Muslims, and here it is combined with Communism. Can you imagine such a mixture? In Kosovo, the Albanians are developing a national consciousness, they are damaging our churches. They have 15 or 16 children, and they want the land. They will not rest until the last Serb has been driven out of Kosovo, and all the land is Albanian.' [The Albanians of Yugoslavia, most but not all of them in Kosovo province, are the third largest nationality in the country after the Serbs and Croats; and their birthrate of 34 per 1000 is said to be the highest in Europe.] 'For us Serbs, who have only one or two children', Lakicevic adds, 'it is a question of survival.'

Isn't this Serbian xenophobia? 'Maybe, but xenophobia against the Serbs is growing also. Yugoslavia is breaking up. In such a situation everyone is becoming xenophobic.' But I thought socialism was supposed to have overcome the 'national question', I say to him. 'It was supposed to have overcome every problem,' he answered.

*

'A state of emergency has been declared,' announces a boozed-up British journalist (falsely) at the reception desk of Belgrade's Hotel Moskva. How do you know? 'It is coming over the wire,' he replies, holding on hard. (What wire?) In a corner of the lobby two tense Spanish journalists are helping each other with their copy. 'How do you spell "Bosnia-Herzegovina"?' one of them is asking the other.

'No one knows what is going on in this country,' says the hotel porter, who studied law at the University of Belgrade and watches Sky Television.

The journalist lurches into the night, in search of a headline.

*

A conversation with a senior western diplomat in his embassy. 'The sense of crisis is exaggerated,' he says, urbanely – or complacently – setting his face against the tide of opinion. 'There may be sheer confusion here', he continues, 'but there is also a freer atmosphere than anywhere in eastern Europe, Hungary included. For example, there were no guards around Mikulic [the prime minister] when he came here the other day to an embassy reception. Have you seen that anywhere else?'

But what about the Serbian imbroglio, Milosevic and so on? Isn't the upsurge of nationalism an ugly business? 'It isn't nationalism, it's populism. It's a case of the Serbian pot calling the Albanian kettle black. All I hope is that we don't have to choose between them,' he added, flicking with a mannerly hand at the sharp crease in his trousers.

*

In fact, finding your political balance in Belgrade has become very difficult. Thus, in Marshal Tito Street you can buy your own photocopier, something unheard of in the rest of eastern Europe, while Solzhenitsyn's *Gulag Archipelago* and the novels of Milan Kundera are in the bookshops. Milosevic, a man with an illiberal record who likes using class language, is said to want both a stronger centralized State and a freer, deregulated market. With inflation at South American levels, old people can be seen picking over street garbage; nationalism, or populism, is on the rampage; and the Yugoslav republics are ganging-up with, and against, each other as the political vacuum widens. Even good minds seem to be unhinged by the complexity of the crisis.

The Serbian preoccupation with the behaviour of the Albanians of Kosovo is stoked each day in the Belgrade media, which are said to be under the thumb of Milosevic. 'Super-Slobo', whose rallying cry is 'No compromises, no concessions!' promises his followers that Kosovo will be 're-taken', its autonomy ended, and the Serbian minority there ('our people') 'protected', by being brought back within the fold of Serbian administration. At a stroke, the Albanians themselves would be turned into an embattled minority within a Greater Serbia.

The propaganda is intensive, and demonizes the Albanians. They are legatees of the Ottoman usurpers; polygamous and over-breeding Muslim primitives; secessionists ready to join up with Tirana; swarthy and violent rapists of flaxen-haired Serbian women, including nuns in their convents. They are charged with having driven out the Serbians – since 1981 perhaps 30,000 have left Kosovo – by bidding up local land prices, by 'fostering ethnic strife', by 'terror'. Portrayed as heathen desecrators of the shrines of Serbian Orthodoxy in the province, they have even been accused of 'spraying Serbian houses'. Indeed, the Albanians – first cousins to the 'lustful Turks' of our own barrack-room ballads – seem to have been charged with every 'atrocity' except the posting of excreta through Serbian letter-boxes.

It is the price of glasnost and a high one. As with Armenians and Azeris in the Soviet Union, so here in Yugoslavia different ethnic groups are now free to say openly what they have always said in private about each other. The result is not yet civil war; civic uproar, rather, and a giddying swirl of hatreds.

*

Not everyone has been swept into the whirlpool. Lazar Stojanovic, the Belgrade film director, describes himself as an 'undeclared Serb'. 'I used to tell people I was an Eskimo when all this started.' Is the situation dangerous? 'Potentially, very.' Does the man-in-the-street think so? 'No. But it reminds me of how we were torn apart in the war.'

Why is it happening? 'We have our north-south problem, like the Italians. We have deep religious divisions. Political confusions are total. Most of the intelligentsia wants capitalism, most of the working class wants socialism and the State is trying to hold the balance [laughter]. Since the death of Tito, federal authority has been decaying. Above all, these are the Balkans and we are a mass of diverse people. In Bosnia, for example, the Muslims are in a majority and they are real Muslims.' [Last year, three Muslim fundamentalists were jailed in Sarajevo for 11 years, after calling for a *Jihad* to make Bosnia a theocratic Muslim State.] 'In Kosovo, Islam as a force is weaker. There are between 100,000 and 200,000 Albanians in Belgrade. But they do many things, including being our bakers. Out in Serbia their situation is worse than in the city; when something violent happens in Kosovo, they get their shop-windows broken.

'In the past our problems were always resolved by force. That is what makes me so frightened at the present hysteria.' But what will the Serbians actually gain in the end by all this agitation? I ask him. He taps his head. 'Nothing. Every few decades the Serbs suffer from these theatrical obsessions. It will be another victory which is merely Pyrrhic. They are ready to lose thousands to gain something which is nothing more than a symbol. They see themselves as heroes. This kind of thing has always been typical of the Balkans,' Stojanovic added gloomily.

What is Milosevic actually after in Vojvodina and Kosovo? I ask. 'It is like Hitler's push into the Sudetenland. Everyone thought he would stop there, but he didn't. In terms of his own obsessions, he was achieving something.' Where could Milosevic go next? 'Montenegro, where the people are basically Serbs [and were ruled by the Serbs from 1912 to 1941], Macedonia, part of Bosnia.' Is he a fascist? 'Basically, yes. He is a corporatist, he is a demagogue, he plays on the sense of Serbian betrayal by Tito, and he has established a direct relation between himself and the masses. They shout "Slobodan, we are with you!" They adore him, he claims to follow them, and they think him the liberator of Serbia.'

What has all this to do with socialism and Communism? 'Nothing,' he said.

*

Who, in your opinion, has greater justice on their side in this conflict, the Serbians or the Albanians? I had asked Stojanovic. 'The Albanians are pretty primitive', he had replied, 'but they are 95 per cent in the right. Kosovo is a very poor region and they are the most politically deprived people in Yugoslavia. They are our *üntermenschen*. But they are also armed and they would make proficient guerrillas. Kosovo is their land. They are the owners of it. Many of the Serbs are merely settlers who went to Kosovo in the 1930s.'

Would you say this on a Belgrade bus? 'I wouldn't dare to say it.' Why not? 'I'd probably be beaten.'

*

At 6.30 a.m. works buses – from local tractor factories, a 'thermo-electric' plant and sundry 'kollektivs' – are parked, engines idling, in Belgrade city centre, waiting for their employees. You can see them approaching along the damp pavements from different directions, mostly singly: pale and bleary-eyed, coughing, yawning. They clamber aboard the buses wordlessly, feet thumping on metal, and sit down in silence, staring.

*

'Of course, any intra-ethnic conflict is irrational,' says the depressed Kosta Cavoski, a lawyer and admirer of the philosopher John Locke, whom he has translated into Serbo-Croat. 'But the Albanians of Kosovo breed like rats,' he adds, briefly losing his head in the conversation. Rats? He laughed, shrugging me off as if there were no more time for scruples.

'They do not learn Serbo-Croat and no one can understand their language. They could start terrorist actions.' His mood is almost apocalyptic. 'They are organized in family clans. They fight vendettas for family honour, and they buy up the land together. That is why the Serbians are so weak there; thousands have packed their bags and come north. In Kosovo, the Serbians are individuals, but they must face a whole clan if there is a personal quarrel. To the Albanians Kosovo is like Palestine for the Jews, a homeland. They are striving for unification with Albania,' Cavoski insists, though there is precious little evidence of it.

'Their aim', he says, 'is to break up Yugoslavia.' Fifteen years ago he was sentenced to five months in jail, suspended for two years, for criticizing the Yugoslav legal system. Today he sounds like a patriot; there is deep anxiety in his voice about the fate of Yugoslavia. 'Even the opposition here is Balkanized, divided by ethnic difference and fighting each other. There is no organized homogeneous force in Yugoslavia which can keep the country together. Serbian nationalism is moving to fill the vacuum.'

This is precisely what Tito feared might happen after his death. 'For the Serbians, Kosovo is a point of pride. Like the Falklands for Mrs Thatcher,' Cavoski added.

*

An escape from the smog-laden city. In its light and landscapes the countryside might be Italian; after all, Croatia faces Venice and Emilia Romagna across the Adriatic, and Bosnia the Abruzzo and Molise. But despite the rural depopulation of central Italy, there the neat vines are hung with grapes this October, the serene autumn fields at rest after another (overworked) season of plenty, the *contadino*'s wood stacked in good order for winter.

Here, too often, even the fertile Serbian lands are visibly mismanaged and neglected, the good earth left to indifference or dereliction. Here, green meadows have been turned over to thistles, and hillsides – once terraced – lie tangled in bedraggled underbrush and bracken. Here, there were once thriving farmsteads; now there are fallen walls, copses of unruly acacia and rank elder. It is as if Yugoslavia were separated by the Adriatic from what it might have become, if Communism had not taken over.

★

He suddenly produced my book, *Against Socialist Illusion*, from his drawer as I sat down to talk to him and placed it on the table between us. Professor Branko Pribicevic, a former member (from 1968 to 1974) of the Serbian Communist Party's praesidium, is now a member of the International Commission of the central committee of the Yugoslav Communist Party; he has the reputation in Belgrade of having 'waged ideological war' from 1968 to 1971 on student dissidents, of whom Kosta Cavoski was one. When he was Belgrade University's vice-chancellor, he was said to have declared himself 'the Husak of the campus'.

'I hope you agree with at least half of what I wrote,' I bantered, chancing my arm with him. 'I agree with all of it,' he said briefly. (What?!) He handed me his copy and watched as I leafed through it. The pages were covered in underlinings, exclamations and annotations. I gave it back to him; evidently even the one-time Stalinists here are aboard the post-Communist bandwagon.

'We are in a transitional stage,' he continued, carefully putting the book away in his drawer. From what to what? 'From something to something else,' he replied, chuckling, 'but no one knows what. It is a rather dramatic situation,' he added; and catching my eye, laughed uneasily, as if a political abyss were opening. 'Our problem is that we are the most heterogeneous State in Europe, and there are still no real Yugoslavs in Yugoslavia. We are still Serbians, Croatians, Slovenes and so on. Thirty-five kilometres north of Zagreb [which is twinned with Birmingham] is the border between Croatia and Slovenia. Here, all trans-European express trains have to stop to make technical adjustments. Why? Because for twenty years these two "sovereign States" have not been able to agree on a common electrical power system.

'The most radical changes are needed. They are still being obstructed. We must have more centralization in Belgrade, but what happens? Our Slovene friends become obsessed with the old pre-war syndrome about Serbian domination. An explosion is coming', he went on, 'because an autonomous civil society has begun to develop, while at the same time nationalistic feelings have been kept suppressed for too long in this country.'

By what? 'By Commie fascism,' he suddenly said in fluent vern-acular English. By Commie fascism? 'By Commie fascism,' he said again, for the record.

*

'You may think I am xenophobic', Pribicevic had also said to me, 'but Kosovo is the least developed part of Europe. Serbian women cannot walk the streets there. Last week, two young Albanian soldiers on home leave molested a Serbian girl in the street, beat her, and started to strangle her. Ten metres away, a group of Albanians stood with their arms folded. The local Albanian police do nothing.' [There are armed Serbian vigilante groups now in some parts of Kosovo.] 'These are backward, semi-educated people,' he declared in anger. 'What is happening to Serbs in Kosovo is a disgrace to western civilization,' the central committee man added.

Quite apart from old Serbian accusations against them of having collaborated with the Nazis, the Albanians have for some time been giving hostages to fortune which rankle with every Serbian. For example, in October 1987, only four months after Kosovo Serbs had marched en masse all the way to Belgrade to protest against Albanian 'terror' in the province, Fadil Hodza, the seventy-seven-year-old Albanian Communist Party patriarch in Kosovo – and a former federal vice-president of Yugoslavia – was expelled from the Party for saying in a public speech that statistics of rape in Kosovo would fall if local Serbian women were allowed to practise prostitution. 'Albanian women', he declared, 'will not do it, and Serbian women would like to do it. So why not let them?'

Later, he said that he had only been joking.

*

It is plain enough that this is a country struck amidships by glasnost and rising expectations, which is attempting to find its way simultaneously out of socialism and a prostrating third world economic crisis. In May 1988 seventy sets of Lenin's huge *Collected Works* were found at the Belgrade city dump; the scandal, such as it was, was short lived. At the same time a feeling of need for a strong leader has been growing, especially in Serbia.

None of this is really surprising; Yugoslavia's riches and energies have been squandered, and its people are confused and tired. The social and economic system – described by the Yugoslav Communist

Party as a system of 'socialist self-management, based on social ownership' – is collapsing. Yet to the democratic socialist in the West, this kind of thing is (or was) a favoured alternative model to centralized or Stalinist state socialism, also a failure. What a fiasco!

*

This is not Prague, yet he too has a plainclothesman hanging about in the doorway. Milovan Djilas, a Montenegrin, Yugoslavia's leading dissident and one of the great survivors of the Stalinist period, is now in his late seventies. Purged from the Yugoslav Party in 1954, he spent nine years in Tito's jails branded as a traitor, despite having been his comrade-in-arms during the Second World War, and after. His crime was that he had criticized Tito and attacked the 'new class' of privileged apparatchiks which had come to rule over eastern Europe.

Today, he has a passport and is free to travel. 'Everything is changing; not exactly as I would wish, but at least it is changing. The whole social structure of our Communism', he declares – calling it a 'crude system', and waving his hand dismissively in the direction of the dark window of his Belgrade flat – 'is disintegrating. The conception of single-party rule cannot be reconstituted.' He talks easily, his manner youthful. 'Marxism', Djilas goes on, 'had its roots in the Enlightenment, but its aims were mystical and ideal. It refused to recognize human nature, or to understand that private property cannot be eradicated. Nearly everyone here can see that the impact of Communism has been predominantly negative.'

What is Communism? I ask him. 'It is essentially a system of industrial feudalism, characterized by unusual forms of oppression which place a heavy weight on the whole of society,' he answered promptly. 'Here in Yugoslavia our particular form of it, the Titoist legacy, is disintegrating on a nationalist basis.' Isn't it hysteria? 'There is some hysteria over the question of Kosovo', Djilas replied, 'but the Serbians have real grievances and just reasons for their anger. Albanian chauvinism [he also called it oppression] is driving them from the region. And in what mass movement is there no hysteria?'

His gaze is steady, his bearing upright. 'This Serbian rebellion also has many positive features. It represents a struggle not only against the bureaucratic apparatus but against the disintegration itself. It is a reflection of the deep crisis in the system. But I do not think there will be serious disorders, except perhaps some incidents in Kosovo

when the Stalinist leaders there are removed from office. The autonomy of Kosovo may even be liquidated,' he added, suddenly relaps-
ing into purest Stalinist terminology, as if (despite everything) to the
manner born. 'But so far not a single car has been set on fire, and
not a single window has been broken.'

This is not how film director Stojanovic saw it. 'Though there are
aggressive groups in the Serbian movement, this is Communist
nationalism', said Djilas, 'and it is highly disciplined. The protests
of the Serbians are controlled ones.' Controlled by whom? 'The
Serbian leadership,' he answered. So these protests are not spontaneous? 'We can call them spontaneous. But it is partly organized
spontaneity,' he replied, with some amusement. Is this an old Communist's cynicism, or ironic good humour?

Then why all this talk of civil war? 'Exaggeration is inevitable in
our situation, though anything is possible in the Balkans. The Serbian
revolt is the revolt of an offended people, and Kosovo is patriarchal,
tribal and feudal [Stalinist categories again], with a very high birth-
rate.' But isn't some of this just racism? 'Yes,' he replied, without
flinching. 'But it is mainly one chauvinism pitted against another.
Down there in Kosovo there are also young intellectuals who think
they are the purists of world Communism. They are under the
influence of Albania,' he said with distaste, 'the ideology of Enver
Hoxha.' Djilas described this ideology as 'Stalinist nationalism,
hostile to Yugoslavia'; indeed, Radio Tirana regularly denounces
Milosevic, while there are alleged to be several clandestine extremist
organizations in Kosovo following 'the line' from Albania.

On Djilas's bookshelves, which fill the room from floor to ceiling,
are the Soviet dissident Grigorenko's memoirs, Solzhenitsyn, and the
journal *Survey*; as well as Mary McCarthy, and Ross Terrill on China.
And what of Milosevic's allegedly proto-fascist ambition? I ask him.
What do you think of the slogan 'Slobo-Duce'? 'It is too early to call
the Serbian leadership fascist,' he replied. (Djilas avoided using
Milosevic's actual name throughout our conversation.) 'There is no
separate Serbian paramilitary organization, for example. The new
Serbian leadership, whose economic conceptions are liberal, is trying
to use Serbian anger about Kosovo to reinforce its position in Yugoslavia.'

In which case Milosevic is an opportunist? 'It is always so in
politics,' he replied coolly. But under a reformed Constitution, could
not Milosevic become leader of Yugoslavia in the future? 'Serbian

rule over the rest of Yugoslavia is out of the question,' Djilas said flatly. 'The real issue is different. We are in a transitional period towards a market economy, with private economic activity, changes in property relations, and increasing foreign investment. Every Communist country is in this situation, except North Korea, Romania and Albania. But our federal institutions are too weak to manage this transformation. So there is pressure for centralization, which is creating these tensions. Everything is in upheaval.'

But how do you bring about greater centralization and greater democracy together? 'They are not contradictory,' he answered. 'In the end, but not easily, a democratic system will come to Yugoslavia, and not only to Yugoslavia.' How can you be so sure? 'Because we are going towards the market economy and democracy. Multiple parties and so on must be part of it.' Isn't this a transition from socialism to capitalism, a capitalist restoration? 'What is this "capitalism" you speak of?' Djilas responded in some agitation. 'Can we compare today's capitalism with capitalism in the days of Marx and Lenin?' I should think so, yes. Why not? 'You mean', said Djilas, 'that the system which you call "capitalist", with its huge organic historic development since the thirteenth century is not continuously changing?' Yes, I said, it is changing, but only within certain limits.

Djilas sighed. 'Capitalism is not a very merciful system, I agree.' (I had said nothing, one way or the other, about mercy.) 'But I am an anti-Communist, not an anti-socialist.' What is a socialist? I asked. 'To be a socialist, means to be social,' he answered. (Earlier in our conversation he had also described himself, in passing, as a liberal.) 'I am also one of the most defamed men in history,' he said quietly. 'Because I have lived so long, I have been slandered for thirty-four years in succession. But now the cult of Tito is weakening, and they no longer attack me in the old fashion. I am convinced that I shall be morally and intellectually rehabilitated.' He paused. 'Even that has some importance.'

When I left, he stood at his door, a spry figure, waving briefly from the landing. Outside, the plainclothesman emerged from the shadows, and asked me for the time in good English. Ten minutes later I returned, to see him looking up at Djilas's lit window.

*

Djilas had said that the cult of Tito was weakening. Doubtless it is. But the little ditty 'Comrade Tito, We Pledge To You That We

Will Not Swerve From Your Path' is still being sung in party circles. Nine months ago, a café singer was jailed for refusing to sing it.

*

At a wayside petrol-station near Nis, deep into Serbia on the main north-south highway, a battered white Volkswagen camper is parked in the shade. It has German licence plates. Beside it, two dark men are kneeling on prayer-mats, lips moving silently and bowing towards Mecca.

And here, just across the border from Serbia proper into the autonomous province of Kosovo, is a roofless Serbian Orthodox church in open country, its cemetery still in use, the building abandoned. In its long-ruined nave, the grass grows among the tumble of masonry and fallen roof-timbers. At the still-tended graves are wreaths of plastic flowers, with plates of sweets, mouldering apples, and even a small jar filled with coal, left for the departed. Of a resurrection – for Serb and Albanian alike – I can see no prospect; not amid such ruins.

*

These are ancestral lands beneath the village minaret; the men in white close-fitting caps, their women in baggy trousers tapered to the ankle, stooping in the fields together. Young children tend the cattle. A little over seventy-five years ago, Kosovo, with its 290-mile border with Albania, was part of the Ottoman Empire; today the old ploughman struggles with his wooden plough and autumn seed is cast, to an old rhythm. Stand by the roadside, and you hear the cawing of crows and the creak of the wooden carts passing. Kosovo, waiting for the Serbian axe to fall – or so it believes – could be the Punjab.

Pristina, the nervous provincial capital, with its mosques, its 30 per cent unemployed, its dog-browsed mounds of refuse, squatting men and smell of woodsmoke, is full of western newsmen – some with green Pentel pens and filofaxes – waiting in hope for the fighting to begin between Serb and Albanian. It was in fields two miles from Pristina that the Ottoman invaders defeated the Serbs six hundred years ago, and in Pristina that there were bloody riots during the 1981 insurrection, when Kosovo Albanians demanded in vain to have full status as a constituent republic of Yugoslavia, and to be free of Serbian tutelage.

It is the dense life of the oriental market that is in full non-socialist, and non-Slavic, swing here; the Muslim artisans in their warrens cobbling, working their filigrees, and bent over their stitching. The paparazzi pass by, with their zoom lenses, looking for trouble; the sound, however, is that of meat sizzling on charcoal and of slow, bristling brooms on the muddy, cracked pavements.

*

Outside, there is the dusk haze, bluish-pink, of a dusty Indian city at nightfall. He calls himself 'Jim' for safety. A scared Albanian Muslim who speaks passable English, he is in his mid-thirties and earns about £28 a week in a responsible service job in Pristina. ('What do you do, steal or starve?' he asked me.) He carries a gun when his work takes him to a Serbian village.

'They think', he said, 'that because they have 8 million people in Yugoslavia they can do anything [to us]. Before, it didn't matter to me if a man was Serbian or Albanian, Muslim or Christian. What is the difference? Now, at the bus the Serbs must come before, the Albanians second. In the past, such things did not matter. It is a great tragedy for everybody. We are the majority, eight to one, but they do not speak our language. They want us to be second. But Albanians support each other. We are very close to our families, to our friends, to our relations. Why not?' Would you marry a Serbian girl? 'Definitely not', he said recoiling, 'better an Albanian wolf than a Serbian lamb,' he added. (There is not much fun in this, though he began laughing.)

In the street, I cannot myself distinguish a Serb from an Albanian; some Albanians are spruce and fair, some Serbians are swarthy and unshaven. How can you tell a Serb? I asked him. 'From the face, the hair, the clothes', he answered, 'and', pausing to find the word, 'behaviour.' He was silent for a few moments. 'They want to destroy us.' Why should that be? I asked. He shrugged his shoulders, as if it were obvious. 'Only old people go to the mosque, I never. But we are Muslims. That is the first reason. Also, we work hard. We are hardworking,' he repeated. 'Our money comes from work. They [the Serbians] are mostly in shops, offices, teachers. We are good farmers. We have some good businesses also. They want to take them. That is the second reason.' And thus it is that 'market forces' provoke and exacerbate 'ethnic tensions'.

'Third, we build houses. We need houses, because we have fifteen children, every nine months like a factory. My father six, my uncle eight. This also they do not like. This is the third reason.' And land prices in Kosovo are now said to have risen to five times the average for the rest of Yugoslavia. 'But this is our land', he declared fiercely, 'and we are ready to fight, we are ready for whatever happens.'

Don't they accuse you of wanting to separate from Yugoslavia? 'I have never been to Albania in my life,' he answered heatedly. 'Educated people do not like what they know about it. Ninety per cent of us are not interested to join with them.' Why not? 'Here we are democratic enough. Why should we? Are they free? Can anyone get out of that country?' And in Albania, Islam has been officially abolished.

Are things getting worse here? I ask him. 'Now the Serbs shout at us in the street, in the market, if we brush them, "You touched me! Why did you touch me?!".' He looks to me for a response, sitting four-square and impassive at the table.

★

In Pristina's Grand Hotel, I overhear a London journalist phoning in a report to his foreign desk for next morning's paper. Reading loudly from his notebook, he is talking of 'menacing crowds of Albanians and Serbians gathering on the street corners of Pristina'. There is no sign of this whatever.

At the hotel doorway there are small ragged children, carrying smaller siblings, begging; and young shoeshine boys rapping the backs of their brushes on their wooden foot-stands.

★

The room is drinking sweet Turkish coffee; at the doorstep stand a line of dusty shoes and slippers. This is mud-walled Gadimlje in the dry Zegorac hills, 80 miles from the border with Albania, and the house of one of the village's farmer patriarchs, Musli Tasholli. 'There are no Serbians in Gadimlje,' said one of his sons, lying on a mattress covered with fleeces and cushions; we are in the *oda*, a room for meeting guests, from which, traditionally, women and children under eighteen were excluded.

They tell the family history in Homeric fashion, to set Serbian hearts quaking. 'One hundred and twenty years ago, we started here from two brothers. When there were forty-two people in one household, so they divided. Today, eighty houses' – half the houses in the village – 'are of our clan brothers'; I learn later that 'some' of them have two, or even three, wives each. There is some money here, too, from labouring employment in Germany, Switzerland, France and Belgium; one third of all adult male Albanians in Kosovo province are working abroad in western Europe. There are also new brick houses a-building in the dry stubble; and plenty of guns around, most likely.

Tasholli, a man of sixty-four, has five hectares and seven married children; he also has a cataract in one eye, a bristling moustache, and teeth part-consumed by caries. 'The Serbs', he declares, 'used us as shepherds, used us for digging. President Tito gave a chance to everybody. But they were happy to keep us in such a position. They did not want us to be educated.' The room murmurs in approval, as more family-members – three generations of women, one carrying a swaddled baby – emerge from an inner room and take their places; a granddaughter can even speak a few words of English. 'But now we are more educated, we are more civilized, we are not closed now, we are open to everybody.' He has a cigarette-holder, a watch-chain, black striped trousers, and a hand-stitched brown waistcoat. He smiles affably, his eyes closing.

He leans closer to me, the room attentive. 'We are weak in our hearts. We are not against anybody, or against any other nation. Whatever comes is from God, to Serbian or Albanian. But they are threatening us, they want to take everything from us.' 'It is a dirty game,' one of his sons added in an undertone. 'They say,' Tasholli continued, '"Put away your flag, this is not Albania."' (The provincial flag of Kosovo bears the double-headed eagle of Albania.) 'In the market, wherever you go, since last year, you must be careful about everything, how you speak to them. They are making out they are afraid of us.

'But if people are not united, the things which are happening will happen. There are weak ones among us. These troubles have brought our people closer. In the past, Albanians killed each other. Today, we are not against any other nation,' he repeated. 'But now we are all up to our heads, and ready to do it.' Do what? 'Whatever is necessary. We wait and see,' he replied, smiling again.

Outside, in the autumn sunshine, he poses for the camera in his white cap, hands stiff to his sides and shy of his cataract. On the wall, the heavy fragrant roses are deep red, their heads hanging.

6

Hungary, January 1989: hara-kiri

'The Hungarian Communist Party is decomposing,' says Gaspar Tamas, smoking a cigar at his table in Budapest's *Jugendstil* Cafe New York – the pre-war name recently restored. Even the red star, so rumour has it, is to be dropped from the national blazon, in favour of the apostolic crown of the old Hungarian Kingdoms.

This is my second meeting with Tamas, the forty-year-old Budapest University philosopher who was sacked in 1982 for 'oppositional activity'. Twenty months ago he was saying that 'any madness could happen', that the reformers were 'not securing reforms of substance', that the situation was 'incoherent'. Now an honorary fellow of St Antony's College, Oxford, he is also a member of the steering committee of the Free Democratic Alliance, one of the embryonic political parties expecting to take part in Hungary's general election in 1990. During the last year he has divided his time between leading protests in Budapest – dressed in a camel coat, black gloves and bow-tie – and writing in his London flat, sometimes for the *Spectator*.

'People in Budapest don't yet trust what is happening. They say, "It's all talk", or "They're all bastards".' But change there is: diplomatic relations are soon to be restored with South Korea, and even the Boy Scouts are back in business. At the next table two middle-aged men are discussing how to fiddle Hungary's new tax system.

'Hungary is a great scoop,' the former sceptic Tamas continues, posing for a photograph against a convoluted column. 'It is chaotic, the country is not being governed, and we need to hurry. But a profound transformation is going on which the West is underestimating. They simply don't realize how important these events are for Europe. The whole position', he calls out, changing position for the camera, 'is moving very quickly. The Germans are coming back to their old sphere of influence. They want our market and cheap labour, but here they are the great power.'

He returns to his table, walking in the ghostly steps of the literati who once frequented this place, before Stalinism turned it into a vegetable warehouse.

'Orwell's *1984* is coming out in a few weeks. *Animal Farm* has already been published. An interview with Djilas has just been printed. And the official press is pinching everything, taking our *samizdat* translations without paying us a penny. Even Koestler's *Darkness at Noon* has been officially published. It has gone so far that they are trying to make Koestler into one of the new saints of the regime. He has become the good leftist, who not only saw through Stalin, but was of Hungarian extraction into the bargain. These are desperate means to prevent the demise of the system.'

In the *Spectator* Tamas has written on theological questions, recommended High Toryism to eastern Europe, and last June tried to lead a march through Budapest demanding the rehabilitation of the victims of the 1956 Soviet invasion.

'Most of my friends in the Free Democratic Alliance are to the left of me,' he adds, elegant amid the mirrors and gilding of this restored *fin de siècle* setting. 'But in Budapest we are all regarded as westernizers.' Isn't it, I asked him, a new kind of élitism? 'The oldest in Hungary,' he answered. For years, Tamas – the son of Communists – has been regarded as the archetypal bourgeois intellectual. Now he is stirring back to life, cigar in hand, in a post-Communist limbo.

*

'They will rehabilitate Imre Nagy soon,' Tamas had said, referring to the hero of the 1956 revolution, executed in 1958. 'But I don't want them to do it.' Why not? 'Because it is our cause. They are going to steal even that from us.'

*

The press attaché at the Hungarian Embassy in London had been unwilling, or unable, to shed any light on the meaning of events in his own country. At ease in the new world of bonhomie created by glasnost, and behaving in a self-consciously 'normal' fashion – like the Soviet Union's new breed of sophisticated spokesmen – he had shrugged away my question as if the whole thing was beyond him.

'Who knows where we are going?' he said, relaxed and almost lolling in a gilt embassy armchair. There are some on the left here, I said, who really regard all this as a counter-revolution. 'We are not trying to please the western left. We are concerned for our people.' The left is getting rather confused by it. 'That is not our problem,' he commented.

But if people like you don't know what is going on, then I shall have to ask a few dissidents, I chaffed him. 'What dissidents? There are no more dissidents,' he countered swiftly. Does that mean you are 'all reformers now'? I asked. His answer was good-humoured laughter; an opaque response, dating from the time before Gorbachev had set his cat among the pigeons.

*

At the slick, white-carpeted offices in Mayakovsky Street of the new weekly tabloid *Reform* – all tits, bums, jokes and political scandal, and owned by a new joint stock company in which the Hungarian Communist Party (the HSWP) has a '15 per cent' holding – the Budapest upheaval becomes stranger.

The start-up deal between the Hungarian Credit Bank and the Party was fixed, says *Reform*'s editor Peter Töke, by the central committee secretary and ideological strongman of the regime, Janos Berecz. With a circulation of 250,000 after only a handful of issues, the swinging reformism of the 'first independent paper in Hungary', as it calls itself, was described by Gaspar Tamas as a 'disgusting secret police stunt', and 'like *Sunday Sport*, with politics added'.

Rotund and dishevelled, Töke (pronounced 'Turker') sits beneath the arc lights of a visiting West German TV crew, surrounded by black MFI-style furniture, mini-skirted dolly birds, mirrors and red telephones. 'We want to catch the eye with 40 per cent rumours, sex and sport, 30 per cent pluralism and reformism, and 30 per cent advertizing', he says, grey-faced. 'We want to compete with television.'

The place looks like a unisex hairdresser's in the Fulham Road. 'This was a fashion boutique before we took over, and we got their furniture,' explains Töke, who has a journalistic staff of twenty-five, four of them (but not him) Party members, one of whom joined *Reform* from the Party's moribund daily paper *Nepszabadsag*, whose circulation is plunging. Around him, as he talks, there is a crush of denim, TV cameras, red fingernails clawing at sheaves of papers, and black leather; the blow-ups on the cabin partitions are of sultry women in silk underwear.

Isn't this style unusual in a socialist country? I ask in the bedlam. What's it all about? 'We are a capitalist enterprise', Töke answers, 'with shareholders: some banks, the Rubik [cube] Foundation, the Party. They want a profit. We are the first independent paper in Hungary, a bit similar to the *Independent*.' The West German Springer Group, which is planning to set up its own newspaper printing-plant in Budapest, is showing an interest; Springer publications fill *Reform*'s street-front display windows.

Töke broke off for a brief TV interview, leaving me with his art director – who was trained at Springer – and a couple of luridly-illustrated back numbers; they included articles on multi-party democracy, women's mud-wrestling, Romanian agricultural policy and the Hungarian-Italian hard-porn star, Cicciolina. ('*Kulissza Tit-kok*', ran an alarming headline.) 'Pretty sexist,' I said to the art director. 'You must be very puritan,' he answered.

Töke came back, sweating profusely. They say in Budapest, I tell him, that this is some kind of trick by the regime, which has been scared into trying to co-opt and confuse the reform movement. 'The Party doesn't need such tricks,' Töke replied testily. 'Nobody tells me what to publish. They have their own papers.' That is not an answer. 'Then people can say, if they like, that we are the secret weapon of the Party, and perhaps we are. But I am being physically threatened, I am on a Stalinist liquidation list, and we are getting very dirty fascist letters.' (I was later shown a scrawled note received at the paper after it had carried a travel article on Israel: 'Do you want tattooed numbers on your arms again, like the last time?')

In this Hungarian vortex whirls an old violence; there are many political scores to settle, and new ones being added daily. Töke has lately had threats for publishing – amid the splayed thighs and technicolor buttocks – interviews with leading opposition figures. His next issue features Karoly Ravasz, leader of the pre-war Smallholders' Party. Would you call yourself an opposition paper? 'Opposition to what?' asked Töke sharply. To the Hungarian socialist system, for instance. 'No, it is not an opposition paper.' So this is a capitalist enterprise, which supports socialism? Here, quite justifiably, the hard-pressed editor of *Reform* became impatient. 'This is a joint stock company. Money doesn't know if it is socialist or capitalist. Our first aim is to tell the truth, and make a profit.'

Deeper into this Party-licensed sleaze it was not possible to go: of Marxism stripped to the buff, and Leninism in frilly knickers.

*

Since the fall of Kadar in May 1988, after thirty-two years in power, there has been a cascade of reforms both enacted and promised, non-persons have been rehabilitated, and taboos have been lifted. Karoly Grosz, Kadar's successor as Party general secretary – whom Gaspar Tamas described to me as a 'neo-Stalinist' twenty months ago – has called it 'breaking through ideological barriers' and 'trying to meet the requirements of western markets'.

Now, the Hungarians have got VAT and an embryo stock exchange, Big Macs, Mormons, foreign TV commercials, and faction-struggles between conservatives and progressives as fierce as the wars of the Spanish succession. In a single day I have passed puce-haired punks in Lenin Boulevard, read an official description of Stalin as 'a dictator whose victims numbered millions' and seen a newspaper report of thousands of members – 60,000 last year – leaving the Party. Eight weeks ago, fifteen Hungarian skinheads were jailed for an attack on ten Cuban 'guest-workers' at a Budapest tram-stop.

The Party daily *Nepszabadsag*, which has called for a 'new ideology' in Hungary, has even begun to blame the last forty years on 'leftists' who in 1945 'stood up with the demand for the dictatorship of the proletariat'. And, according to a recent announcement, even a Disneyland-style 'Fanni-Park' is threatened in Budapest; this is either a 'Funny Park', or the *coup de grâce* for socialist feminist culture.

*

Yet more bleak economic statistics, and appeals for belt-tightening, have come in today. A resumé of them makes grim reading, on a cold January morning, in the office of the chairman of Budapest's new Stock Exchange Council. Real wages have fallen to 1973 levels; basic consumer prices – for transport, meat, milk, medicines – have leapt yet again, in some cases by as much as 90 per cent, as 'market pricing' of goods and services takes over from state subvention; average pay in 1988, net of new income tax and pension deductions, was a miserly 6,700 forints (about £75) a month; and there is the highest per capita hard currency debt in eastern Europe.

In addition, about 20 per cent of Hungary's 10 million population live below the official subsistence level; food consumption is expected to fall by 10 to 15 per cent in the first six months of this year; and unemployment, especially in Hungary's old heavy industries, is gradually rising, as subsidies paid to loss-making State enterprises tumble. 'We will not guarantee jobs, unless workers work efficiently. We want profitable work,' Karoly Grosz declared on the day of his elevation as Party general secretary.

From 1 January 1989, the new Company Law came into operation, permitting Hungarian private entrepreneurs to employ a workforce of up to 500, and allowing western capital to set up wholly owned firms without Hungarian participation. The law, which in effect legitimizes the 'private ownership of the means of production', passed unanimously – without a single abstention – through a Parliament of 367 members, 250 of them members of the HSWP.

'Market forces', Grosz announced in Japan the other day, 'will now be allowed to apply in Hungary with few restrictions.' 'No one form of ownership', the prime minister Miklos Nemeth has said, 'should have advantage over another.' Some call this the restructuring of the socialist economy; the restoration of capitalism, say others.

Zsigmond Jarai, the Budapest Stock Exchange chairman, walking soundlessly across the Budapest Bank's pile carpet, is a bland, smiling fellow. 'The government', Jarai says, 'is pushing us to have a real stock exchange linked to the international market. Under the new Company Law, private investors can now buy shares in new issues. But in practice there are only ten joint stock companies on the market, mostly financial institutions. We meet once a week, and for the rest do business by telephone.

'Total trading in 1988 amounted to 20 billion Hungarian forints [$400 million]. Our problem is that we have no experience in these matters. I have already made serious mistakes with the domestic bond market.' (It nearly collapsed in November 1987 in a wave of panic selling, investors withdrawing their savings and transferring them to gold and consumer durables.) 'So far only one company has made a new share issue which the public can purchase.' This is very small capitalist beer, as the socialist economy staggers.

Nevertheless, real privatization is in the air. 'We need a very substantial reduction of the State sector,' Jarai continues. 'The government is trying to force, or to press, some State-owned compan-ies to reorganize themselves as joint stock companies.' What is preventing it? 'The middle-level bureaucracy is working against this process by creating complications. This is the key problem,' says

Jarai. You mean the bureaucracy is resisting the restoration of capitalism? 'I am personally not interested in the word capitalism,' Jarai answers smoothly, immaculate in his managerial suit, shoes gleaming. 'I am interested only in the process of creating a capital market.'

Ah, I see. So what is going on, Comrade Jarai? Do you want to see the privatization of the whole economy? 'That is not the solution. Very few people want a 100 per cent capitalist system,' as he puts it. 'We have to try to create a third sector, neither State nor private, in which ownership rights belong to pension funds, investment trusts, insurance companies and so on. The social security fund could be a large investor in such a market.' (He called it, variously, 'quasi-private', a 'dangerous way' and 'very complicated'.)

'The government must also create a good environment for foreign investors. However, they will not invest unless they can also sell on a Hungarian share market.' But how long is all this going to take? 'It will take five to ten years. First we need a new legal system, stability in the economy, a reduction of bureaucracy, an information law, a securities law, and a convertible currency.' This is a tall order, but Jarai was still smiling blandly.

'At the moment we are in a dangerous and complex situation of transition. Most people in the street believe the reforms will not work, or that the reformers are not serious. I do not blame them. I also think we could fail. To establish a political democracy and a new economic system at the same time is very difficult.'

Can it be done at all? 'It may need a dictatorship of democracy,' he answered, smiling still. Whatever this means, it is not the dictatorship of the proletariat.

*

Freezing under deep snow, the huge, juddering steelworks at Ozd – the Ozdi Kohaszati Üzemek – in the Borsov region of rural northern Hungary, close to the Czech border, is a working-class world away from Jarai's stock exchange, and his thick pile carpet. Here, last year, 3,000 workers (with more to come) got their cards, as economic reform struck its first blows at the Soviet-built megaliths of the Stalin era; but there is no alternative work in the area.

This is a smoking, black Leviathan, beached, rusting and roaring with flame; the weary helmeted workers at its guard-rails, or climbing about its frozen iron rigging, look like the crew of a broken-backed colossus of the steam age, caught in pack-ice.

Without its own ore, without its own coal, Hungary is nevertheless lumbered with Ozd's redundant and uneconomic steel-making capacity, fathered upon it in the 1950s; the plant is now merely a sink of subsidy, making poor quality rolled steel with poor quality ore imported from the Soviet Union. But steel, throughout the socialist world, was always more a matter of ideology than of rational manufacture: a species of heavy-industrial machismo.

Underfoot, the snowy ground vibrates with it.

*

Laszlo Steiner employs 140 other Hungarians in his medical electronics firm; it produces cardiac intensive-care equipment and computer-controlled dialysis machines. It is a private joint-venture company, with 30 per cent of its capital from West Germany – yet again – and Canada, and he is its managing director, with a 2 per cent holding. 'Really good employees are offered shares', and bonuses depend on profits. His annual turnover is around £5 million. 'I am a self-made man,' he says in his discreet modern office.

Is this capitalism, and is capitalism developing in Hungary? I ask him. 'It is,' he answers, without batting an eyelid. 'Janos Berecz [the Party's ideology chief] would say, "No." After all, he must say, "No", but I am in a different position. I can say, "Yes, why not?" Didn't your social regulation in the West come mostly from socialist ideas? So why shouldn't we learn something from you about capitalism and markets?' he asks in a forthright, confident manner.

He was born in 1947; his father, manager between the wars of the Hungarian subsidiary of General Motors was, in Steiner's words, 'put into the shadows in the Rakosi period, because of his American connection', and died in 1958. Steiner, a man with a small, grey-flecked black moustache, looks brisk and bristling in his shirtsleeves. What about the unions? 'Here there are no trade unions. In any case, the trade unions have practically no real supporters now. It is not for us a political question: we concentrate on our jobs and our profits. There is no reason for trade unions in this company.' Why not? 'Because we offer stable work and pay better than other places. To our employees, it seems like a family enterprise.' (Later, he admitted using wage-cuts, of up to 40 per cent in one case, as sanctions for slack individual performance; or, as he put it, 'if we are dissatisfied, we decrease wages.')

You sound like a ruthless paternalist of the pre-war days, I say to him. 'I don't deny it,' Steiner answers coolly, doodling on a piece of graph paper. 'After forty years of socialism, we all know that there is no future in it. We have come to a few metres from the end of a cul-de-sac with our economy, and we recognize it. We have to go back to the entrance.' Where is that? 'Maybe even back to the 1930s. Instead of paying salaries for work without value, it is time to start paying a little unemployment benefit,' he adds ruthlessly. 'It could be very uncomfortable for everybody. But what is the alternative? There is no other route for us.

'For forty years we have lived in a tin can which has suddenly been opened,' Steiner continues. 'The bureaucracy has brought us nearly to ruin. They tried to control things which were uncontrollable, while we looked for holes in the rules and tried to find the easy way out of every problem. At school and university I learned the theory of socialism; what I am telling you is socialism-in-practice.'

But what about the decadence of capitalism? 'I have been through Amsterdam's red light area, and it was not interesting to me,' he says briefly, doodling still. That is not the point, I say. 'All right, for you it may be a wider social question. But I see it as a question of personal culture. If the family is strong, then this "decadence"' – Steiner treats the term with distaste, concentrating on his drawing – 'can be defeated.' That is still not the whole point. 'For us, in our conditions', he explodes, pushing aside his doodle with sudden irritation, 'how can we think about such matters?!'

Yes, but aren't you increasingly going to run into our kinds of social problems? 'It will be a very difficult operation,' Steiner says, still hot under the collar. 'But if we open our doors to the West, Hungary could become a very nice place in Europe. Here we could make for you a special custom-designed non-mass production system. In the Far East labour is very cheap but it is very far away. The brain of our industrial workers is cheap, better than the Oriental [or "more tricky", as Steiner also puts it] and much closer to western Europe.' You mean you want Hungary to offer cheap labour for western exploitation? 'Yes,' he answers bluntly. 'It would be better than the present situation,' he adds without expression.

An unemployed steelworker in Ozd wouldn't think much of what you are saying. 'Yes', Steiner says, looking me in the eye, 'at first he would be angry. But in a year or two the results would begin to convince him. In the past these people have heard only orders and slogans. If you explain to him carefully, with kind words, why he should do something,' he said earnestly, 'then the worker from Ozd would understand.' (I am beginning to withdraw from the conversation, and Steiner is quickly aware of it.) 'Mine are the special opinions of a rather uneducated person', he says apologetically; then adds, 'but there are a lot of similar-minded people.'

He starts to doodle again in the silence. 'Socialism created great cultural and social problems. Our people have not been taught the values of work. They have not been taught, under this socialism of ours, even the values of other human beings.' So where is 'socialist man'? 'There is no socialist man,' Steiner answered, shaking his head over his own reply. 'There is only a man. People are people,' he added, rounding off his drawing on the graph-paper.

*

'For the West to solve the Hungarian economic problem would be peanuts,' Steiner had said. 'If they decided to do something, a Marshall Plan, they could do it. Hungary is not India, Hungary is like Austria, with the same customs and habits. It is a market of 10 million Europeans. It is not Libya, it is not Africa, it is Europe.' Who thinks Hungary is Africa or India? 'We are Europeans,' Steiner repeated, ignoring the question.

*

'Do you know who Baden-Powell was?' he asks me.

On the table before us is a jumbled assortment of Boy Scout manuals and memorabilia. Outside, snow threatens. 'My scout name', says the middle-aged electrical engineer Jozsef Ormay, 'is Toci [pronounced "Toshi"].' His friend, who wears a green scout badge in his lapel, is Imre Sinkovits, a well known Hungarian National Theatre player. Now in his early sixties, Boy Scout Sinkovits is also a member of the steering committee of the Hungarian Democratic Forum, which describes itself as an 'independent spiritual-political movement'. Nationalist in its sympathies, and allegedly inhospitable to dissident Jewish intellectuals, it is at present the biggest of the alternative political associations, with '3,000 branches' already established across Hungary – a 'non-ideological' Christian Democratic Party in embryo.

Sinkovits and Ormay turn the pages of a 1933 Hungarian Scout Jamboree album, proudly showing me a picture of Baden-Powell standing alongside Hungary's right-wing regent of the time, the autocratic (or worse) Admiral Horthy. Abolished in 1948 as 'national chauvinists with imperialist-capitalist connections', the Hungarian Boy Scout movement, which in the 1930s had several hundred thousand members, has also been rehabilitated. About a dozen small groups are now legally in existence – in Pecs and Szentendre, for example – some of them meeting on Catholic church premises; old bonds are being re-established.

'It represented happiness, the intense romanticism of late childhood, and a relationship with nature. It was all torn away,' declares Sinkovits, who was denounced in Stalinist times as a 'clerical reactionary, attracted to right-wing youth movements'. The room is very cold. 'In Budapest we kept safe in three wooden boxes the relics from those times, our flags, our books and ties, our Boy Scout belts and badges. For forty years they remained hidden in deep caves in the Buda hills.

'Every New Year', he continues, his voice resonant, 'a small group of our brotherhood met in deserted places without our uniforms. We went to greet the forests, asking the bare trees for a return of Nature's pleasures, in order to preserve the spirit of the Boy Scout movement.'

Ormay, a small grey man jailed in 1956, sits silent and trusting beside his troop leader. The room seems colder than ever; the two elderly boy scouts' noses are red with it. 'For forty years we have been waiting for this moment. To us, the Boy Scout movement gave non-political ideals, it gave the truest fraternity.' In what way 'truest'? 'Did Stalin know about fraternity?' Sinkovits asks angrily. 'Our fraternity was not forced upon us. We were moral, the Communist Young Pioneers were atheists. We were taught to be humanists, while the Communists killed even their own comrades. We were declared an illegal organization, and they called us fascists. There were Boy Scouts in working-class areas, but they accused us of being an "élitist movement of the intelligentsia".'

Then what were you? 'We were an irritation. We were voluntary, we were independent, we were healthy, we had love for our homeland. We were patriots, so they called us "national chauvinists". And because scouting is English in origin, they accused us [laughing] of "imperialist connections". They wanted to create a Communist pioneer movement, so many Scouts were banished and sent to prison. We supported their wives, cleaned their apartments and gave presents to their children.'

Why are they allowing you back? I ask them. 'I don't mean to be reactionary against them', says the actor, striking his chest, 'but they are in trouble. The regime is very weak and they are seeking support from everybody. It is not so easy for Communists to create a democratic system in order to stay in power [laughter]. They have problems with young people, and the Communist youth movements are failing.' Yes, but how many of the Hungarian younger generation are going to join the Boy Scouts?

'Look', says Sinkovits, his voice dropping, 'there are many people in high places who were once in the Hungarian Boy Scout movement. They too remember how things were in the old times.' Boy Scouts in the politburo? I ask in jest. There is frosty laughter in unison; two pairs of eyes look at me intently. 'Karoly Grosz was himself in the Boy Scouts [more laughter]. I have seen his membership card', says Sinkovits, grinning like a schoolboy, 'and a photograph of him pulling a boy scout cart.'

What was in it? 'Tents,' they answer together, laughing.

Cold fingers pluck at the faded albums. Outside, a light snow has begun falling. 'After forty years, romanticism is coming back,' Sinkovits added.

★

Dr Karoly Ravasz is a slight, white-haired figure. His party, the Smallholders' Party – which was the strongest democratic opposition party in the pre-war Hungarian Parliament, and won 57 per cent of the popular vote in the last free Hungarian elections of 1945 – is one of the opposition groups waiting in the political wings; it seems set to make a comeback, though on what scale it is hard to judge.

With the aid of unpaid volunteers, it has re-established '34' branches in various parts of the country, with some 3,000 members. 'But we never dissolved ourselves,' says Ravasz; 'we held illegal meetings of the Party leadership, mainly former members of Parliament, once a year from 1960.' The Smallholders stand for the small farmer, the small entrepreneur and the self-employed artisan; for free enterprise and competition; for modest welfarism and a 'solidarity with the weak, so that they do not fall by the wayside'; above all, for a 'smooth transition to parliamentary democracy'.

The cultivated Ravasz, educated in Pecs and Vienna, is the Party's general secretary. A lawyer, economist and former diplomat now in his seventies he was jailed in 1944 for his part in the Resistance. Today, he thinks that a coup within the Party or in the country, against the reforms, is still possible. 'Things have not yet reached the point of no return. There is a death-list. There are forces in place in the police, the army and the middle ranks of the Ministry of the Interior. They could end everything in one hour.'

These are also the anxieties of an elderly man, who, after spending years in exile (in Austria, Britain and Australia), fears that his dream of a democratic restoration could yet turn into a new totalitarian nightmare. Ravasz left his country in the last days of 1948, crossing the border into Austria at night, after having been recalled in May of that year from the Hungarian legation in Prague where he was serving. He was dismissed from the diplomatic service for 'political unreliability'. Given the option of joining the Party he had declined, rejecting both its ideology and its economics.

'I told them during their investigations that it was not possible to plan an economy centrally, and that I could not accept the Marxist theory of value.' Why not? 'It is a primitive fallacy. No economy based on it could work, and if the economy does not work, any party with a monopoly of power is bound to look for scapegoats for the failure, and oppress them. I also told them I did not want a return to the pre-war semi-feudal society under new Communist management. I left Hungary with the determination that I was not an emigrant, that I would return if there was useful work to be done.'

Why did you not stay? 'Because I would have had to suffer things which I preferred not to suffer. Most of my friends were either interned or given jail sentences on trumped-up charges. I also knew that if I stayed I would have to do things against my conscience.' What, for example? 'Be an informer, be obliged to bear false witness, take part within the Foreign Ministry in carrying through policies absolutely against our national interest. But I made one error of judgment. I did not think all this would last forty years; I thought it would end sooner. For the rest, I could say "I told you so". But I have very mixed feelings seeing the condition of my country. And nobody likes a wise guy who says "I knew it would happen".'

You mean that, apart from the length of time the system has survived, nothing surprises you about what is happening? He raises a bony index finger. 'One thing only. That a man like Gorbachev was able to hide his views until he came to power,' he answers. (Now there's a thought for you.)

'But all these changes are a terrible headache, very explosive stuff,' he continues anxiously. 'They are making people in Hungary realize that, in addition to the economic hardship, for forty years their lives have been wasted.' He leans forward, an old man reanimated. 'Imagine, you have a Communist Party using its monopoly power to restore capitalism. To say, "This is impossible!" is an intellectual's response. But ordinary people cannot understand it either. It is not that they don't want the private ownership of the means of production. They simply don't trust the Party which led them into this in the first place. They ask, "Are they tricking us?" But the ideology and the economic system are sinking together. So the Party leaders are trying to find a way out of it, while retaining their personal positions. On a practical level of realpolitik, it is perfectly comprehensible. The problem for them is that because of the democratic pressures, they are at the same time having to get themselves into a shape where they can face elections.'

He laughs drily at Communist discomfiture. 'The only thing they could do is to get rid of their neo-Stalinists and turn themselves into a social democratic party.' But don't you think they have already done a great deal? 'If they are really doing what they seem to be doing, it will be the end for us of the post-war era. We will be able to say an epochal change is occurring.'

Ravasz leaned back in his chair. 'At least, we hope so,' he said, as Hungarian doubt returned.

*

I had asked Ravasz, who described himself as 'in many respects a classical liberal', what he thought about *Reform* magazine. 'It is not to my taste, and it is not right to call it *Reform*, but if people want it, it is legitimate to have such a paper,' he had answered. 'It is the price of a pluralist society, and we have to pay it if we don't want anyone to tell us what we should read or see. This is also a Catholic country, so such things seem like forbidden fruit, as in Spain after Franco. *Reform*'s sexual freedom, or licence, is being thrown at the people. If the Party cannot give them bread', he added bitingly, 'at least it can give them a circus.'

*

An unexceptional and silent market town, set in an uneventful landscape, 70 miles from Budapest. It is up to its ankles in frozen slush, under a louring, heavy-burdened sky. Fur-capped townspeople and their country cousins struggle, purple-faced, along its pavements.

As well as a baroque church, with its unswept steps snow-laden, there are a few shops, fewer vehicles, crumbling stucco. Putnok is central Europe at its most humdrum; except for a harsh 25-foot high end-terrace mural abutting the church square, painted on a bright-white ground and advertizing a local brand of cotton fabric. It depicts a young tousle-haired woman – her eyes staring strangely – half-reclining in black bolero top and mid-calf boots, with a zebra-striped mini-skirt riding high on her thighs, and pin-up legs wide apart at the mural's epicentre.

The branches of the still trees are lightly snow-dusted; she is wearing matching knickers; a farm-cart passes, in its own fashion. The Hungarian cultural revolution has reached Putnok. A Ravasz may have his doubts, but an end-terrace wall tells its own story.

*

The long-discredited Central Council of Trade Unions [SZOT], used for forty years to doing nothing very much as the torpid creature of the State socialist system, is slowly waking to a new situation. The turn to the market – and the entrepreneurism of a Lazslo Steiner – is threatening to bring the oldest kind of class interest back into circulation.

The Council's apparatchiks in their Budapest headquarters have also begun to reconsider the ruined history of the Hungarian trade unions. 'One hundred years of our tradition', said one of them, 'were destroyed by our autocratic, centrally-planned economic system.' 'We lost our functions to the government, and our character as a movement to the Party,' said another, equally bitter. 'We are faced with a changed economic system,' declared the Council's secretary, Magda Kovacs, more cautiously.

You mean capitalism? 'I would call it a market-orientated system,' she said, flushing at the question. But aren't you opposed to it as trade unionists, as representatives of the proletariat? There was a moment of fluttering hesitation; these are, after all, historic post-socialist conundrums. Obedience to the Party-line of reform – even if it dictates walking the plank – the renewed stirring of socialist commitment to workers' interests, old Stalinist habits of thought and language, and the wild temptations of market freedoms are plaited together in an ideological cat's cradle.

'We *want* to establish a market-orientated system,' she replied without conviction, plucking at the first strand of it. 'In the past everything was socialist property,' she continued, toying with the second. 'Now, of course, some employees will become real employees,' she said, going back to the first. 'But this does not mean that there will be contradictions between the employers and the workers,' she added, moving over in reflex to the third.

But I have just spoken to a Budapest entrepreneur with fifteen hundred employees, I said to her, who uses wage-cuts as a disciplinary measure. He does not want anything to do with trade unions, and says that his company is like a family enterprise. 'He is unusual,' she said defensively. He thinks he is a model for the new order, I told her. 'If the market situation becomes more general, then things could change in this way,' she said uneasily, being on unfamiliar ground.

'Our first task is not to obstruct but to assist the process of reconstruction. We must also be careful not to frighten foreign investors.' (Her more militant colleagues remained silent.) 'We will of course oppose wage-cuts' – miners have already struck over them – 'and job-losses. But we do not want to be blamed for future economic problems.' But will you take the workers' side if their interests clash with those of foreign investors, or if there is a working-class backlash against the reform programme? Will you be organizing for the Hungarian class struggle?

'We think that in the new system workers should have an inalienable right to strike,' she answered, carefully side-stepping the question. 'And in the sense that the trade unions must look through the eyes of the workers, we shall have to represent the victims of reorganization,' she added, without relish. And the Hungarian class struggle? 'I do not accept the expression,' she said, lost in an ideological no-man's land, without a compass.

*

The eve of the great debate. Tomorrow morning (10 January), Professor Kalman Kulcsar, the minister of justice – an affable non-Party academic in built-up shoes and pin-stripe suit – is to present to Parliament his bills to restore the rights of assembly and association to the Hungarian people, as the pace of things quickens. In addition, a new constitution embodying 'European legal culture' and a new bill on political parties are being drafted under his aegis. In Budapest he is regarded as the legal midwife of the reform process; by Gaspar Tamas he is described, intemperately, as 'a liar with a bad 1956 record, whose new career depends on the liberalization'.

1 Demonstrators carrying a portrait of the Serbian nationalist leader, Slobodan Milosevic: Pristina, province of Kosovo, Yugoslavia, October 1988

2 Milovan Djilas, veteran Yugoslav dissident and former comrade-in-arms of Tito: Belgrade, October 1988

3 *Above left*   Janos Berecz, member of the Hungarian politburo, after speaking in the National Assembly on the restoration of civil liberties, Budapest, 10 January 1989

4 *Above right*   Kalman Kulcsar, Hungarian minister of justice, during a recess in the Assembly debate, Budapest, 10 January 1989

5 Session of the Hungarian National Assembly, Budapest, 10 January 1989

6 *Above left*   Gaspar Tamas, dissident philosopher and Hungarian
   opposition leader, in the Café New York, Budapest, January 1989

7 *Above right*   Peter Töke, editor of *Reform*, at the weekly's offices in
   Budapest, January 1989

8 The Hungarian cultural revolution reaches Pultusk, 70 miles from
   Budapest, January 1989

9   Father Petkin in his vestry, Church of the Mantle of the Virgin, Sofia, April 1989

10   Nikolai Kamov, secretary of the central committee of the Dimitrov Youth League, Sofia, April 1989: 'The forms of our work cannot be the same as they were before'

11   Leninism at the end of its tether, Sofia, April 1989

With Kulcsar, glasnost Hungarian-style has few limits. He is frank to a fault. 'It was impossible to continue in the old ways', he declares, 'we had no choice but to change direction.' Contrary to Tamas's astringent judgment, the justice minister appears to be an advanced prototype of the post-Communist liberal democrat now arriving in high places here and there in eastern Europe. He was appointed in June 1988, replacing Imre Markoja, a Kadarite stalwart; and makes no pretence in our conversation of being a socialist, let alone a Marxist. Instead, he believes society's progress depends on the 'creative minority', on 'selectivity' and on the 'spirit of enterprise'. He cites Arnold Toynbee with approval and is opposed, in Thatcherite fashion, to a 'system of dependence which does not favour autonomous responsibility and action'. He has also written recently that 'popular jealousy' does not provide a 'social medium favourable to enterprise'.

What Kulcsar has to say today sounds as momentous as the fearful Ravasz was hoping. Hungary, which he describes as being 'on the eastern periphery of Europe', has been taken by socialism into a 'side-road of history', and under socialism is unable to go further. 'Without the development of democracy in Hungary, we cannot modernize,' he says, citing numerous third world development theorists. 'We have to change this authoritarian political system for economic reasons. It has not given us sustained growth, and it has not permitted creative forces to develop. We must therefore detach ourselves from it and adapt ourselves to the European political and economic situation' – code for gradually drawing closer to the EEC and other European institutions, which are waiting for Hungary across the Danube, and for gradually turning away from Comecon and the Soviet Union.

Contrary to the demand of Party conservatives that new parties should have 'socialist' or 'progressive' aims, there will be no loyalty oath to 'socialism' under the new rules Kulcsar is preparing. 'Tomorrow', he declares, 'I am going to propose to Parliament the setting up of a new constitutional court, whose task will include the registering of political parties. The only question will be whether such parties accept the new Hungarian Constitution', now under preparation. What will it contain? I ask him. 'It will enunciate some basic principles and values', Kulcsar answers, 'but it may not use the words "socialist society", and will take a new view of private property.'

In which case, it will also end forty years of socialism's ideological imperium in the country. It would, for example, legalize – and legitimize – the commitment of the Smallholders' Party to a parliamentary democratic system founded on private enterprise. These are crucial steps both for the history of socialism and the history of Europe. 'I myself was astonished', Kulcsar continues, 'that Parliament unanimously accepted the new Company Law last October'; 'something new' he calls this counter-revolution against forty years of socialist endeavour, which opens up a broad path to private enterprise. 'It was an historic step. I think they didn't understand what they were doing,' he says, laughing.

What about the risks of this revolution? 'The real danger in this time of transition', Kulcsar answers, 'is of economic collapse and a call for a return to authoritarianism. There is growing nostalgia in some quarters even for the 1950s, for the discipline of that period.' (The anxious Karoly Ravasz had told me he was afraid of people beginning to murmur: 'In Rakosi's time, there were stable prices'.) Despite such apprehensions, the demotion of the HSWP from its position as the 'leading force in society', protected by the Constitution, is now, says Kulcsar, 'under discussion'. Imre Pozsgay, one of the Party's leading reformers, has described the HSWP's monopoly of power as 'an unfortunate historical accident'.

You mean it will lose its guarantee of power? 'Yes,' Kulcsar says. 'Of course, there is no unanimity on this in the Party. But we don't want to maintain the special position of the present ruling party in the new Constitution. I believe that the HSWP should be able to rule in future only if it can command a sufficient parliamentary majority by election.'

Aren't these changes suicide for the Hungarian Party? An historical *hara-kiri*, like the Spanish Falange committed after Franco? 'It could be. I don't know. Much depends on what happens outside Hungary also.' Where? In the Soviet Union? 'Yes,' says Kulcsar. 'Grosz is confident that no situation will arise where the HSWP would have to surrender power after a general election, though it might have to share it in a coalition. I myself think that a coalition is inevitable.' You mean Grosz doesn't believe that the HSWP would be decisively rejected in an election? 'Hungarians have never had a great sense of reality,' Kulcsar replies; it is the boldness of a man who considers himself to be lighting the way out of Hungary's darkness.

What is the name of this system you are creating? 'Nobody could give you the answer. We have to restore continuity with our historical traditions, without going backwards. We have to create something new, but I myself don't know what this "new" is.' What are to be the limits of this reform? I ask him. Will there be any? 'There is no decision,' he answers.

At parting, Kulcsar inclines his head in a stiff bow, and clicks his heels together.

*

Next day, the atmosphere in the packed Hungarian National Assembly is electric, and appearances more bourgeois than proletarian. Under dustsheets for decades and fallen into dullest political shadow, the gilded neo-Gothic chamber – chandeliered, ornately vulgar – glitters once again in its late nineteenth-century parliamentary splendour. From the press gallery, I observe phalanxes of dark suits, animated women, a bemedalled general and a grey uniformed police chief; a stern rabbi in his skull-cap and a timid-looking clergyman in his dog-collar. Parliament, ablaze with light, may once more become the focus of the Hungarian political system.

'There can be no further economic development in Hungary', the minister of justice tells the hushed, crowded benches, 'within an authoritarian political order. Our type of political system is incapable of handling the tensions which arise in the process of modernization.' The rows of dark suits stir, as if a breeze were blowing through them. 'Hungary', Kulcsar continues, 'needs a new constitution, a new constitutional court, the independence of the judiciary ["beyond debate"], the separation of powers, the rule of law, the protection of civil liberties, and the filling of other gaps in our legal system', in the name of what he calls 'our reintegration into the history of European constitutions.'

His terms are elementary and the reasoning simple; it is as if the unknown principles of liberal democracy were being explained to children. But there is iron in it also; the shadows which are being dispersed are totalitarian. 'At the most primitive level of our political culture', he roundly declares – the benches again stirring – 'demonstrations have always been regarded with hostility and suspicion.' Against such 'primitivism', Kulcsar cites the International Convention on Human Rights, describing 'the rights of association [in order to 'advance one's interests'], of assembly and of demonstration as 'inalienable' and 'every citizen's due'.

'Demonstrations', says Kulcsar, as if conceding points to the alarmed authoritarians on the benches around him, 'may give more room for demagogy than contemplation. Demonstrations may damage, it is true, the interests of other people walking the streets. But they serve as a warning to power, and whatever the inconveniences of human rights', he adds sardonically, his voice remaining steady in the renewed silence, 'they cannot be subject to arbitrary approval or disapproval, but only to rational limitation.'

The dissentients – who read their prepared speeches – are 'worried about the fate of the country'. Former foreign minister Frigyes Pulya is 'anxious' about the right of association, wanting to exclude the possibility 'for one more year at least' of the formation of new political parties. 'A vigorous debate between many parties would not help our country. This haste', Pulya declares with passion, 'could lead to political instability and danger'; out in Budapest, the '5,000' strong Ferenc Münnich Society – 'mostly made up of old soldiers and retired policemen', according to Gaspar Tamas, and dedicated to the 'struggle against counter-revolution' in the name of a notorious 1956 hardliner – has been denouncing the reforms with straightforward Stalinist invective.

The debate becomes more intense. 'Where is the end of the tunnel?' Pulya cries out. A short-haired police chief from Bacs-Kiskun weighs in with worries about public order, expressing fears of 'anarchy and extremists'; opposing him, a fiery young woman doctor makes uncomfortable use of Hungary's rising child mortality rate – 'the highest in this part of Europe' – to warn against any backsliding in the reform process. 'Our country has many times stood on the threshold of democratic transformation, but we have never succeeded in getting across it. Now', she ringingly declares, 'the people of this country expect it.'

Into the maelstrom, and silencing the dissenters, steps the bull-like Janos Berecz himself, central committee secretary, tainted Party historian and commissar for ideological questions, who throughout 1988 marshalled the defence of the one-party system and led the attack on 'bourgeois radical and liberal forces'. The intervention of 'the most conservative member of the politburo' is decisive. 'Dear members', he tells the Assembly, 'there can be no question of playing for time. The only question is whether Hungarian society is ready for a modern form of democracy, guided by socialist principles.'

There was an inhaling of breath from various places in the

Assembly, which almost sounded like hissing. 'But do we not need to lay the foundations, now, of a modern state, democratize ourselves and renew socialist society under the rule of law? My answer is that we do. It is a matter of the up-to-date exercise of power. The HSWP, which recognizes realities, is against any postponement in the drawing up of a new law on political parties. In fact, we are keen on such a law; we are partners in the exercise. It is a landmark in our progress.'

Again there is a rippling along the benches: it is the beginning of the end for the one-party Hungarian People's Republic. When he resumes his seat, loud applause greets him.

*

Still high from his speech in the chamber, Berecz – small-eyed and broad-shouldered – comes into his room accompanied by a saturnine apparatchik (who describes himself on his visiting card as 'Central Committee Head of Section'). As he sits down, Berecz puts aside the text of his speech, and the copy of a magazine.

Eyes ranging about the room, he describes the moment as 'historic', and with unexpected gusto dismisses 'forces which wish to slow down the reform process because they think they can avoid the changes'. To some, Berecz is a brutish hardliner in disguise – or Stalinist wolf in sheep's clothing; to others he is the 'weather-vane of the reform' and a calculating opportunist. 'Restless and unpleasant' was Gaspar Tamas's description of him. 'His insistence that the 1956 uprising was a counter-revolution from the first minute has made him unacceptable to nearly everybody in the country', was Karoly Ravasz's harsh judgment.

Is this a democratic revolution against socialism? I asked him. His manner is bluff and breezy, his eyes sharp with cunning. 'It is a period of revolution, which we can manage', he says foxily, 'with the help of a reform programme.' Reform to what end? 'Towards the construction of a modern legal State, with mixed ownership of the means of production, adapted to the workings of the market.'

Is this socialism? 'Can we remain the conservative party of this country?' he asks. 'It is a modern concept of socialism based on an empirical recognition of the situation.' Yes, but to any non-socialist, or anti-socialist, this would seem like a confession of socialist failure, I say to him. 'By all means. But it is a failure of the kind of socialism we used to support, based on the omnipotence of the State and in which only one party can hold power. This kind of practice has failed. The second failure is that we did not direct commodity production to the market, and took the path of egalitarianism instead of freedom.'

The rest of the room is listening in silence. It has just heard him disposing of the cornerstones both of state socialism and socialist values.

Until recently, I say to him, you have been opposed to this degree of revision. In previous months you have repeated the slogan of 'pluralism within a one-party State', warned against 'anti-socialist opposition groups', and described a multi-party system as 'unrealistic'. Today, you have said something completely different.

He looks at me, smiling, eyes narrowed. 'If we were better off', he says, 'we could continue to think of a one-party system. But in the last twelve months the economic situation has deteriorated. It has sharpened social conflicts and is creating new forces which must find expression. We have to get out of this nadir.'

I ask him if the Party is being 'driven by panic', at which he guffaws loudly, pulling at the knees of his trousers and revealing highly-polished black ankle-boots.

'At the moment, we are taking off all our political clothes, and trying on new ones.' Whose? Mrs Thatcher's? 'I would not like to enter too far into that question,' answers Berecz. The room laughs uproariously together, Berecz's eyes almost disappearing into his head; the magazine remains on the seat beside him. 'The situation cannot be resolved by a few hundred Party members,' says Berecz. 'We need the help of the people.' Even he has written recently in his Party daily of the need for a 'new national understanding'.

What if the Party lost its guaranteed leading role under the new Constitution? Could you accept it? 'From the formal, legal point of view, yes. But, politically, I shall work hard to maintain the Party's position.' What if you lose an election? 'Potentially, that is part of the situation,' he replies vaguely. 'We will see when the time comes,' he adds, standing up with his 'head of section' to return to the debate, and gathering up his papers, the latest issue of *Reform* among them.

It contains articles on the Stalinist Terror, I-Ching, Budapest prostitutes and the funeral of Christina Onassis; page 23 carries a photograph in colour of John Lennon crouching naked on top of Yoko Ono. Outside in the corridor, editor Töke, still sweating, is distributing copies of *Reform* to eager parliamentarians, from a plastic bag. 'This issue is really hot stuff,' he said to me, as Berecz re-entered the chamber.

*

Kulcsar's bill was carried overwhelmingly. Last-minute fears among the extra-parliamentary opposition groups in Budapest that 'loyalty to socialism' might be made a criterion of legality for new parties were not realized. Even outright anti-socialist parties – previously an anathema – could become a legitimate political option in future, provided that they express their opposition 'within the law', and agree to accept the new Constitution.

Indeed, failing Karoly Ravasz's nightmare of a neo-Stalinist coup, the old socialist order, its legitimacy ebbing, appears to be ending in a democratic counter-revolution; 'democracy without a qualifying adjective', is what Imre Pozsgay, the leading Party liberal, says that he is seeking for his compatriots.

But out of this is coming something complex and dangerous: a clash of beliefs, at the heart of which there stand opposed, broadly speaking, the politics of old socialist conservatism – the politics of reaction, mainly proletarian in inspiration – on the one hand, and the politics of civil liberties and the free market, espoused by mainly non-proletarian radicals and progressives, on the other. It is bringing together, on both sides, the strangest of bed-fellows. On the first side, the side of reaction, are to be found old Stalinist tribunes of the interests of the proletariat, military veterans, anti-semites, and died-in-the-wool servants of the apparatus; on the second, the side of progress, are to be found potentially ruthless entrepreneurs, human rights activists, full-time anti-Communists, men of the cloth and Party reformers, with each side claiming that its own ends correspond to the 'real interests' of the nation.

However, if what is afoot proceeds further, it will represent an historic reversal of the Marxian dialectic, which was always predicated on the transformation – aided by a Communist 'vanguard' – of an exploitative capitalist 'realm of necessity' into a post-capitalist 'realm of freedom'. But the transformation did not happen. Instead, the inmates of the 'realm of freedom', with many of their leaders too, have now begun to retrace their steps, after forty years in a wilderness of vain endeavour. It is as if Moses, having failed to find the Promised Land, had decided to go back to Egypt.

7

Bulgaria, April 1989:
One step forward, one step back

The two guards at the Dimitrov Mausoleum in Sofia – a sacred place for any Bulgarian – are smart in their pink dress-uniforms, a single plume in their nineteenth-century shakos. (A few streets away there is a long queue outside a shoe shop waiting for Hush Puppies.) Motionless, wearing white gloves and presenting fixed bayonets, they stand facing each other at the double bronze doors like a pair of armed bell-hops at an elevator entrance.

Inside, in the spotlit pitch-dark of the guarded vault, face and hands waxen in his glass sarcophagus, lies the printer Georgi Dimitrov. Head of the Comintern from 1924 to 1944, main defendant in the Reichstag fire trial and accomplice of Stalin, he was the first general secretary – there have been only three in all – of thc Bulgarian Communist Party, from 1945 to 1949.

A faint smile upon his lips, he is smartly dressed in a black lounge suit, white shirt and maitre d.'s black necktie; his head rests on black velvet, grey hair ruffled, one of his fingers flexed slightly. Outside, in the spring sunshine, where the hissing currency dealers are at their furtive business, handsome girls and youths pass in stone-washed jeans and trainers.

*

The mausoleum stands in September the Ninth Square, the date of the 1944 'revolutionary uprising', or seizure of power, organized by the Communist-led Fatherland Front to coincide with the Red Army's crossing of the Danube from Romania into pro-Axis Bulgaria. It is also the date from which real time begins for Communist Bulgaria, and marks the national boundary with the prehistoric.

After 9 September 1944 and under Georgi Dimitrov, the usual

salami tactics, the usual trials and the usual executions of the leaders of other parties followed, until the People's Republic was set up in business in December 1947.

★

Southern Balkan land of Cabernet Sauvignon, attar of roses and 9 million people, of electronic equipment for the Soviet space programme and economic stasis, Bulgaria has borders with Romania, Yugoslavia, Greece and Turkey. Subject to nearly 500 years under the Ottoman yoke – 'a time of humiliation and horror', as official publications describe the period between 1396 and 1878 – Bulgaria has a deep-rooted peasant economy, and a long tradition of autocracy and political violence. After the June 1923 fascist coup which overturned less than four years of democratic rule of Bulgaria by the peasant Agrarian Party, its fiercely anti-monarchic leader, Alexander Stamboliski, was not merely tortured and murdered but decapitated, and his head (so it is said) presented to the Bulgarian Tsar, Boris the Third, on a platter.

Thereafter, until 1944 and following an orgy of executions and murders between 1923 and 1925, Bulgaria experienced a bewildering variety of Mussolini-inspired fascistic dictatorships, military coups, vestigial democratic moments and, after November 1935, direct personal rule by Tsar Boris, who was in fact a German. Indeed, support for Nazi Germany was never seriously in question, Bulgaria joining the Axis powers in March 1941, while at the same time ambiguously refusing to declare war on Russia, its other traditional ally.

Boris, who is said to have died by poison, ruled from 1918 to 1943; the seventy-seven-year-old Todor Zhivkov has been leader of the nearly 1 million-strong Bulgarian Communist Party (BCP) since 1954, a period of autocratic rule ten years longer than that of old Tsar Boris.

*

In a back-street Sofia market, there is a mêlée of dark gipsies and the smell of strong tobacco; nearby, the crowded stallholders' cafe is at its greasy commons. Here are kerchiefed peasant women and men with two days' growth of stubble, selling radishes and spring onions; dried fruit, walnuts and honey; flowers, and a sprig or two of herbs and heather.

At this stall, in the aroma of food, earth, tobacco and bodies, there is even some old sense of poor well-being, as the coins pass from hand to hand, and into an apron pocket.

*

In his thirty-five years of power, Todor Zhivkov – the peasant from Pravets – has even-handedly espoused Stalinism and (now) anti-Stalinism, iron-fisted reaction and (now) 'open-minded' revision. A statue of Leonid Brezhnev, to whom Zhivkov gave the medal of 'Hero of the People's Republic of Bulgaria' on three separate occasions, was removed from Sofia in September 1988, as Gorbachev's star rose in the heavens.

Zhivkov has also impartially ousted both reformists and Stalinists from his politburo, as well as cutting down – at roughly five-year intervals – every likely dauphin who has threatened his position. They have included Mitko Grigorov in 1962, Ivan Abadzhiev in 1967, Boris Velchev in 1977, Alexander Lilov in 1983, and most recently the fifty-two-year-old Chudomir Alexandrov, Bulgaria's leading Gorbachevite reformer and Soviet protégé, who was purged in the summer of 1988, after himself calling for a purge of the dead wood in the politburo. (As he fell, he was smeared in characteristic fashion; his father-in-law was denounced as a pre-war fascist.) Today, half of Bulgaria's population has known no other leader than its present Grand Vizier.

Like his Romanian neighbour Ceausescu, Zhivkov, a widower, prefers his own family and close family cronies around him, although not on the heroic Romanian scale; fellow ex-partisans are included in Zhivkov's praetorian guard. His eccentric daughter Lyudmila – who spent a year at St Antony's College, Oxford in the early 1970s, much of the time allegedly buying antiques while Bulgarian embassy staff wrote her essays – was promoted to the politburo at the almost unprecedented age of thirty-six as minister of culture. An anorexic patron of the Bulgarian arts, Lyudmila is said to have lived on mashed potatoes and to have been increasingly attracted to arcane forms of mysticism (she began to speak of 'beauty' and 'light' rather than class struggle). She died in unexplained circumstances four years later; some say following a car accident, brain damage and surgery in the Soviet Union. Others suggest, more fancifully, that she had become an embarrassment to the regime and was murdered, in the Byzantine fashion. The Lyudmila Zhivkov Palace of Culture built under her auspices in Sofia – but which since March 1988 has no longer been called after her – is decorated with the motif of a blazing sun and is said (by some) to have been 'constructed upon cabbalistic principles of architecture'.

Today, Zhivkov's thirty-six-year-old son Vladimir is deputy minister of culture, science and education; his granddaughter Evgeniya, the elder of Lyudmila's two children, is a member of the central committee of the Dimitrov Communist Youth League, or Komsomol. This is merely continuing a tradition of nepotism: Vulko Chervenko, Zhivkov's predecessor as Party general secretary from 1950 to 1954 – and affectionately known in those days as 'Little Stalin' – was himself Georgi Dimitrov's brother-in-law. It did not help him with Zhivkov, who in 1962 presided over Chervenko's expulsion from the Party.

*

By 1957, under Zhivkov, 'complete' collectivization of a peasant land had been achieved. It was followed, from 1958 to 1960, by a Mao-inspired 'Great Leap Forward', and then by a 'New Economic Mechanism' of modestly liberalizing bureaucratic reforms in the

1960s, halted after the shock of the 1968 Prague Spring. Economic reforms were resumed from 1970 with the setting up of very large, and initially successful, agro-industrial concerns; there was further cautious tinkering with managerial reforms in the late 1970s and early 1980s, as the economy continued to make limited progress. (Some Bulgarians even point to their present $6 billion foreign debt as proof of it; it is a mere third of Hungary's, with roughly the same population.) By the mid-1980s the economy was treading water.

Throughout this period, Bulgaria – unlike Romania and Yugoslavia – had remained loyal to Moscow. Liberated from the Ottomans by the armies of Tsar Alexander II in 1878 and from the Nazis by the Red Army in 1944, Bulgaria, paying its dues, took part with a will under Zhivkov in the 1968 invasion of Czechoslovakia. In September 1973, Zhivkov, who speaks fluent Russian, even described the Soviet Union and Bulgaria as 'one organ, with lungs and circulatory system in common'; some 60 per cent of Bulgaria's trade is with the Soviet Union. Bulgarian computers, robots and laser optics make it a useful enough partner.

It has also found itself politically split asunder by the Gorbachev reform process, the deeply conservative political instincts of Zhivkov's politburo at odds with an equally deep instinctive readiness to do the Soviet Union's bidding. In the past, Zhivkov has deferred to every Soviet leader; to Khruschev, with (so it is said) 'alacrity and ostentation'. There are still those who see Bulgarian zeal for an imagined Soviet cause in the 1981 attempt on the Pope's life, despite the Italian acquittal in 1987 of the Bulgarian defendant in the matter. Even Chudomir Alexandrov, the leading Bulgarian Gorbachevite (whom Zhivkov purged in 1988), tried to square the circle, or combine the reformist with the deferential impulse, by calling on Bulgaria to 'become a laboratory for the economic and social experiments of the Communist Party of the Soviet Union'.

Zhivkov's own rhetoric of reform has at times been so enthusiastically radical as to suggest that he was attempting to outdo Soviet perestroika; in 1987 it alarmed Moscow, and led to a warning to Bulgaria in January 1988 to 'proceed by stages'. Yet it has characteristically been combined with reflex rearguard actions which, Gorgonlike, have turned each reform measure to stone, so far.

★

On 20 February 1989, Zhivkov summoned 'representatives of the intelligentsia' – the 'strike-force of restructuring', he called them – to an extraordinary session of the politburo, in order to 'brief them on topical problems and consult with them'. ('More culture, more humanity, more intellect, that is what we need today,' Zhivkov had proclaimed seven months earlier, at a central committee plenum.)

The moment, he now declared to an audience composed of representatives of the media, creative unions and scientific institutions, was one of 'crucial importance to the development of socialism and of the world as a whole'; a time for engaging in 'essential innovations'; a time when the working class had 'lost some of its classical features' and technological change was 'increasing the role of the intelligentsia'. Addressing them as 'esteemed comrades', and insisting that 'the Party has always treated our intelligentsia with respect', the 118-page text of his speech is an appeal for the co-operation of intellectuals in the 'processes which are underway in our country to transform it into a highly-developed, civilized socialist State'.

The Party, 'in a truly Communist manner', was 'subjecting its own work to an inexorable self-evaluation' of its 'mistakes and omissions'. There had been inner-Party persecutions and reprisals in Bulgaria in the 1950s; worse still, Zhivkov declared (in what he called a 'digression'), the 'terror and arbitrary justice' meted out in the Soviet Union during the 1930s had claimed 'over 1,000' Bulgarian victims (mainly Communist political refugees from Bulgaria's inter-war despots), 'of whom 600 were killed', including 'leading figures'. 'Comrades', he declared – entirely avoiding the fraught question of Dimitrov's involvement in Stalin's purges of exiled Bulgarians – 'all this belongs to history. Everything that is being carried out under the sign of restructuring in our countries is thanks to the new policy being implemented by the present Soviet leadership, led by Comrade Mikhail Gorbachev.'

And in Bulgaria? 'Our policy, our strategy, our enthusiasm, coincide with what is occurring in the Soviet Union. Irrespective of its ebbs and flows, and the zig-zags of its course, the essence of our policy is restructuring.' Why? Because of 'knots' and 'distortions' which had 'damaged the vital interests of the workers'; because of the 'stagnation of the past period'; because of (unspecified) 'gross violations of the Party's leading role'; because of the 'alienation of the people from the organs of power'; 'and so on and so forth', Zhivkov added.

The solutions? Nothing less than the 'rejection of the previous model of socialism, which has exhausted its possibilities', 'giving up very many of our established ideas and ideological prejudices', and 'going to the very end in the cause of revolutionary restructuring. Comrades', he repeated, 'everything, absolutely everything, must pass through the purgatory of revolutionary renewal.'

Zhivkov even declared in his speech that although 'no one can deny the importance of socialism as an historical stage in mankind's development', nevertheless 'so-called Marxist political economy' had been based on 'unscientific foundations' and was 'in a state of crisis'. In consequence, Bulgarian intellectuals must now 'analyse the new characteristics of the capitalist world' and 'discover the internal mechanism of capitalism's regeneration as a social system'. The name of Marx himself was invoked by Zhivkov to authorize this endeavour. 'Marx used to say', Zhivkov asserted (without giving a source for the bogus attribution), 'that for a people to prosper it has to repeat in one or another form the experience of other countries that are advanced in their development. This postulate applies to us,' he added.

'Why,' Zhivkov asked the Bulgarian intelligentsia, 'are the advanced capitalist countries developing at such a fast rate? Why, despite unemployment in certain western countries, has the level of employment been so high? Why is there a clear trend in developed capitalist countries, despite the ups and downs, for inflation to decline? Of course, this does not mean that we should repeat the development of capitalism with its peculiar features and contradictions. Our task instead is to borrow and adapt, within the shortest possible period, those achievements of human civilization without which progress is unthinkable, and regardless of where they come from.

'Our society needs new and fresh ideas,' Zhivkov proclaimed (while, out in Sofia, dissidents continued to be hounded). 'Let there be disputes, let there be different and even alternative visions. We are advancing towards a new type of democracy,' he told the assembled intellectuals.

*

But within a few pages in the text, Zhivkov is warning that 'restructuring cannot be accomplished without appropriate preparation', that 'socialist property must be regarded as single and indivisible', and that 'the working class remains the leading social force'. A few more pages, and Zhivkov is insisting in familiar fashion on the hegemony of the Party; dismissing 'so-called political pluralism'; menacingly condemning 'nihilism', 'social parasitism' and 'all negative attitudes to socialism, the fatherland, and our country's traditions'; and calling (in true Orwellian style) for 'constructive excitement' only.

On the one hand, glasnost is described in religiose terms as a 'sacred and immaculate value'. On the other, Zhivkov declares, in ugly Stalinist fashion that 'we will continue to unmask the efforts of those who rely on the political dregs and degenerates of this country', and 'will protect our society from demagogy and political contamination'.

It is not difficult to interpret. It is the creed of the professional totalitarian, doubling as enlightened reformer; where the search for new Truth is presided over by old Falsehood, and grizzled reaction supervises a nation's progress.

*

During the course of his speech, Zhivkov also denounced the personality cult, which he described as 'incompatible with Marxism-Leninism, the principles of socialism, the traditions of the BCP and the humanitarian ideals of a new society'; of the fact that Zhivkov has presided over such a cult-of-himself since 1954 there was no mention.

In August 1987, the politburo itself described 'official Bulgarian life' as 'marked by vanity, hypocrisy and airs of grandeur', and called for an end to 'parades with little meaning, empty occasions and the public display of leaders' portraits'. But 'empty occasion' is the very stuff of Sofia's political existence, and there are countless portraits of Zhivkov. Orwell's Winston Smith stares from the wall of every office.

*

Do people admire her in Bulgaria? 'Yes, many people admire her.' The left doesn't in Britain, I said. 'Why not?' asked Lyuben Genov, the burly new editor of the Sofia trade union daily *Trud* (circ. 300,000), ham-fists resting on the table, and intermittently popping a chocolate into his mouth with pudgy fingers. Because of her anti-trade unionism, among other things, I answered.

'The working class here is very conservative also,' he said. 'Here,

too, new technology can only be introduced in a forceful fashion.
One must be a realist. Many of the things which have happened in
your country must happen here also. Her greatest success', he told
me, 'is making the workers co-partners in the economy.' In darkest
Bulgaria too, Mrs Thatcher's name is evidently a totem.

Is Marxism dead then? I asked him. 'If one doesn't have a perception of the real situation, one is lost,' he replied obliquely. Does
Marxism provide such a perception? He laughed, without answering
me directly. 'Here', Genov said, 'we have relied on posters. We built
things up. We made pictures of what we wanted.' What do you
mean? 'We mistook our desires for reality, and ignored our real
condition. We wanted equality and welfare for everybody. Instead,
without doing anything for it, people got used to getting money from
the State, as if it were a milch cow,' he said, taking another chocolate.

'They waited for the State to solve every problem. As a result we
have great deformations among working people. That is how they
became alienated from labour,' he added. (This sounds like the most
radical post-Marxism, even here in 'immobile' Bulgaria.) What is
the solution? 'We have to get back to traditional motivations,' he
answered, his jowls moving. 'We have to get rid of useless workplaces. We have serious problems in our economy. Two days ago,
the council of ministers discussed new trade union proposals for
social benefits for the jobless and the redirection of labour. These
things are not very pleasant, but in Bulgaria too we have to have
them.

'If we don't make real political and economic changes, we will
become not just part of the third world, but of a fourth world not
known yet. Our enterprises cannot sell their products, workers cannot
use the technology we have imported, there are shortages of raw
materials. The ideal of the previous generation was enormous plants
with steaming chimneys' – big black steam, he called it – 'but this is
not the same as genuine economic power. We have to solve these
problems ourselves; the solution cannot come from the West or
the Soviet Union. But our labour force is cheaper here', he said
unexpectedly – sounding like Laszlo Steiner in Budapest – 'and could
be beneficial for western companies.'

If there are real moves to a market economy, what of the resumption
of the class struggle? I asked Genov. He seemed taken aback by the
question. 'What class struggle could we talk about now?' he answered,
fumbling. 'When we are speaking of a common European home,

it would be unthinkable. We will of course need trade unions to defend the interests of our labour force, but the concept of class struggle is an anachronism,' declared the editor of Bulgaria's trade union daily.

Tell me, I said to Genov, is all this some kind of new orthodoxy? 'What orthodoxy?' he asked sharply. Party-ordered glasnost, but without real perestroika, I answered. 'Party bureaucracy is still very strong. There are many obstacles, old laws, old habits,' said Genov. 'There are new arts which the State must master, but the desire of every human being is to be freer, to decide for himself, and to get rid of unnecessary limitations.

'Everybody is ready for change,' Genov asserted, his hairy wrist, in a heavy gold wrist-watch, resting on the edge of the table.

*

How do you know everybody is ready for change? 'Every newspaper is getting letters from its readers,' said Genov, '*Trud* also. They are saying they are tired of the old images and slogans. We have had meetings recently with some of them. In one meeting they told us they were sick of hearing only about strikes in England, and only good things in Bulgaria. They are right. In the past, such criticism was treated by the Party as an ideological diversion. Today we cannot continue to disparage what is done in the West in such an automatic fashion. We have to learn to tolerate each other without ideological preconceptions, the way we tolerate our wives and husbands. For forty years we were taught not to believe in such a thing as human nature', he added, 'but it is never too late to give up false teaching. There are still many layers to be exploded, but we have had enough of empty concepts and phrases,' Genov said, biceps bulging in his jacket, a framed portrait of Zhivkov on the wall of his office.

'This is a sort of renaissance period,' he continued. 'It is like the most beautiful moments in Bulgarian history.' (There have not been too many.) 'Today, for us, there are no forbidden areas. Now, the only question is truth.' The warm breeze stirred the curtains behind him. Are you saying that you are free to publish what you want? Can you, for example, criticize corruption in high places? Here, his geniality waned a little; Genov's predecessor as editor of *Trud* was dismissed in March 1988, after publishing an article on corruption which named members of the Mihaylov clan, friends and protégés of Zhivkov.

'I told you that it is a question of truth,' said Genov. 'When a journalist starts criticizing, he cannot insult human dignity, or simply curse someone. The question of truth is also a question of civilized standards. A journalist cannot hold his pen the way a monkey holds a ribbon,' he declared obscurely. 'It is a question of self-limitation.' You mean self-censorship? There was silence, as he weighed his answer; but glasnost triumphed, even in Sofia. 'When journalists write something critical', he said quietly, 'they are still not free of administrative enforcement' (code for police action). 'It is a struggle,' he added. (A new press law to 'protect investigative journalism' has been promised frequently – like so many Bulgarian reforms – but with no outcome.)

Is the regime frightened of its intellectuals? I ventured. 'If they are, it is normal. Authority must be frightened of intellectuals,' he said boldly; he himself is the son of a teacher. 'Stalinism – thirty years ago', he quickly interposed for the record – 'practised terror and violence against intellectuals. Now', he said, retreating into his fox-hole, 'nobody is deprived of the right to work because of what he has written.' This was false; Stefan Prodev, the editor of the leading Sofia weekly *Narodna Kultura* has been dismissed for republishing items from the Soviet press, including an article from the liberal weekly *Ogonyok* which came close to raising the issue of Dimitrov's role in Comintern-inspired repression in the 1930s. 'The scum and filth of Soviet glasnost', Zhivkov is said to have called such re-publications.

'At our recent Congress of Journalists, those who spoke in the old way were hand-clapped and forced to leave the podium,' Genov continued. 'There is greater intolerance now for the old generation of Party journalists, for the years of trite words, stereotyped phrases and dogmatic opinions. All our papers for years have looked the same, but we cannot remain in this cage indefinitely. It is necessary for us to say goodbye to the old approach, and change our way of thinking,' he said, re-emerging from his fox-hole.

'We must be allowed to express our opinions, good or bad, freely. But I have colleagues', he said, dropping his voice and losing himself in his private labyrinth, 'who have been put on trial for criticizing individuals and institutions. Of course, if they tell lies, they cannot have immunity. But newspapers must be free to criticize, even to criticize the Party. It is very difficult. We started on a new path only a month ago, and some colleagues are against it. They could provoke trouble, but things are changing. Now, we are in a market of ideas,' said Genov, choosing another chocolate.

*

What do you think of Hungary? I asked him. 'The euphoria there is temporary,' he answered. 'Now they have sex shops, according to our information, like in Amsterdam. I have been in Amsterdam,' he said, going off at a tangent, and again sounding like the Budapest entrepreneur, Steiner. 'I have seen families taking their children into sex-shops there,' he added. (This is a new one.) 'They consider it pretty normal. It is part of the psychology of the Dutch people. If we had sex shops in Bulgaria, God forbid, it would be the cause of great troubles.'

Why? 'Because there are no such traditions. People would go mad over it.' Why? 'Because we don't have the culture to perceive sexual facts normally,' he answered. Why not? I asked him. 'Because here questions of morality have been made too ideological. Virtue, including sexual virtue, is ascribed to socialism, and vice, including sexual promiscuity, to capitalism. This is a fabrication. Here, crime also increases, but our statistics do not show it,' he admitted casually.

What about more important matters in Hungary, like privatization? 'For us, too, the market and the mechanism of private interest are the most important questions in the country. Here in Sofia with our private restaurants [leased by the State to their existing employees, in return for a share of the profits] the effect in some cases has been tremendous. Their profits have even increased three- and four-fold, they fix their own salaries and menus, they take care of their customers, and they have become very self-assured places.' The Italian Restaurant in Sofia, for the last year a self-managing, semi-private enterprise of this kind, is now impenetrably crowded.

'In the USSR', he went on, 'they say that the leasing system will save them. But private interest also has negative aspects,' he said, retreating again. 'Those who work in identical State enterprises and see what is happening in the private sector are deprived of their will to work. They ask, "Why should I work so hard, doing the same job, and earn less?" Or take those with private plots in Bulgaria. They produce 50 per cent of our vegetables on 5 per cent of the land,' Genov said, oddly exaggerating the officially published figures – 41 per cent of vegetables from 13 per cent of the land – or perhaps blowing the true position. 'But they also travel all night to market, and go to the factory in the morning to catch up on their sleep there.

At the moment, there is tolerance of this, but it cannot last for ever.'

Comrade Genov, these are rather trivial responses to the scale of the Hungarian changes. You know as well as I do what is afoot there, I said to him. What are people in the Party saying about it? He offered me a chocolate, took one himself, and considered the matter.

'Those who want a return to the ways of the past', he answered, approaching it crab-wise, 'are especially dissatisfied with the Hungarian situation. But such people are losing ground, they are a minority.' (What, in Bulgaria?) 'But we cannot underestimate them. We have a right wing too,' he continued, his bold self gaining the upper hand. 'They use high-sounding ideas and language to defend their interests. At the moment they are appealing urgently for a return to the methods of the Stalinist period. In those times, they say, there was iron discipline. And they tell the reformers, "You, too, want to betray socialism, just like the Hungarians."'

How many people in Bulgaria agree with them? He hesitated, as if sniffing the air. 'Maybe 20 per cent. But those who cry "betrayal of socialism" do not say who would be betrayed by it,' he added.

*

At midnight I passed the Dimitrov Mausoleum, in September the Ninth Square. Closed to traffic, brilliantly-lit and bounded by the former royal palace and marmoreal government buildings, the square was deathly silent, the expanse of polished cobbles shining. The guards, presenting arms through the long night and almost asleep on their feet, were swaying slightly, starting and checking themselves; then whispering to one another across the mausoleum's bronze entrance, their eagle plumes nodding. From a barred side-window of the vault shone a pale, blue-grey light, the colour of a cadaver.

*

For years, the regime's watchwords in decree after decree have been 'flexibility', 'decentralization', 'enterprise independence', 'self-management' and 'democratization'; like Ceausescu, Zhivkov claims to have been restructuring his country since the 1950s. Yet, today, Bulgaria faces flagging agricultural productivity – in 1987 even potatoes had to be imported – a decline in energy generation, basic shortages, environmental deterioration, a falling birthrate and gradually rising inflation.

Yet the radical decrees continue. Indeed, they are more radical

than ever. Thus *Decree 56 on Economic Activity*, a *'ukaz'* issued by
the State Council on 9 January 1989, appears to permit joint stock
companies, limited companies, 'personal companies' or 'autonomous
citizens' firms (with a maximum of ten employees), remission abroad
of foreigners' hard currency profits from joint ventures, and even
free-trade zones. The scope of the Decree is almost Hungarian, on
paper; but, as ever in Bulgaria, the new 'freedoms of the market' are
bound in the sticky red tape of the State's planning apparatus.

New enterprises, whatever their form, will be regarded as 'part of
the unity and indivisibility of socialist property.' Furthermore, State
institutions will 'guide the companies' business by a co-ordinated
system of economic levers', and even 'act as their partners' in the
'fulfilment of the State plan'. The aim of the Decree, ostensibly
free-market inspired, is to 'promote socialist economic competition',
while 'company formation', and 'company [?capitalist] culture', will
be 'integrated into existing socialist relations of production'. Even
'individual ownership' is to be regarded, zanily, as a 'socialist form
of management'; while the terms private ownership and private
enterprise are sedulously avoided.

The result is a stalemate, in which change is encouraged on the
one hand, and its implementation stifled (or even punished) on the
other; in which form is given priority over substance; and in which
for every tentative step forward, there is a firm step backward, in
compensation.

★

The faded former residence of the Papal Nuncio to Sofia now
houses the weekly journal *Pogled*; or *Look*, when roughly translated
from the Bulgarian. Nikolai Todorov, its studious-looking new editor, has an awkward, convoluted manner; he is a man with whom it
is hard to come to grips, in another labyrinthine encounter. He
describes his paper as 'the most independent in Bulgaria'. It is owned
not by the State, but by the Union of Bulgarian Journalists, though
you would hardly notice it. Using the same words as Genov, he too
describes these times as ones in which there are 'no forbidden areas';
'Bulgarians', he says, 'are now seeing through the old deceptions.'

His manner, however, is strangely diffident, and seems to belie
what he is saying. Which deceptions? I ask. 'We saw man as someone
to manipulate, a mere abstraction', he answers anxiously, 'while the
working class saw themselves only as producers. Today, things are

coming into their right places and the correct focus. Before, we used to absolutize things, during the period of great class contradictions.' What do you mean exactly? 'We used to say', he replies, fiddling with the end of his tie, 'that everyone who was not with us was against us'; the old Hungarian Stalinist slogan.

'We say now that ideologies can co-exist without a life-or-death struggle.' There is a silence. 'We accept the practice of the capitalist countries. We think that the social systems are moving towards .convergence. I am very interested in your Mrs Thatcher', Todorov adds (he too); 'her realistic approach to policy arouses certain sympathies with us,' he says, pushing his spectacles back to the bridge of his nose with an index finger.

Is this change of perspective a matter of choice, or necessity? I ask him. 'It is a choice which is the result of necessity,' he answers. Then it is not a choice, is it? 'Yes,' he says, shaking his head from side to side. Do you mean no? 'Yes, I mean no,' he answers. You mean you have no choice? 'Yes,' he repeated, drawing me into the labyrinth.

*

'The trouble in Bulgaria', he resumes expressionlessly, 'is that there have always been so many people who behave like automata or robots, who seem to be without their own opinions. They perform their roles with the obedience of clerks, following every order. These same people', he adds, 'have become adherents of the new line without believing in it.' What new line? 'The new line of reform,' he answers, eyes lowered.

But what about non-Party intellectuals? There must be some spark of life in them at least? 'The best of our intelligentsia is already in the Party,' he answers. 'There may be some dissatisfied people who think that reform is going too slowly' – using almost the exact words of Zhivkov's 20 February speech to the intelligentsia – 'and who make their propaganda on the BBC World Service, the Voice of America and Radio Free Europe. The development of democracy will reduce their interest in foreign radio stations.

'Decadence has never succeeded here. Today, there is a very acute interest among certain people in pornographic video cassettes, but they cannot take root in our culture. The Bulgarians have very sober feelings. Symbolist decadence also failed here in the 1920s. We have been limiting the actions of young people through administrative methods [the euphemism, once more, for police action]. But it is hard to stop them. It was easier for us when the Iron Curtain existed.'

Do you mean you'd like to see it return? 'We have not always been behind the Iron Curtain. Now, whatever the risks, it must be taken away,' he answers.

*

What is the name of the Bulgarian system? I ask Todorov. Is it socialist? 'It is not socialist,' he replies. Why not? 'Socialism is democracy, choice, social justice.' But that is closer to liberal democracy, surely? At this Todorov began withdrawing. 'Socialism cannot be a matter merely of a State headed by a Communist Party. But I am not a theorist,' he said, choosing not to go down this track further.

*

I tried again. Why, after so many journalists lost their jobs for offending the authorities in 1988, are all these editorial changes taking place now? Why, I asked, tongue-in-cheek, are the more liberal-minded coming into editorial positions, like Genov at *Trud* and you at *Pogled*?'

He took wing at last, crowing. 'I shall be very frank with you. When I myself was working at *Trud* last year, I published a series of articles under the title "Saying It Aloud". Six weeks ago, I received a summons to a very responsible place,' he says in Kafka-like fashion. 'I said to my kids before I went, "They will probably punish me for it." But I found that they had called me to promote me to the editorship of this paper.' (So much for its independence.)

'A new line has been established', Todorov continues, candid beyond expectation, 'to renew our press. At the Congress of Journalists a month ago [where more liberal figures came to the fore by election], I made a very critical speech. I talked about the manipulation of journalists, how we had been turned into clerks without courage. This was a taboo subject until recently,' he adds, fluffing out his glasnost plumage.

'Tell me', he says, with the intimacy of a man who has just unburdened himself, and abruptly changing the subject, 'what do the British think about Bulgaria?'

*

In Alexander Nevsky Square stands the neo-Byzantine cathedral, which was built – on huge scale – to commemorate the 200,000

Russian soldiers who fell in the Russo-Turkish war of liberation of 1877-78; the war lifted the Ottoman yoke from Bulgaria, and earned Russia undying favour. It is an ornate and ugly confection of South American onyx, Egyptian alabaster, Venetian mosaics and nineteenth-century Bulgarian icons.

There is a loud hum of profane voices; the deity of the place has long been absent. A white-haired sacristan in a black barber's-style apron is lackadaisically straightening the candles in their holders, while two chattering teenage girls, arms linked, stroll the vast nave, their white high-heeled shoes clicking on the Italian marble.

*

Dimitar Deliisky has tortuous arteries at his temples, a portrait of Marx over his desk, and chain-smokes throughout our discussion. A senior Party economist, he is deputy editor of the BCP's grey daily, *Rabotnichesko Delo*, Bulgaria's leading paper. He claims that unlike most other Party papers in eastern Europe in the era of glasnost it has suffered no drop in circulation.

What is the secret of your unusual success? I ask him, avoiding his eye. The room is stale with cigarette smoke. 'New printing technology from West Germany and Sweden,' he answers. 'Our readers have noticed the qualitative improvement,' he adds, deploying a key term of Stalinist verbiage and inhaling deeply.

But are you reflecting the spirit of revolutionary restructuring? Are you passing through the purgatory of revolutionary renewal? He exhales, closing his eyes over the questions. 'If we are asking ourselves', he eventually continues, 'about restructuring, then our paper should address the problems we have been keeping silent about before.' Are you addressing them in fact? Again he inhales deeply, his hand bluish. 'Not so drastically as in the Soviet press, maybe,' he answers.

Why is that? 'Look,' he says, flicking ash from his lapels, 'we have a completely different reality in Bulgaria. We have carried out reforms since the 1960s. We have an 8 to 10 per cent dynamic growth rate. The repression, the stagnation, such things have not existed in Bulgaria,' he declares, lying through his stained teeth, and stubbing out his cigarette.

*

Now that *Pogled* and *Trud* have more liberal-minded editors, I tried out on him, have you noticed a difference in their papers? 'What you heard from them has presented us at a disadvantage.' (Nobody has yet mentioned *Rabotnichesko Delo*.) 'They do not act in a correct way. They view themselves as heroes. But none of them has put his hand deeply into our problems. They do not possess the competence for real economic or statistical analysis. It is we who are raising the problem of inflation,' he adds, his match flaring.

What is the rate of inflation in Bulgaria? I ask him. 'We don't have the method to find out the rate,' he replies. (But there seems to have been less difficulty with the growth figures.) 'We don't know what it is, 2 per cent or 15 per cent. But it exists. This we are saying.'

The phone rings and, standing beneath his august portrait of Marx, he speaks with roughened voice to his caller. Do you read western newspapers? I ask him, as he puts down the receiver. 'I listen to the BBC, Deutsche Welle, the Voice of America,' he replies, returning to his chair. 'Until eighteen months ago they were jammed, but now I listen.' What do you think of them? 'We have ideological differences with such radio stations. The Voice of America and the BBC carry out their attacks on us with great professionalism. Radio Free Europe does it in a very crude fashion. They do not see a single positive or good thing in our society, they have no respect for our country.'

He gets up and goes to his cluttered desk, returning with a wad of papers which he tosses down on the small table at which we are sitting. What are they? I ask him. 'They are transcripts of RFE broadcasts.' Do you read them? 'I read them.' And? 'And whatever they say [raising his voice] about our country, or our Party paper, or whatsoever' – this with a sweeping gesture of rejection, cigarette between his nicotined fingers – 'we are entitled to defend our ideology. This', Deliisky adds, stabbing the table, 'is an ideological Party paper!'

Nevertheless, he too presents himself as a reformer. 'We cannot follow the old paths, because of the lack of enterprise in our economy and the slow pace of technological innovation. So we must create the legal basis for a closer economic relationship with the advanced countries, for western capital to enter Bulgaria, for setting up new companies and so forth. Some of the old Communists are saying that we are trying to restore capitalism.'

Are you? 'We are creating the conditions', he answers, putting up a smokescreen of Party gobbledegook, 'for the freer influence of objective economic laws.' Do you mean for a freer market? 'It means that we do not see why the market should not function in a socialist society, as well as in a capitalist one. We have decided that there is nothing criminal in it.'

No, but how long can you go on pretending that private enterprise is socialism? At this, he laughs loudly. 'I am hesitating. But wherever the Communist Party is the ruling party, and bases itself on objective laws, it could not permit a capitalist restoration,' he said, still deep in the ideological bunker.

*

On the subject of Mrs Thatcher, there were (once more) no bounds to our Party editor's approval. 'It is my point of view', Deliisky declared, 'that she is one of the greatest post-war political figures.' There do not appear to be many votes in these parts for the western left's nostrums; but then Mrs Thatcher seems to have set the agenda for the counter-revolution which is under way in most of the Soviet system.

'Thanks to her logic', said Deliisky, 'serious economic prosperity and dynamic development have come to Britain. We too want to create the conditions in Bulgaria for a total economic renewal.' It seemed churlish to dampen his ardour; and it turned out to be no use interposing remarks about cuts in public provision, assaults on the unions, our foreign trading account, or the condition of the education system. 'But Mrs Thatcher has won the support of the people,' he interjected.

I fell silent. 'These are dramatic times for us also,' he said, smiling.

*

Kremikovci Steel Works, near Sofia: the clank of rusting coal wagons, distant snow-capped mountains, slag-heaps and scrap-iron dereliction. The wind is acrid with pollution. A ragged curtain gusts through the broken window of a workers' tenement building; dark children of Cuban and Vietnamese indentured labourers, socialism's *gästarbeiter*, are playing on the grey pathways as the dust stirs and eddies; flapping festoons of washing hang from window to window, garlanding the discoloured concrete.

Here, the BCP's heroic painted slogans are washed-out, bleached, faded; and trailer wheels bounce in the pot-holes.

*

These two learned sociologists, Professors Petkov and Fotev of the Bulgarian Academy of Sciences, are among the new gurus of the reform process, advisers on social policy and alchemists of a putative new order. For sociology is no longer regarded with the old virulence as the bourgeois alternative to Marxism; Professors Petkov and Fotev have between them recently discovered – or are being allowed to say – that 'Stalin's theories of class are a burden', and that 'belief in monopoly State ownership is a dogma.'

They now declare that they are 'dealing with ideas and language which were previously considered part of a hostile western reality', as they put it. 'Many people are confused and shocked, but now we openly discuss such matters', they say with grave pleasure; it is 'part of the process of overcoming Stalinism' and of 'disassembling the Stalinist model'. But can your work really make any difference? I ask them. 'Within the framework of dogmatic Marxism', they answer, dividing sentences between them, 'desire was confused with reality, and that which in life is truly complex was made straightforward and simple. The logic of life runs counter to rigid dogma. "Theory is dry, but the tree of life is forever green,"' says Professor Fotev, quoting Goethe.

Is the problem one of dogmatic Marxism, or of Marxism itself? I ask them. 'We need a new reading of Marxism', they answer, following the up-dated Zhivkov line to intellectuals, 'which is controlled by observation of the real world itself.' Where would that take you? 'To a new dialectical understanding', I am told, 'in which the essence of things is not reduced to simple polarities between the positive and the negative.'

This was as clear as mud. And where would you be then? I enquire. 'We would be able to see, for example, what is positive in bourgeois democracy,' they reply, like latter-day Galileos gazing into the capitalist heavens. Is this a Marxist activity? I ask of this star-gazing. 'Modern capitalist countries are different from what Marx was researching. Now we can see the rational features of the market system.'

They are also experts on Britain, and (once more) on Mrs Thatcher. 'Your left wing cannot suggest better alternatives to her policies in the present state of the technological revolution. This does not mean we are supporters of Thatcher. For example, as humanists, we feel very close to your trade unions. But they can only become strong if they are a movement for social justice, a movement which does not stand in the way of technical advances. In your miners' strike, the trade union wanted to preserve coal-mines which had no function. It was the last example of the classic class struggle. We do not think there will be another in history. Our own reform process [what reform process?] will temporarily bring more social conflict, but society must be a harmonious unity,' they say, sage as Confucians.

How long have you thought this kind of thing? I ask them. 'That is a dramatic question. Our whole careers have been based on a certain orthodoxy which is now being pronounced an error. Some Academicians are having to go from one extreme to another in order to change their way of thinking. Others cannot find it in themselves to do it and are not altering their positions.'

If you personally believed earlier what you are telling me now, why did you not say it before? I enquire. 'It just wasn't possible. We didn't talk, because we couldn't.' And if everything goes wrong, and there is another change of direction? 'They will blame the economists, not us,' they say, laughing.

★

A question of ethics. I had asked the two professors whether people in Bulgaria weren't sick of ideology in general. 'They are not sick of ideology, they are sick of false ideology,' they had answered. 'They need a real value system,' Professor Petkov had said; 'people will always need real values,' Professor Fotev had added.

What values will they get through a turn to the market? 'Real economies do not exist in an ethical vacuum. If we introduce market mechanisms and abandon our ethics, which contain universal values, we will get the ethics of capitalist production,' said Professor Fotev. But how, I asked him, can you have market mechanisms without market ethics? 'Market mechanisms have to do with such matters as prices, bank lending, investment and so on. The social consequences of a market system are a different question.' Are you saying the latter can be neutralized by administrative methods? 'To achieve social ends through the market we must use socialist methods.' Don't you actually mean anti-market ethics must be introduced into the market?

'These are very difficult dilemmas,' Professor Fotev answered, sighing. 'We cannot fill our shops with ideology. We have nowhere to turn. We must carry out a reform process, whatever its dangers.' At least, I said to him, you have one more choice than us. 'How so?'

he said. You can choose our way, but we cannot choose yours, since it is a failure, I answered.

At this he looked at me briefly, without the slightest expression, and did not comment.

*

I trudge back to my hotel from the Academy of Sciences, past clenched-fisted statuary and lovers loitering in the pale sunset; there are skateboards too, and women queuing at a stand-tap. Night falls, and the streets empty.

I turn on the television set in my hotel bedroom. After a flicker or two I am confronted, in full colour, with Mrs Thatcher, being deferentially interviewed from Downing Street for Soviet television; the programme is being relayed to Bulgaria at peak-viewing hour. For thirty-five minutes she is alternately demure and regal; a Tsarina (or so it seems in Sofia) come among rough *muzhiks*, to praise them for their efforts at self-improvement.

What Mr Gorbachev had seen when he came to power, she confides to the watching millions – the Bulgarian voice-over leaving the English audible – was 'not good enough for the Soviet people'. In consequence he was seeking 'what we have achieved', and 'trying to telescope into a few years what we took decades to obtain, our prosperity and our freedom.'

Sitting self-possessed in what seems to be a gilded chair, she lavishly commends glasnost and perestroika to a socialist world jaded by privation. Outside, the city has fallen into stillness. Mere change of attitude is 'insufficient', she declares; greater wealth, together with 'our freedom of choice in the shops', can be attained only by the 'overcoming of old conservative ways', by the acquisition of new managerial skills and by raised levels of production, while at the same time 'respecting national tradition and culture'.

'But the path of reform is difficult', she says, genteel in pearls, 'and without greater freedom of the individual there can be no economic progress.' It is once again a statement of the post-Communist agenda, and exactly judged; a Queen of the Night's elixir for famished peoples. 'May I wish you well', she adds majestically, with an awkward glacial smile, 'in your search for the greater prosperity which you will surely find.' Outside, the silence was deathly. 'My very best wishes to you all,' she repeated, before her image faded.

*

If Bulgaria cannot isolate itself from developments elsewhere in the socialist world, it is even more intimately affected by events in the Balkans. Thus, Bulgaria – with historic territorial claims on neighbouring Yugoslavia – has expressed its own hostility towards Slobodan Milosevic's 'Greater Serbia'; in particular to his presumed designs on the Yugoslav Republic of Macedonia, once dominated by Bulgars.

Serbian self-aggrandizement, and the possible collapse of the Yugoslav Federation, arouses Bulgaria's grievances about the 1878 Congress of Berlin, which severed Macedonia from Bulgaria and led to a further carve-up of the former between Greece and Serbia. The Macedonian question played a substantial part in determining Bulgaria's support for Germany in two world wars, since she looked to Germany both in 1914 and 1939 for assistance in the restoring of her former borders; indeed Nazi foreign policy included Bulgarian territorial expansion in its war aims.

Today, West Germany – together with the Soviet Union – continues to have most favoured nation status in Bulgaria. In the last two years, there has been a long list of reciprocal high-level contacts between them: Zhivkov was invited to Bonn in June 1987, while visiting West Germans have included Foreign Minister Genscher, Economics Minister Bangemann (twice) and President von Weizsaecker, who in November 1988 paid a four-day visit to Sofia.

On that occasion, von Weizsaecker was told by Zhivkov that his goal was the 'unlimited restructuring' of Bulgaria.

*

Outside the ministries' blank and granite exteriors stand lines of black Mercedes limousines. Gleaming in the sun, they carry the administrators of state socialism through deserted squares sealed to other traffic; only the silhouettes of power are visible behind their white lace curtains.

*

Welcome to the Dimitrov Communist Youth League, the Komsomol of Bulgaria!

'Break-dancers', says the thirty-three-year-old Nikolai Kamov – a sharp dresser and secretary of the League's central committee –

'recently used to gather in the street outside the headquarters of the Sofia Youth League. For them, the Komsomol is an absolute zero'; the decline in its membership is said to be accelerating. 'So we offered them free rehearsal space inside the Youth League Hall, a choreographer was provided, and the Central Youth House bought them some costumes.'

It was not always so tolerant. The Dimitrov Youth League, part of whose traditional function was to organize obligatory youth labour and whose ranks once included 'most of the school-age population', was until recently in the forefront of the Party's struggle to defend Bulgaria against the 'imitation of all things foreign', the 'unscrupulous worship of the Golden Calf' and 'spiritual pollution'. But in 1988 even a British heavy metal rock-group was allowed a fourteen-concert tour of Bulgaria. 'We Have Waited So Long!' read a banner in the audience in Sofia.

Kamov, who simultaneously believes in socialism, the stimulus of private property and the 'unchanging essence of the class struggle', is a sleek fellow, by training a lawyer. In his rimless glasses, with a stylish haircut, expensive moccasin slip-ons and an abstract daub on the walls of his modern office, he is some kind of Party yuppie: that is, a member of the rising class of smiling, bureaucratic reformers.

'When an informal group of young people gathers on the basis of a certain interest, musical, artistic, spiritual, political or whatever', he says smoothly, 'but outside the activities of the Komsomol, it is a very big challenge for us.' Why? 'Because it means we have failed to catch the trends of youth through the activities of the Komsomol.'

But what on earth is the concern of the Komsomol with break-dancing? 'It is a hobby which has nothing to do with political interests, but it influences young people.' So? 'If this interest is being developed independently of us, it could be reduced to something very elementary,' he replies, collapsing into obfuscation; but to Sofia's punks the Komsomol has not a cat in hell's chance of co-opting in this fashion.

Does this then mean, I ask Kamov, that you have given up your struggle against the imitation of all things foreign? 'We have to strike a balance between the preservation of our own values and giving Bulgarian youth access to the cultural traditions of other people.' Have you stopped trying to combat spiritual pollution? 'For the time being', he answers, 'we are not proposing to our members that they carry out any tasks against what we used to call bourgeois ideas.'

Why not? 'Because the world is changing. Modern times are themselves creating the means for young people to acquire knowledge of what is going on in the world. Promoting the image of the so-called enemy, and exposing the ways capitalism propagates its interests, cannot now yield the same results, especially among better educated youth, those who have their own information or have been to other countries,' he declares fluently, gesturing in a waft of after-shave, or perfume.

In other words, the Komsomol is in ideological difficulties, and you are looking around for a new sense of direction? 'There is a decline in our authority, I admit it. I can also admit that it is hard to find ways and means of overcoming it.'

His shirt is grey, and his tie matching; a kind of male twin-set. 'My parents', he suddenly confides, 'nurtured the ideals of our socialist revolution as something sacred. But they cannot be automatically translated into ideals for the younger generation. Our parents once lacked everything. They wanted to give their own children all the material things which they had not had themselves. So their children learned how to choose as a matter of principle. They were taught by life itself to choose', he repeats, 'but the Komsomol never taught this kind of culture.' Yesterday Mrs Thatcher was trying to fill the vacuum.

Aren't you facing a serious ideological crisis? 'I would call it an opening to the world, not an ideological crisis,' Kamov replies with calm assurance. But is a real reform in progress? 'We need to establish a more just and more productive socialist system,' he says, not answering directly. 'I am not over-optimistic that we shall do it quickly.'

There was a brief silence; over his desk he too has a large portrait of Zhivkov. How many members have you lost in the recent period? I ask him. (Total membership of the Komsomol has been estimated at around 1.5 million.) 'We have no statistics on such matters,' he replies, as smooth in the old falsehood as in the new candour.

What did you think of Mrs Thatcher on television last night? 'I admired her answers. She is a strong personality who can defend her positions. But I could not accept everything she said. It was half-truth, a lecture on how nice it is to have one's own work in one's own hands, how nice it is to have freedom of choice, and so on. It was an idealized model of life in Great Britain,' he declares, smiling. Do you think many people were watching? 'Nearly everyone,' he answered.

*

In her official persona, my minder at the Sofia press bureau, the formidable Violeta Stoichkova – formerly a teacher of languages – says to me, over a cup of coffee, 'The important thing is that Bulgarian society is moving.' We exchange sceptical glances. 'If it isn't, it better had,' she added, laughing in her private capacity, and in a deep contralto.

*

The Eastern Orthodox Church of the Mantle of the Virgin, in central Sofia. Fastidious Father Petkin, brown-bearded and of refined gesture, is in the dark vestry, with his plump son, softly setting out a small table with sticky cakes and teacups. On the vestry walls hang faded grey photographs of late nineteenth-century church benefactors.

He does not know how many Christians there are in Bulgaria. (An unofficial estimate has it that 70 per cent of Bulgarians consider themselves members of the Eastern Orthodox Church.) 'I have not asked myself this question,' he adds, cutting a lemon into thin slices. What about baptisms, then, in this church? Are they rising? He pours the tea, taking his time, his hands the colour of alabaster. Spoons tinkle in the silence, his son watching wide-eyed from a corner.

Father Petkin, handsome in his black cassock and the fourth generation priest in his family, carefully takes up the baptismal registers and slowly turns the pages. 'In 1986, 129 children were baptized in this church,' he says, reading from a page of annual totals. 'In 1987, 148. In 1988, 280'; an increase during the last year of nearly 100 per cent.

He turns another page, smoothing it down before reading. 'In 1987, there were 21 marriages celebrated. In 1988, 34.' He takes up an account book, leafing through it page by page to find what he is seeking. 'In 1986', he reads, 'we sold candles to the value of 22,000 leva.' He turns a page. 'In 1988, to the value of 40,000 leva.'

Is there then, I ask, a religious revival in Bulgaria? There is a long silence while he replaces the registers and the account book on the shelf from which he took them. 'A point comes', he eventually answers in Chekhovian fashion, darting a swift glance at the official interpreter, 'when an unbeliever will turn his thoughts to God. What has been hindering him, everyone can say for himself.'

If there is a revival of baptism and church attendance, has it anything to do with a change of political climate? Silently he offers me another cake, the vestry clock ticking loudly, his son unstirring. 'In our country, the Church has never lost the respect of the people.' You mean there has been no real change in the State's attitude to religious observance? He takes his first careful sip from the teacup, soundlessly replacing it in its saucer.

'There is a beginning.' A beginning of what? 'A re-evaluation of values,' he replies, cutting his cake into four neat pieces and placing the first of them in his mouth, dropping no crumbs on his cassock. But what about the harassment and intimidation of radical priests demanding greater religious freedom? He eats the second piece of cake, and sips a second time from his teacup before he answers. 'Maybe in the post-war period such things happened,' he says, darting another swift glance in the direction of the interpreter.

'The Church in Bulgaria', he continues softly, 'has always taught the people to keep to their own places and to do their best, as God's creatures. It is a flower, a living organism, which is watered when it is needed. Only two or three days ago, our Patriarch was received by President Zhivkov. It is a sign,' he adds. A sign of what? 'It is a sign which testifies to the good relations between Church and State in our country.'

Have you heard of the Committee for Religious Freedom? I enquire. (Composed of large numbers of young Orthodox priests, as I have heard, and based in the city of Veliko Tarnovo, it has been demanding, among other things, the opening of new seminaries and rights to promote religion, through the teaching of children and religious publication.) He takes up the third sliver of sticky cake in his fine fingers, the clock seeming to tick louder. 'I have heard about it,' he says. What have you heard? Father Petkin leans down from his chair to a black leather note-case on the floor beside him, and, putting it on his knee, slips the catch, opens the flap and – careful not to snag its long chain – draws out a crucifix. 'The Patriarch will pull my ear if I am not wearing my cross,' he says laughing, pulling his own right ear and replacing the note-case on the floor, propping it against the chair leg. He puts the chain around his neck, adjusting the cross so that it hangs straight on his cassock.

'They should not act in the name of the Church,' he says, swiftly now. 'They are only very few. The Holy Synod is insulted by their actions. There are rules in every Church to be observed. If they had complaints, they should have brought such complaints before the Synod. In a family, the troubled child should always go to his parents to seek assistance,' he declares in the gathering darkness. 'Are people forbidden to attend church? Are priests forbidden to preach sermons? None of this has been forbidden. So what are their problems? No one knows,' he answers, hands clasped together on his chest, nestling dove-like on his carefully-pressed cassock.

When I leave, his tea stands cold and barely a third drunk on the vestry table, and there is a quarter-piece of cake still uneaten.

*

Is there a genuine reform process beginning in Bulgaria, or not? Judging by the new Institute of Economics and Management, set up in May 1988 with a staff of '400' under the auspices of the Ministry of Economics and Planning there is. Or is there? 'Yes,' says the Institute's untidy director, Benko Benev, 'there is.' But then he would say that. Around him, at a long boardroom table, are assembled the deferential stars of this new Bulgarian think-tank, which includes economists, sociologists, demographers, 'planning engineers' and development experts. There is even a philosopher among them.

'We want to create a planning and market economy, both,' declares Benev, tie loosened and slumped at the head of the table. 'To do this, we have to change the function of the plan, and adapt it to the market.' But how? 'We need indicative planning which reflects the necessities of the market,' he answers, using different words to restate his original formulation.

'Our task', he goes on, reading from a note pad, 'is to find the optimum rate of development for the country, restructure the price and tax system, devise policies for the stimulus of technical inno-vation, establish modern information networks, create new methods of management, institute broad levels of computer training and solve the difficult social problems of the development process within the framework of our socialist system.'

Hair tousled, he looks over his spectacles at me, as if for comment, or even approval. This is like God's six-day programme, I say to him. 'But on the seventh day God rested, and we are not resting,' rejoins Benev, heaving himself up in his chair and guffawing. There is polite, glasnost-style laughter, and stifled coughing from a demographer in sunglasses. But why, supposing that this can be done at all, do you want to do it? 'If we want to be a modern State', replies Benev, who has slumped down in his chair again, 'we must interrelate with everything advanced in modern civilization'; almost the exact words used by Zhivkov in his speech to intellectuals.

'We want joint ventures, we want free trade zones as in China, we want to become a rich country, we want to work with you on the basis of new principles, we want to hold you in respect and we want you to help us,' he says flamboyantly, the rest of the table fallen silent. (Is this urgent aspiration, or sound and fury signifying nothing?) I find it hard to get my bearings here, I say to the crumpled Benev. In the West, Bulgaria is regarded as an immobile society, a kind of Dead Sea in the Balkans. 'It is not a Dead Sea. Under the surface the waters are agitated. We are gaining the strength to swim in them at this very moment. It is a very complicated situation, which will be described in the future by historians, philosophers and poets,' he adds with a disorderly flourish.

His greying hair overhangs his ears and collar. 'We must devolve power closer to the people, we must tear down factories causing environmental damage, we must transfer agricultural land to the cultivators, we must restore the beauty of the Bulgarian village,' he announces, waving me down as I try to ask another question. 'Every country is engaged in restructuring, progressive things are emerging from which we too are learning. Why not us also? Does it mean we are flirting with capitalism?' he asks, his notebook forgotten.

'You think there are risks,' he continues, not letting me get a word in. 'Socialism has always been running risks. In Bulgaria we have been losing certain battles. Now we are trying to win the war, we are opening up a new front of struggle,' he says, with an air of dishevelled triumph. What war? I ask him. 'We want to give impulse to initiative, we want to improve the quality of life, we want the law to be sacred like the Ten Commandments, we want a new, creative, Bulgarian personality,' he says, thudding on the table.

He subsides, the room abashed and silent. Is all this hot air, or honest endeavour? In Budapest, I say to Benev, Janos Berecz told me that Hungary had taken off all its clothes and was trying on new ones. 'But first', declares Benev, 'you must wash. Our bodies are dirty.' What do you mean? 'First, we must recognize our errors, Kim

Il Sung, Pol Pot, Mao. Second, we do not have to wear foreign fashions. Third, we need new trousers only.

'But is it not an objective necessity', he asks noisily, struggling upwards in his chair, 'to increase domestic accumulation? As Marxists, do we not have an obligation to be creative? Why should socialism not take some progressive aspects from the capitalist system?' he demands, as if addressing a reluctant politburo. No one moves a muscle. 'For example', he says distractedly, 'we are nurturing ideas about private health care. In the past our health care was absolutely free, but such a system liquidated the enthusiasm of our doctors and alienated them from their patients' medical problems. It is an outcome which, for us, has damaged the free socialist model of health care. We say that if you can choose your own car and your own shoes, why can you not choose your own doctor?'

You sound exactly like Mrs Thatcher, I say to Benev. He took it as a compliment, beaming. 'We understand', he says politely, 'that Mrs Thatcher has worked out her new scheme of health care. We wish to introduce it here in Bulgaria also.' (Can it really be? Or am I dreaming?)

How are you going to restore a genuine market system in Bulgaria? I enquire. By decree? By administrative orders from the Ministry of Economics and Planning? He doesn't appear to hear me, slapping his notebook closed; and seeming to have had enough of the conversation, turns to speak with a colleague. He then rounds on the question. 'The market was destroyed from above', he says curtly, gathering up his papers, 'so it must be restored from above. He who has made the mistake should correct it.'

Does everyone share your views in ruling circles? He stands up in a shambles. 'We have started a process of active searching. We shall get rid of political traditionalism and we shall get rid of dogma. The old system of doctrine-by-order broke socialism. Now we are again coming up against obstacles, but we have declared war on conservatism,' he announces with grim relish.

Can you really make such a bold statement in front of so many? 'People have to get used to saying what they really think,' he answers.

*

A few minutes after my arrival at their dingy flat, Zhelyu Zhelev's wife, hearing the sound of a vehicle, went to the window. 'They have come too,' she says wanly. She is wearing a baggy shift and has a sallow complexion, and he is in old carpet slippers. Outside, a grey van with screened rear windows is manoeuvring into a parking-space. ('They also want to listen,' says Zhelev.)

An historical research worker at a Sofia Institute of Culture, Zhelev is a leading figure in the 200-strong Club for the Support of Perestroika and Glasnost, and one of the 'political dregs and degenerates' denounced by Zhivkov in his address to the intelligentsia. Launched in November 1988 at a meeting held in Sofia University, the Club calls for 'real democratization' and 'free public discussion'; but it can meet only privately, circulating state-ments to the newspapers, the radio, the TV, 'even though', says Zhelev, speaking in French, 'we know they will not be published.'

It is modest work. But spying on those who belong to the Club – by tailing, by phone-tapping, by bugging apartments – is intense and constant; my assignation with Zhelev, arranged by telephone, has brought the police van along also. BCP members who have had the courage to join have been expelled from the Party; others, Party and non-Party members, have been harassed by house-searches, and several thrown out of their employments. The regime is even going to the lengths of disbanding Zhelev's Institute, where there are a half-dozen Club activists, 'merely in order to break up our group', says Zhelev; he has been told by the authorities that the Institute will be re-formed, with personnel changes. 'It will deprive the six of us of the means of living,' he adds; Club members in work will contribute to a levy to support them, as is already being done for others.

From the small kitchen, there is a rough clatter of pans and a dull thud of gas as the cooker is ignited. 'They are putting pressure on me to leave the country', Zhelev says – enforced exile being regularly employed by the authorities in order to rid Bulgaria of dissenters – 'but I have no intention of going. I refuse categorically to accept their propositions,' he adds, as the room fills with the smells of cooking. 'Ten members of another group have recently been expelled to Vienna. There is a permanent danger hanging over us. It weighs upon the heads of all those who are working for genuine reform in Bulgaria'; indeed, the Bulgarian Penal Code makes propaganda and activity against the Bulgarian socialist system, as well as the 'spreading of information that weakens the Bulgarian Communist Party', crimi-nal offences.

Zhelev, a small grey-haired man in his late forties, lives in straitened circumstances, his apartment stale and frowsty. The reformers in

Bulgaria, he says, are demagogues and hypocrites; to him, the initiatives which they announce from time to time have no real content. 'The man-in-the-street', he continues, taut with the stress which his own opinions bring him, 'does not believe in all their so-called reforms and innovations, since they always come to nothing. Their manoeuvres are well known in Bulgaria. How can you have genuine perestroika without democratic changes? The political conditions simply do not exist in Bulgaria for a real reconstruction. Here even public debate is forbidden.'

So what is real in Bulgaria? I ask him. 'Only the scepticism is real,' he answers, going briefly to the window, and returning. 'They know their socialism has failed, but they will not admit it,' he says, sitting down again in his battered armchair.

Is there nothing new in the situation? 'Yes. They are now speaking of reform with greater vigour. The outcome will be no different.' But how do you know? 'Because they don't believe in reform themselves,' Zhelev answers. And how do you know that? He laughs. 'Because they speak about the reforms in a different way when they are with their friends in the apparatus.' How do you know? 'I know,' he answers, without elaboration. 'In any case, do you really think they would endanger their own interests by permitting a genuine reform process? And if there is such a process, why are they continuing to persecute us?'

He has a halo of hair like Harpo Marx; grandparents, children, animals live together in the small apartment. 'The authorities do not even permit translations into Bulgarian from the Soviet press. Soviet glasnost is too much for our Bulgarian reformers,' he adds wrily. 'Fortunately, the intelligentsia here understands Russian well. It is fantastic to think that the Soviet Union should have become a source of intellectual freedom. We exchange *Ogonyok*, the *Literary Gazette*, *Moscow News* and *Novy Mir* among us. Whoever has a copy passes it on quickly. Together, Soviet publications and western broadcasts have become like a force of nature,' he adds, briefly jolly.

What about the Bulgarian press? Are you saying there are no signs of glasnost in it? Editors have been speaking to me in a relatively open fashion, I say to Zhelev. 'For the critical intelligentsia here, which first of all wants the true history of our country since 1944, there is no glasnost. There is too much to hide, too much from the time of Zhivkov himself. They cannot afford to reveal it.'

Yet hasn't Zhivkov just told intellectuals that Marxist political economy is unscientific? Isn't that a victory for candour? 'Not really,' Zhelev answers. 'He merely wants to create the impression that he too is part of the discussion that is going on everywhere in the socialist system.' But isn't there a faction struggle going on between conservatives and reformers as in other East European countries? 'No. Here, there are only rival bureaucratic interests in competition with one another. Here the struggle is based not on principles, but on ambitions.' Then why is Mrs Thatcher cited with such approval by leading figures in the Party? 'Because her toughness and strength of will, her method of governing Britain without bending, is seen by our bureaucrats as a model of authoritarianism which is useful to their interests.' So are you saying that the economic changes which have been announced have no substance? 'Fascism also combined a totalitarian State with private property,' he answered fiercely.

They shared their poor evening meal with me: a glass of home-made wine, and a little rice with two small cubes of meat, mainly gristle. A cat – tail in air – prowled for a left-over morsel. What is socialism? I asked him. 'I do not know,' he said simply. Then what do you have here? 'In Bulgaria, we have a police-dominated system of bureaucratic human domination, which is called "socialist" by its own agit-prop department,' Zhelev said flatly.

Out in the dark street – 50 metres from the unlit grey van with its screened windows – a second vehicle was parked, containing (said Zhelev straightaway) four plainclothesmen. It drew away from the kerb as we approached. Zhelev, accompanying me to the taxi rank, was still in his slippers.

*

It is the first day of Ramadan, and Sofia's city-centre mosque is crowded; in its doorway, swarthy men in corduroy or baggy trousers push forward, with darting eyes, towards their devotions. Strolling Bulgarian passers-by fastidiously avoid the alien throng, stepping into the roadway without a glance at Islam's faithful.

Officially, and to the great anger of the government in Istanbul, no Turkish community as such exists in Bulgaria. Instead, they are regarded as descendants of ethnic Bulgarians forced into Islam during the centuries of Ottoman rule from Constantinople. Some 900,000 in number (around 10 per cent of the population), they have been fiercely resistant to Sofia's policy, accelerated since 1984, of forcible assimilation; but they remain in the eyes of the regime errant Bulgarians.

Turkish-language schools have been closed in the name of a 'patriotic education for all', mosques (though not the Sofia mosque) shut down, Muslim cemeteries ploughed over, religious instruction banned, circumcision prohibited as a 'criminal interference with children's health' – and even the use of Islamic or Arab names made illegal. In February 1988, the UN Human Rights Committee singled out Bulgaria as one of seven countries 'systematically preventing the peaceful practice of religion', even though Bulgaria's own penal code makes it a crime to 'prevent citizens, by the use of force or threat, from performing their religious rites and services'.

To the authorities in Sofia, the Turks of Bulgaria are Bulgarian citizens of a 'unified socialist nation'; but when racial trouble flares they quickly become a 'potential Nato fifth column' or even a 'Turkish Trojan Horse in Bulgaria'. Settled mainly in underdeveloped rural areas of north-eastern and south-eastern Bulgaria, with poor educational facilities, a conservative Islamic culture, chronic unemployment and a high birth-rate, many find work as seasonal migrant labour. ('The question of the Turks is a very sensitive issue, a taboo subject with the authorities. They are the great demographic problem of our future as a nation,' even Zhelyu Zhelev had said, with an unexpected flurry of passion.)

In December 1984 and January 1985, at least forty and perhaps one hundred people died in the violent crushing of protests against the assimilation programme; in Kardzhali and Momcilgrad in southern Bulgaria even tanks were used (so it is said) to put down what had become an ethnic minority rebellion, as Turkey rattled its Ottoman sabres across the nearby border.

After the revolt was suppressed, the protagonists received their various deserts: the hardline BCP boss of Kardzhali, Georgi Tanev, who earned his spurs in the Momcilgrad street-fighting, was promoted – after a decent interval – to be minister of the interior, and the local Imam, Nedyo Gendzhev, who all along insisted that Bulgarian Muslims possessed complete religious freedom, is now the Chief Mufti of Bulgaria. Acts of sabotage, committed at the time in the name of resistance to assimilation, were punished with execution.

*

The chandeliers in the silent palazzo of the State Council – of which Todor Zhivkov is chairman – are a-glitter, the long identical corridors a receding vista of unmarked closed doors and red carpets, where every footfall is muffled. Behind one such door, the same as all the others, is Deputy Chairman Yaroslav Radev, sitting at a long council table; on the wall hangs the largest portrait of his Leader I have seen in Sofia.

The web of Bulgarian State power, in which Zhivkov places his intimates in key positions, is a complex one. It is also totalitarian. Thus, the State Council – formerly called the praesidium – not only supervises the governmental council of ministers, but also, as the 'representative of the national assembly', has its own direct legislative powers. It is able to issue decrees, or Balkan ukases, with the force of law when the Assembly is not meeting – which is most of the time. These legislative decrees are then approved, usually without much discussion, at the next brief session of the Assembly, of which there are usually three a year. A proposal of July 1987 (typically put forward by Zhivkov himself) to abolish the State Council and give greater authority to the Assembly has come to nothing, like other putative reform measures in Bulgaria.

Yaroslav Radev, a pugnacious old man with a limp, white hair and intermittently drooping eyelids, is said to be one of the principal supervisors of Bulgaria's reform process. 'A conception is being worked out for legislative changes', he says gruffly, the interpreter's voice trembling; 'changes in the responsibility of various State institutions, changes in the legal system, changes in the management of the economy, changes in local government administration.'

He proceeds, eyelids drooping, to a didactic twenty-minute account of details of the existing system; talking me down when I try to ask for particulars of the changes which the State Council has under consideration, the interpreter a-flutter. But he finally claims, at length and in a surly basso, that Bulgaria is intent on creating a 'socialist legal State' with 'safeguards for citizen rights', and an 'independent judiciary, elected by the National Assembly'.

Why do you want an independent judiciary? I eventually manage to ask him, the interpreter quaking. 'No matter what the social order, in the constitutions of other countries it is a principle that judges obey only the law, and should be independent of the bodies which create the law.' (This too sounds almost Hungarian.) But if the Assembly is given the power to elect the judges, how can they be regarded as independent of it? I enquire.

'Through these measures', he continues, ignoring my question entirely, 'we will guarantee the judges' independence. We are still discussing whether they should be elected for life or for fixed five-year terms, and what procedures should be adopted if they do not impartially fulfil their duties.' A detailed description of Bulgarian legal administration follows.

He sips from a glass of water; a space opens. What did you mean by a socialist legal State? I ask him. Is the present State not legal? He looks at me with hooded eyes, fists on the table, as if unused to being directly questioned; the voice of the interpreter, anxious at the *lèse-majesté*, wavers. But stalking even this red-carpeted labyrinth is some kind of glasnost. 'At recent plenums of the central committee', he answers slowly, 'I have repeated that a socialist legal State must be one in which democratic principles are continuously developed, and where there is precise' – 'or meticulous', adds the interpreter, offering me another option – 'observation of the laws which govern the rights of the individual.'

Are they not observed now, then? There is a brief pause, the interpreter's eyes in her lap, hands folded. 'Ever since 1944, I remember things,' Radev surprisingly replies, his curmudgeonly manner beginning to soften. 'Ever since the socialist revolution [what socialist revolution?] in Bulgaria, there have been violations of the laws.' In which areas? 'We have failed to defend the rights of the citizen consistently, and we have broken the law in the law-making process itself.' How? 'By permitting too many different State authorities to issue laws, decrees, administrative acts and regulations. Now we even have direct ministerial law-making. It has produced a normative jungle, in which neither the judge nor the citizen can make his way. It has permitted the over-breeding of regulation. I have told the central committee that the law is for the citizen, and not vice versa.'

What of changes in property law? I ask him. Here he begins to withdraw; both candour and *preustroistvo* (as perestroika is called in Bulgaria) have their limits. 'Personal property is already permitted under the Constitution,' he replies without expression. Yes, but what about the private ownership of the means of production? The interpreter translates, and waits. 'The new economic *ukaz* has already introduced the idea of personal property in the means of manufacturing.' But will you introduce a new view of property into the Constitution? 'The majority of property will remain in the hands of the State or in co-operative ownership.' So there will be no structural economic reform of substance? 'We shall see what are the effects of the earlier economic changes,' he answers, his eyelids drooping.

*

In Sofia, I said to Radev, some people say your reform is unreal, without substance and will come to nothing. 'They can say what they like,' he replies abrasively. How far have you really gone with it? I ventured. 'We have prepared our conception for the restructuring of institutions.' You suggested earlier that the conception is still being worked out. 'It is almost completed,' said Radev.

But what is meant by conception? Do you mean you are considering some kind of philosophy of change? 'It is more concrete. We are working out the general direction of changes to State bodies, the legal system and so on. The preliminary work is urgent. It is also the most difficult,' he said with a flash of irritation. Why is it difficult? 'Because we have to define the direction of development. And if we change one thing we have to change another, yet everything which is good needs to be retained and only the bad discarded. All this must be understood and considered carefully beforehand.'

Some people think you are making a few economic adjustments, but do not intend to carry out real structural changes. He did not respond. People say that it is all talk, I added, venturing a step further, the interpreter blushing.

There was a few moments' silence. 'The laws and the Constitution cannot be changed in piecemeal fashion. Some know-alls, or know-bests, out there [jabbing in the direction of the window] think we are hesitating,' he said aggressively. 'Or so you tell me,' he added. 'But to ensure stability in Bulgaria needs serious study, an assessment of all the components in the situation. You cannot make a machine from a design of only one of its details. Can an architect make a plan of the first floor only? We must go from the general to the particular in a steady manner, without haste, assessing the likely consequences of each one of our actions.'

How long do you think all this will take? 'Did your bourgeois society become a reality at once, without clashes?' Radev returned swiftly. 'Did you not have your Levellers, your Cromwell, your English Revolution? Napoleon, Hitler and Stalin all tried to impose their systems on the world', he said hotly, 'but they ended in failure.' (This I took to be an oblique, or unintended, reference to Gorbachevism also.) 'I have told my Russian friends', he continued pugnaciously – the interpreter being swept along – 'of the negative consequences of what they are doing, of the great risks that their own citizens will disturb the system in an increasingly undemocratic fashion, of the impulsive nature of their new election laws and of other similar changes.'

You mean there will be no multi-party system in Bulgaria? 'We already have multiple parties in Bulgaria,' he said dismissively, his Stalinist persona taking over, 'the BCP, the Agrarian Union, the Fatherland Front, the working collectives, the public organizations. But perhaps Mrs Thatcher', he said, smiling suddenly, 'should tell us how many parties we should have in Bulgaria, according to her understanding of the matter. If she thinks we should have five, then tell her to introduce three more parties in Great Britain.' There are already five, I said. 'We have our own traditions,' he interrupted, waving me away and brusquely talking down the interpreter. 'The West has only one idea, that our dissidents should be in power.'

He looked at me impassively. 'But in our world there are still two different social systems, with two different ideologies, strategies and tactics. What do you, for example, think your right-wing theoreticians are aiming for? Do you have no ideas about it?' he demanded, leaning forward across the council table; the interpreter murmured her translation into the silence. 'Their aim is to prove to working people that they live in the freest and best of all democratic worlds, and that if they struggle to change their system they will lose their freedoms. And what is that?' he asked, looking from me to the interpreter, and back again. 'It is a strategy', he answered, stabbing the air, 'for the self-protection of their system. I too have listened to your Mrs Thatcher,' he said, leaning back in his chair and gazing at me.

Why? I asked him. He took another sip of water.

'Because when you create the principle of glasnost, you have to listen to all opinions,' he replied sardonically, eyeing me idly. 'But in Britain and the United States your opinions are controlled by the State authorities and the press owners,' he continued, brushing aside my objections. 'Here, with glasnost, there will be all sorts of opinions, everybody will put forward his own programme. We will break the habit of issuing and responding to orders. We will give initiative to the people. We will create the conditions for competition between talented and gifted people,' he declared with a rough bravado.

So the democratic revolution is underway in Bulgaria? Radev looked vaguely at me, as if pursuing his own thoughts, or tiring of the conversation. 'The broadening of democracy can take many forms, and has many dangers,' he said quietly. 'To admit incompetents leads to anarchy and other distortions.' There was a brief silence, during which he gave the impression of a man benignly musing. 'At every historic stage, as in the French Revolution, illiterates, semi-literates and demagogues have become involved in political upheavals,' he declared in Olympian fashion, beginning to collect up his papers. 'In the USSR, semi-literates now write even in *Izvestia* [the newspaper of the Gorbachevite reformers],' Radev added brutally.

He stood up, and became more genial, as if he were relenting. 'I cannot yet say exactly what changes to the electoral law and the Constitution will be adopted. But we will probably introduce such changes at the end of 1990, when there will be the next National Assembly elections. I do not want to offend you, but one thing is certain. We will not choose a monarch, nor an upper house with lords in it.'

At this he smiled broadly, beneath the framed portrait of his Leader, his eyes closing.

*

Is the State Council to be abolished? I asked him as we moved towards the door. He laughed, taken aback by the question, which he understood before it was translated. 'They will have to shoot us first,' he answered. Who are 'they'? I enquired. He did not reply, shaking me warmly by the hand and glossing over the moment with laughter.

*

The cowering provincial town of Momcilgrad, shabby scene of the violent troubles with the Bulgarian Turkish minority in December 1984 and January 1985 – approached past unmanned roadside police posts – is grey and sullen. As dusk falls and the poor shops close, the very town seems to emit a cowed sigh of weariness, or boredom.

Here, a mere 25 miles through the Rhodope mountains from Thrace and the northern Greek border, are paved streets ending in cleared lots like old bomb-sites; derelict or ramshackle stone houses; jerry-built apartment blocks; and sheep browsing amid rubble and nettles. As the joyless streets empty of their last hurrying figures, a

Bulgarian militiaman with fierce curling moustaches sets out on his patrol, boots ringing on the cracked pavings.

*

The sun itself seems to quiet the landscape of rolling, open pasture along the almost deserted road from Harmanli to Elhovo, which runs parallel with the Turkish border. You can hear, on this blissful day, sheep's bells tinkling in the sunny stillness, and the buzzing of an insect in the bell of a wildflower; from the nearby hamlet of Bogomil come the sounds of children's voices and a woman talking.

No more than 180 miles from Istanbul, it might also be rural central India; Bogomil's thorn hedges are like a stockade, its beaten paths sandy, its movements sun-stifled. The small grey mosque – with its old central cupola, and its porch set upon graceful stone columns – is derelict, the stucco broken. But here at least there is no heroic statuary, nor muscular granite, and not a whisper for or against glasnost. Only the sound of larks, and a tethered ass's agonized braying.

*

On the way to Sofia airport, the young taxi-driver said 'Gorbachev super. Here, perestroika very little,' pursing his thumb and index finger at 70 miles an hour. 'Bulgaria theory, da; Bulgaria practice, nix,' he added, taking both his hands off the wheel for the flat, scything gesture.

8

Poland, May 1989:
V for Victory

There are horses drawing the wooden plough at the city boundary as
we drive eastwards out of Warsaw. 'We can wait fifteen years for a
telephone', my photographer Wittold Krassowski is saying, 'and
twenty or thirty years for an apartment' – even thirty-five years in
some places. The allocation of toilet rolls is said to work out at eight
per person per annum, or one every forty-five days, on average. 'With
you, the fact that you have an efficient State has isolated people from
one another.' He drives along in silence, a light rain falling. 'Here,
the problem is different. It is socialism itself that has demoralized
us,' he says, waving vaguely at the drizzling landscape.

*

Night and Fog, *Nacht und Nebel*, in Lublin. On this mist-wreathed
road through the heart of the old Nazi charnel-house of eastern
Poland a sign points into the darkness to the camp of Majdanek;
between 1942 and 1944, 360,000 people died there. Krassowski
points in the opposite direction. 'This used to be a big field', he says,
gesturing at a passing building site, eerily arc-lit, 'where Pope Wojtyla
said Mass [in June 1987] during his visit.'

Here are ghosts of past annihilation and martyrdom, million upon
million; no less than 6 million Poles died in the war (or some 17 per
cent of the entire population), of whom 3.3 million were Jews, 90
per cent of the Polish Jewish population.

Now the socialist phoenix too has fallen back into the ashes.

*

'Left' and 'right', like the word 'socialism' itself, have lost their
meanings in Poland. No wonder, when you have a proletarian move-

ment led by a former shipyard electrician who is often on his knees to the Black Madonna of Czestochowa, and which for a decade has been struggling for 'democracy' and 'freedom' against the exploitation – by state socialism – of Polish working people. The movement, moreover, has been aided in its search for progress by a hierarchical Roman Church, strong in Poland for a millennium, with a profoundly conservative social policy and unshakeable working-class support; and it faces a Communist Party led by an army general, Wojciech Jaruzelski, whose coup in December 1981 was intended to rescue Poland from the 'anarchy' threatened by a workers' trade union.

To cap it all, the stiff-necked general himself is said to be of the Lublin aristocracy and Jesuit educated.

*

After the declaration of martial law, Solidarity – which, by 1981, had some 10 million members, and was more than three times the size of the Party – was suspended and its activists, including Lech Walesa, interned or driven underground. In October 1982, the union was formally dissolved by law. In December 1982, an alternative labour organization, OPZZ, was set up by the State, membership of which became a precondition of employment; the Third Reich had employed a similar method to break the pre-war German labour movement.

In July 1983, martial law was lifted, though the army remained effectively in command of Poland, its continuing purpose to restore the authority of the Party and its institutions. An amnesty for many of Solidarity's leaders and advisers was declared in August 1984, though some remained in prison until 1986 and others underground until as late as 1988. In October 1985, in order to legitimize his regime, General Jaruzelski called 'elections', Solidarity called for their boycott, and perhaps two-thirds of the electorate voted. At the tenth Party Congress in June-July 1986, Gorbachev's reform policy was endorsed, and Gorbachev in return endorsed Jaruzelski's rule in Poland. In September, 225 more political prisoners were freed.

Throughout 1987, the beginnings of change made their tentative appearance. Jaruzelski visited the Vatican; US sanctions against Poland, imposed in the wake of martial law, were lifted; and at the end of the year plans for reform – trading political liberalization for public acceptance of an austerity programme – were put to a referendum. But it was all very slow moving.

*

More recent events have moved quickly. In October 1988 students were being arrested in Warsaw for protesting about housing conditions, and General Jaruzelski was arguing that there would be 'no pluralism' until Poland had 'achieved economic recovery'; but Adam Michnik – one of Solidarity's leading intellectuals – was insisting, for his part, that it was Solidarity which gave 'real life to our society'.

In November Jaruzelski, Walesa's former jailer, was telling Mrs Thatcher on her visit to Poland that a 'new phase of democratic humanistic socialism' was emerging. In December 1988, a national Citizens' Committee of over one hundred representatives of the opposition, set up by Lech Walesa, was sneeringly described as a 'petty Parliament' by Wladyslaw Pozoga, the deputy minister of the interior. In fact, a situation of dual power was already in existence.

The same month, as the politburo was reshuffled and hardliners ousted, Prime Minister Mieczyslaw Rakowski – a Jaruzelski appointee whose first wife and two sons had defected to the West themselves – declared that 'democracy can be developed without Solidarity'; in December 1980 Rakowski had famously described

Solidarity's advisers as 'little shits' and Lech Walesa as a 'devious and ignorant peasant'. But by January 1989, a central committee plenum was recognizing the 'role of pluralism in our political system', as the Party, its authority and confidence ebbing, restated its aim to 'create a modern version of socialism in Poland'. In the same month, another two politically turbulent priests were murdered.

In February, the Round Table talks between the government and Solidarity began, Walesa calling for a 'reconstruction that will make this one-party State into a State that belongs to society and to the nation'. At the same time students were being tear-gassed in Cracow while demonstrating for an independent students' union; Rakowski was telling *Le Monde* that 'the majority of Polish society is interested neither in Solidarity nor in the Round Table'; Jerzy Urban, the government's chief spokesman, was exclaiming, 'stop pushing us against the wall, we are proposing sweeping changes!'; and Jaruzelski himself was 'prepared to call in the army to quell any anti-government attempts to destabilize the country'.

By March 1989, basic agreement had been reached in the talks, and on 5 April they ended. The next day accords were signed; the day after, Parliament – the *Sejm* – was agreeing to legalize Solidarity, to amend the constitution and electoral laws, and to provide both for new *Sejm* elections and the setting up of a freely-elected Senate. Twelve days later, on 19 April, Lech Walesa was in Rome paying homage to the Pope. On 1 May the traditional May Day parade – 'too long, boring and expensive' – was cancelled.

*

Food, as well as freedom, has been for twenty years and more at the centre of popular grievance. Past food price increases have led to strikes, to riots and even to the fall of Party leaders, as with Gomulka in 1970, and Gierek ten years later. Walesa's shipyard protest movement was born in the uproar which greeted a steep rise in meat prices in July 1980, while in 1988 Prime Minister Rakowski tried (in vain) to tempt the nation with a 'Polish table groaning with food' in exchange for obedient consensus.

The poorly stocked shelves continue to mock the window shopper's dreams of plenty. It is a life, for many, of cheese-paring; a sallow life, or half life; a life of waiting.

*

There is only a month to go before the 4 June general election. In the horse-deal struck (under Church tutelage) at the Round Table talks, it was decided that contests for the newly created 100-seat Senate were to be fully democratic, pitting Party candidates, constituency by constituency, directly against candidates of the opposition. But as far as the *Sejm* is concerned, the Party has been assured 65 per cent of the 480 seats, and the opposition – who will be calling themselves 'Independents' – 35 per cent; indeed without such an undemocratic 'guarantee' to the Party, it might have been on a hiding-to-nothing.

This artifice will be managed in very complicated fashion by allocating to each *Sejm* constituency, depending on its size, a certain number of seats. In a given constituency, two seats, say, will be reserved to the Party and one to the Independents, a disproportion which overall will produce the 65/35 per cent division. (Even the 35 per cent total the Solidarity negotiators had to fight for.) In such a constituency, the electors will be presented on polling day with separate lists of *Sejm* candidates – Party candidates on one list and Independents on another – and will vote for the candidates of their choice on each list separately.

An anti-Communist elector will be able to refuse his vote to all the candidates on the Party's list if he chooses; another elector could give his votes both to Party and Independent candidates, marking first one list and then the other. But there will be no democratic contest between them. [Indeed, in the final reckoning and if the Independents do particularly well, it could turn out that the 35 per cent Independent members of the new *Sejm*, though fewer in number, have been elected with a larger national total of votes than have been gained by the 65 per cent block of deputies elected for the Party.]

There is a further complication: if, in any constituency, and whether in the election for the Senate or the *Sejm*, the winning Independent-list candidates or the winning Party-list candidates fail on 4 June to gain more than 50 per cent of the votes cast for their list, then there will have to be run-offs a fortnight later to find the winners.

The effect of all this complexity, especially in the deeper countryside, is substantial confusion. Nevertheless these are also the beginnings of the establishment of parliamentary democracy in Poland, whatever happens.

★

In a farmhouse near Przemysl, in the far corner of south-eastern Poland, the tired midnight talk among the local Solidarity campaign workers is of organizers' phones which have gone mysteriously on the blink, of tailings by plainclothes security men and other 'normal harassments'.

They have a short period in which to canvass, the parliamentary democratic process is unfamiliar to the electors, and the area is largely rural, with a peasant culture and traditions. Moreover, there is a shortage of campaign funds ('We have no money'); there is even a shortage of paper for their technically still illegal leaflets, banned under electoral rules which allow the Solidarity programme to be distributed but forbid further 'propaganda'. In addition, anything at all which is published in more than 1,000 copies must still be submitted to the local censor, a rule which is being openly flouted in Przemysl.

A low-powered light shines over the kitchen table; in its dim aura are beards and pullovers, weary eyes, a crucifix at a throat, carefully handled Solidarity publications. Down the road, nine miles away, is the Soviet Union, and 50 miles further into the Ukraine is Lvov, which was once a Polish city.

Przemysl itself had a mixed Polish, Ukrainian and Jewish population in the old times, when it was a minor outpost of Austro-Hungary. Today, dairy-farming, timber-processing, the manufacture of artists' paints and the making of prefabricated housing provide the main employment. At the border rail-head to the east of the town there are marshalling yards too, and a flourishing cross-border traffic in smuggled Soviet colour-TV sets and gold, and Polish clothing.

The group at the table consists of members and supporters of the local Citizens' Committee, a branch of the national electoral-front organization set up by Lech Walesa last December, and which is working – despite internal ideological differences – to support the Independent candidates in Przemysl for the *Sejm* and Senate. The Przemysl Committee includes local Catholic intellectuals, 'independent farmers', members of the Workers' Solidarity movement in the area, and representatives of a local cultural organisation which describes itself as 'loosely conservative in inspiration'. Even the local Scouts and an Association for the Friends of Lvov – which says that it wants to 'preserve Polish cultural traditions' in the nearby Soviet city – are represented on the Citizens' Committee.

Two of its leading lights are young Marek Kuchinski, a self-employed market gardener who grows organic tomatoes and reads Hayek, and Jacek Mleczko, the local primary school teacher, who is secretary of the committee. 'There were some quarrels', says Kuchinski, 'about who should be our candidates, but in the end we decided that we couldn't afford personal fights and that the interests of the particular groups on the Przemysl Citizens' Committee should be put to one side. It is not the time for such division.' Excluded from the Committee were 'those who did not fit this time of tolerance', as well as those considered to be 'too great individualists, wanting to fight for their own personal causes only.'

*

At stake in the voivodeship, or province, of Przemysl – one of 49 such constituencies in Poland – are five seats in the *Sejm* and two seats in the newly created Senate. Three of these five *Sejm* seats have been allocated to the Party (the Polish United Workers' Party) and its allies, and two to the Independents.

The anxious talk at the kitchen table is of the pseudo-Independents, crypto-Party nominees and placemen, who have got themselves on to the Independent candidates list for the *Sejm* in Przemysl, as they have throughout Poland, 'in order to kill the opposition'. All that is required for a candidacy are the nominations of 3,000 local electors (5,000 are needed for anyone wishing to run for the Senate) and if the ruse succeeds, so the weary voices around me say, it could mean a pro-Communist Trojan Horse on the opposition benches after the election; at the least, a splitting of the Independent vote, and the failure of some Solidarity-backed candidates to obtain the 50 per cent of votes polled which are needed to avoid a run-off.

Coffee mugs and Xeroxes, cigarettes and matches pass across the table from one fraternal hand to another. The camaraderie is that of the western left in the late Sixties. But here it is fiercely anti-Communist ('we call them Reds'); anti-socialist, too, for many. And here it is the fiat of the tough local bishop, Ignacy Tokarczuk, not the imprimatur of Mao or Trotsky, which governs the actions of these bearded, jeans-clad, radical figures.

Before their names were submitted to Solidarity headquarters in Warsaw, all four Independent candidates chosen by the Przemysl Citizens' Committee – two for the *Sejm*, two for the Senate – 'had to have the prior approval of the local Curia', as Jacek Mleczko admitted; 'the Church chose four,' Kuchinski added. You mean Bishop

Tokarczuk selected your candidates for you? 'Not the Bishop, but the Bishop's council,' said Kuchinski. 'It did not select them, it approved them,' he added in matter-of-fact fashion, as if this degree of Church management of the democratic process could not possibly be an issue.

Instead, Kuchinski is preoccupied with the bugging of their phones, and with plainclothesmen 'circulating around our office in Przemysl'. Nevertheless, says Mleczko, 'the police don't know how to handle what is going on.' Party members in Przemysl, however, are complaining noisily about the unusual neutrality of the local newspaper. 'We have heard that they have been putting pressure on reporters, demanding to know why their reports on our activities are so friendly.'

Thus the anxious conversation continues, in narrowing circles of hope and doubt, into the small hours. The flowers of free-thought are beginning to bloom in what were once the killing-fields of Galicia.

*

A small, dilapidated premises in the forecourt of the town's nineteenth-century railway station – a setting for Chekhov – is decked out with Poland's red and white colours and pictures of the four Solidarity-backed Independent candidates, the national flag fluttering in the cold spring sunshine. 'Vote for the Solidarity Opposition' and 'Votes Used to be Taken from You, Now you Must Vote for Yourselves' read the slogans in the old shop-window. It is the headquarters of the Przemysl Citizens' Committee; a bell tinkles as the door opens and closes, the bare floorboards sagging.

*

The railings of Holy Trinity Church, Jaroslav – like those of every church in the district – are hung with the familiar banner of 'Solidarnosc', red-lettered on a white ground. The sun shines fitfully, the clouds scudding. A priest at the gate greets each latecomer. We are 22 miles from the Soviet Union.

Under the white-flowering acacias of the Reformed Franciscans' large walled garden a silent, reserved crowd of about three hundred people – some standing, some sitting on chairs and benches – is listening raptly to the candidates' platform speeches. 'How many cops do you think there are here?' I asked one of the organizers. 'Probably about ten,' he whispered.

'These elections are not yet fully democratic. But if you don't vote', Tadeusz Ulma, one of the two Solidarity-supported Independent candidates for the Senate, is saying into the mike, 'you will give power to our enemies to rule over us.' Ulma, who introduces himself as the son of a craftsman, was a teacher at a local college of education who lost his job when martial law – or a 'state of war' – was declared in December 1981, and Solidarity outlawed. He was then detained without trial.

On his release and in common with other Solidarity activists in Przemysl, he was taken under the wing of Bishop Tokarczuk, as a catechism teacher. There is no understatement at this meeting about the historic nature of the occasion: it is being made plain to the crowd that a vote for the local Curia's nominees to *Sejm* and Senate is a vote to change a world 'ruined almost beyond redemption' by socialism's failure in Poland.

'Brainwashing', Ulma continues in the silence, his audience almost stock-still, 'has created a total emptiness in our heads. Our economy is sick and our nation wounded. This is a maimed generation. We have 1.5 million alcoholics, and 40 million Polish babies have been murdered by abortion. The satanic crime of destroying our nation did not stop after 1945, but has continued.' (Ulma raises this issue despite the Church's falsely disingenuous instruction to candidates not to make abortion an issue in this election.)

'We offer you a new world, in which we shall defend the moral power of the people against all the forces which hamper us. Your representatives will speak the truth and restore Poland's honour. Ours is a will to serve the nation, a nation which believes in God. Such values are timeless.'

In the distance is the sound of a provincial town's traffic; a woman, on the margins of the crowd, gently rocks a child back and forth in its perambulator. It is as if everyone were sleep-walking in this backwater; or dreaming, in this church garden, of finding some other way, any other way, of living. And who would not? The foreign debt is $39 billion, life expectancy for both men and women (in a population of 39 million) is falling, meat is rationed, '95 per cent' of the nation's water is said to be undrinkable, subsidies take up nearly half the national budget and each year there are some 20,000 new cases of tuberculosis.

In the front rows of benches, set on the freshly cut grass, are thick working hands folded in laps, a priest, a tired woman holding a small sprig of white lilac, and square-set peasant faces. To the right of the platform a group of young men, some stocky and others thin-chested, stands, arms akimbo, under the acacias. 'We are fighting for the rule of law,' says Ulma. 'We are fighting to become masters of our country, for democracy without adjectives, for freedom from fear, for personal freedom, for freedom for the masses to change the system.'

The crowd, seen from the platform, is pensive, leaning forward to listen. A few nod their heads in agreement, but most are unmoving. The pram rocks gently back and forth in its own rhythm.

'Today', the grey-haired Ulma declares, his voice rising to a conclusion, 'we must listen to the voice of the nation. For me, this voice is the voice of the Church and of Solidarity. It is not the voice of a hierarchy. It is the spirit of the scriptures!' The applause is sudden, hard and unexpected, the faces in the crowd as set as ever, the smell of cut grass fragrant.

*

The next speaker, Jan Musial – the second of the Citizens' Committee candidates for the two Senate seats – is a journalist in his late thirties. He spent time in prison in 1970 following student riots in Cracow. A man with a fastidious intellectual manner, Musial is a conservative Catholic believer in the free market and former high-school teacher, who went into hiding after martial law was declared in 1981, emerged to get a job as a warehouse watchman, and from 1984 was employed by Bishop Tokarczuk as his librarian. Still on an employment blacklist, he is editor of the local diocesan weekly, *Rola Katolicka*.

'Three or four existential experiences mark my private philosophy,' he announces in lofty fashion. The crowd, silent once more, gazes up at him. 'My experiences as a journalist have taught me that we must fight constantly for freedom of expression. My experiences in Solidarity have taught me how precious is freedom of association. My experiences as a nightwatchman have taught me that a fully planned economy is an absurdity,' Musial declares obscurely, avoiding disclosure of his real belief in a free market. 'And my experiences as a teacher have taught me that an independent education system is needed in this country, free of political indoctrination.

'These things are still in the realm of wishful thinking', he says airily – the crowd dead silent – 'and I do not believe that you trust us fully. But we have to ask what is needed to change a system which has made us all captives. My answer', he declares, with a refined gesture, the sun clouding over, 'is that we must finally break the State's monopoly of truth, and secure full representation in the highest State bodies. The Senate may even become our own independent representative body. [It did, by 99 seats to 1.] Whether it does, depends on you.'

When he finishes – with a polysyllabic peroration – rough hands politely applaud him.

*

The crowd has grown, the blustery day becoming colder. Tadeusz Trelka, a tough-looking, bearded peasant (in a dark blue suit) from the Rural Solidarity movement, is standing for the *Sejm*. Declaring himself to be a 'militant opponent of abortion like the Professor [Ulma]', he tells the audience how he was interned from December 1981 to March 1982, followed by six years underground until as late as May 1988; in the crowd's sombre expressions, you may see – or think you see – the beginnings of anger.

'We are going to fight in every way for the life of the nation,' he shouts, burly fists clenched, the crowd applauding, some brows furrowed and anxious. 'There is no equipment for farmers in this damaged country and no prospects for agriculture.' (More than half the holdings in Poland have no tractor.) 'I come from among farmers and this is an agricultural country. The farmer must become master of his own land! He must decide for himself about his culture!' he cries out. 'If you give me influence, I shall fight to restore the dignity of the cultivator. I shall fight to restore his morale, so that our children will abandon the countryside no longer. Everything [shouting] begins with the farmer, everything which stands on the table of the intellectual and the worker!'

Once, such sentiments would have been the ground of a Marxist call-to-arms against feudalism and landlordism. Here in Poland, after more than forty years of ravages done to the system of production in the name of the proletariat, the class struggle has become a struggle against the socialist order, waged on behalf of the producers. 'The ethos of the family farm has been ruined by the Communist system,' Trelka says desperately, the grim crowd applauding him with a matching desperation.

*

It is the brisk and self-confident fifty-one-year-old Janusz Onyskie-wicz, a small fair-haired man in grey flannels, an English check-shirt and blue blazer, who is the star of the election show in the district. 'Young Poles', he was to say later with a fine fluency, 'need more than their present bleak visions of a pension at retirement, and more than their poor hopes of an apartment before they become grandparents.'

Married to a granddaughter (who was born in Wimbledon) of Marshal Josef Pilsudski, the autocratic ruler of Poland from 1926 to 1935, Onyskiewicz, a mathematician, has been Solidarity's chief national spokesman since March 1981. Born in neighbouring Lvov, and wearing in his lapel a Solidarity badge of the Madonna of Czestochowa, he is – judging from the applause which greets him – the voivodeship's favourite local son. In today's circumstances, his family connection with Pilsudski (who himself carried out a coup in 1926 against Poland's infant parliamentary republic) gives him a legitimacy beyond the bounds of Party.

Yet an almost-racist whispering campaign in the constituency, variously thought to be the work of the secret police or of the Party, has abusively labelled him a 'Ukrainian from Lvov'; and round here memories of wartime atrocities committed on the Poles by local Ukrainian collaborators are still vivid. (There are some 200,000 Ukrainians in Poland, making them, with the Byelorussians, the largest minority group in the country.)

Onyskiewicz deals, or is driven to deal, with the allegation at once. 'Yes', he says defensively, 'I was born in Lvov. But on my father's side' – it is his father who is accused of being a Ukrainian – 'we originally came from Lubaczow [nine miles on the Polish side of the present border with the Soviet Union]. My roots are near this spot,' he insists. 'We lived in Przemysl. And until the end of the Nazi occupation we remained in Przemysl. That is why I wanted to renew my contacts with this area, that is why I am standing for the *Sejm* from Przemysl.'

Eyes pink-rimmed from lack of sleep, he deftly refers to his own wider reputation. 'Now I am Solidarity's spokesman. But I am also in touch with the world of international politics. I have spoken with Mrs Thatcher.' From the platform, I can see a mixture of mistrustful eyes and gap-toothed, hopeful smiling. His slogans are the 'national independence of Poland', 'economic independence', 'local self-government' and an 'independent, Christian culture'. ('We have to develop the idea that our central European culture is basically Christian,' he repeated later.)

'My politics is to fight for our rights as people. Our country', he declares to a great round of applause, speaking swiftly and pugnaciously, 'no longer belongs to us. It belongs to the Party. How many non-Party generals are there in our Polish army? Not one. How many non-Party heads of enterprises or hospital directors? All this has to change. [Loud applause.] The Party says that it also wants change. It may be true. But we must watch them closely. [Laughter.] Yet watching is not sufficient. [Nodding and smiling.] We must have independent associations and independent parties. [Loud applause.] Why? Because real rule is rule which becomes our responsibility. It is rule by us. When the Party uses the word 'democracy', they mean something entirely different. On 4 June we cannot speak of winning a majority in the *Sejm*. That has not been permitted. But the election is a step forward. We will regain part of our country. In the election after, we will regain the whole of it.'

A few of the young men under the acacias are not joining in the loud applause. 'We are on untrodden ground,' Onyskiewicz says to me at the end of the meeting, as the throng presses around him.

*

'I am blind,' a Tolstoyan old man had called out from the crowd during the question period, frailly grasping a white stick and being helped to the microphone by two stewards.

'You speak of Solidarity, but I walk in a town where everything is money. You speak of Solidarity, but in the streets people call me names as a blind man. Some say that the Communists have destroyed our values. Do not the scriptures command us, still, to love our neighbours as ourselves?' There was a silence, the acacias stirring.

'Why has society become so cruel?' he asked, staring out sightlessly at the unmoving audience.

*

The meeting's organizers are stacking up the chairs and carrying away the benches; the crowd mills about the church gate, talking animatedly, before dispersing into the grey streets of Jaroslav.

At a small shrine in the corner of the Franciscans' walled garden, recovering its old silence, there remains a young man on his knees; head bowed, praying, beside the muddy, trampled pathway.

★

Poland is not a Catholic country for nothing. Under the Jesuitical rules which were invented – after a fierce battle of wills – at the Round Table talks, the democratically elected 100-member Senate will have veto-power over the *Sejm*. But the *Sejm* will have the power to overturn the Senate's veto with a two-thirds majority vote. Since the Party and its allies in the *Sejm* will command 65 per cent of the seats, they will be only a hair's breadth from the two-thirds needed. One or two defectors from the opposition side would permit the *Sejm* to veto the Senate's veto, even if the whole Senate were composed of Solidarity-supported Independents.

In addition, there will be a State president with executive powers to issue decrees, to call referenda, to refuse his signature to parliamentary legislation, to dissolve Parliament, to declare martial law (though only in the face of an external threat and only for a three month period). He will be elected by a simple majority of both houses. The 65 per cent Party representation in the *Sejm* should guarantee that its choice becomes president, even if the whole Senate is opposed to it.

★

The road from Jaroslav to Oleszyce runs close to the Soviet border, over the River San, and through bright yellow rape fields. The farmhouses are wooden and whitewashed. Green meadows, cropped by black and white cows, are deep in buttercups and dandelions. At a wayside church, a Soviet tourist bus has stopped; its passengers are taking photographs of the Solidarity banners. In the fields, kerchiefed women – many old – bend, hoeing. Horses and wooden ploughs work the long, long furrows.

★

The elderly men, stiff-armed and square-shouldered, their shoes carefully polished, sit in the hall in a solid phalanx. 'For more than forty years, the foreign policy of the Soviet Union has been the foreign policy of Poland,' Onyskiewicz is saying. 'When we are in power this whole business will be ended. We have our own interests,' he shouts, as the waves of applause engulf him. 'Your hearts',

Onyskiewicz declares at the end of his speech in the small agricultural town of Oleszyce, 'will tell you to vote for Solidarity.'

The applause is intense, an explosion of pent-up, despairing passion. We are 14 miles from the Soviet Union. The central issue has been presented with a brutal plainness. 'Do not sit and complain any longer. If you are passive, if you are lazy, you will allow the Communists to say that they have won. You will sustain the mafiosi.'

The worried questions from the floor are an unburdening of historic and present emotion: about war pensions, about restitution of past property confiscations, about the complexities of the voting system. 'How do we cross off all the candidates of the Party? With a big cross, or each man separately?' someone calls out, to general laughter. 'Leave our names', Onyskiewicz answers good-humouredly, 'and one by one cross off the others'; in the audience the names of the Solidarity candidates are being written down on scraps of paper, in a hum of voices.

The questions continue – about the plight of young people in the countryside, about his allegedly Ukrainian father (which Onyskiewicz dismisses as 'red propaganda'), about new farm taxes, and about Poland's old territorial losses in the Ukraine and Lithuania. 'If we were to start fighting now for Lvov and Vilna.' Onyskiewicz says, 'then we would also have to be ready to give up our western lands in Prussia and Silesia. We cannot reopen this matter. Our policy is not to move our borders but to make them unnoticeable. We want to create freedom of movement as in the West, where you can cross borders fifteen times a day and no one pays attention.

'We do not want unnecessary conflicts with the Lithuanians and Ukrainians, who share our Christian tradition. Instead', he adds dangerously, 'we must help them in their own struggle for independence.' There is a stirring in the crowded doorway. The police, a Solidarity official reports to the platform party, have stationed themselves at the end of the road, blocking the path to latecomers. 'They are telling people', he whispers behind his hand, 'that there is no meeting, that no one is here, that everyone has been arrested.'

The speakers, unconcerned, brush aside the news, and the questions continue regardless: about 'Russian crimes' in wartime Poland, about family members deported 'to the East' and never seen again – it has been claimed that '2 million' Poles in all were deported to Russia from the area of Soviet wartime occupation, General Jaruzelski's family included – and about the 'big graves' which have been recently discovered.

'The situation is bad, let's face it,' declares Onyskiewicz. 'The past must be openly explained to the nation. But Polish historians do not yet have access to the Soviet archives. This business is ahead of us,' he adds quietly. The anti-Russian feeling in the hall is intense, the hitherto unspeakable now being spoken; and as elderly memory is awakened, there is the shocking sound (amid the drone of platform voices) of stifled weeping.

*

An old man in his late seventies, describing himself as a retired farmer, whispers his answers to my questions into the ear of the interpreter. He is not a member of Solidarity, but says in the hubbub of the departing crowd that he has been waiting for a day like this since 1980. 'I am a very believing Catholic. My wife is a very good woman, and she also is happy. We do not understand everything which is happening', he adds, becoming breathless, 'but we want to understand, and we want the changes.'

What about the neighbours? I ask him. 'My neighbours are here also,' he says, chuckling and wheezing, as the crowd jostles past him, making for the doors in high excitement. What changes do you want? 'Freedom for the Catholic religion, and justice,' he replies to the interpreter. (I manage to gather, in the shoving, that he had to hand over his smallholding to the State Land Fund, under a notorious law of 1962, in exchange for entitlement to a pension.)

Will you get justice? 'I am optimistic.' And if you don't? The crowd pushes and presses around him, some listening intently – ears cupped – to our conversation. 'God forbid. People have been through so much here,' he says, faltering. Beside him, an old woman with streakily-dyed black hair wipes her eyes with her fingers; she too has begun to weep.

'I lost my husband and son in the war,' she says, shaking her head. 'I hope they win,' she adds, pushing roughly through the crowd, mouth a-tremble.

*

There are some – usually urban ultras, and perhaps *agents provocateurs* among them – who claim to want no truck at all with the Party, not even for the purposes of negotiation. Their positions are various, ranging from extreme nationalism to a plebeian nihilism which has entirely given up on the political process. There are also groups of rejectionists who believe themselves to be speaking for the 'real interests of the Polish working class'. Honest or dishonest, what most of them have in common is their anti-Communism. Moreover, in this world which is turning upside down, anti-Communism is the ideological starting-point of as many proletarians as intellectuals.

Even in provincial Jaroslav, Onyskiewicz was asked by a young man under the acacias about the 'Fighting Solidarity' breakaway group, which regards Solidarity's treaty with the Party as a betrayal. 'They share our values,' said Onyskiewicz, glossing over matters. 'They too want a plural parliamentary system. But we differ from them about methods. We wanted to make an interim deal with the Party in order to prevent a catastrophe for our nation. They wanted to wait until everything collapses.'

The questioner demurred, shouting back inaudibly in the gusting wind. 'Some people', Onyskiewicz exclaimed in exasperation to the audience, 'want us to be more radical than we are. But what are we supposed to do? Start a revolution?!'

＊

In these parts such impatience – real or feigned – is that of a minority. 'Here, relations are still feudal,' says Mieczyslaw Argusinski, a Solidarity activist and teacher from Lubaczow. 'On the one side the State, on the other the peasants. After forty years of Communism, there is still the old feudal pyramid, with the peasants at the bottom.'

They are still conditioned by what he calls their 'scepticism and dependence'. What are they saying to themselves at the moment? I ask him. 'Many of them are saying, "We are on the State list for a new tractor. But if we support Solidarity, what will happen?". It is at this level that we activists are working, with people who are still afraid and mistrustful. We are making mistakes round here because Solidarity does not have the right people to reach them. In the villages, this is the terrible thing we have to struggle with,' declared the teacher from Lubaczow.

＊

Marek Kuchinski did not agree. Weary at his farmhouse after yet another long day on the road, and surrounded by crates of tomatoes, he believes that Solidarity is heading for a sweeping victory in the Przemysl region. 'The country people see that many of us are

12-15 Lech Walesa addressing a meeting of steelworkers at the Huta Warszawa works, during the Solidarity campaign for the elections of May 1989

16 *Above* Elderly men at a Solidarity election meeting listening to a discussion on the Second World War: Oleszyce, Eastern Poland, May 1989

17 *Below* Janusz Onyskiewicz at the end of a Solidarity election meeting in the grounds of Holy Trinity Church, Jaroslav, Eastern Poland, May 1989

18 & 20 Potsdammer-platz, West Berlin, on the day the Wall was opened by the East German government, 9 November 1989

19 Hans Modrow, East German prime minister, at the emergency session of the Party Congress, East Berlin, 8 December 1989

intellectuals with our own interests. But many of the peasants here are themselves members of Solidarity. The Party is now trying to smear us with its class analysis, its crude anti-intellectualism, its anti-clerical propaganda and so on. But do you think this is harmful to us?' he asked, laughing.

'Today we found out that a new leaflet is circulating saying that Onyskiewicz is the son of an old Ukrainian fascist gang-leader. In villages where we are weak such disinformation can create chaos. But in this area the huge majority is with us.'

If Kuchinski is right, a post-Communist – and even post-socialist – democratic movement, based originally upon an industrial workers' union, is on its way to power.

*

Sunday morning. There is not a lick of paint on the faded and bullet-pocked stucco of Przemysl. The cold wind, smoke-laden, catches in the throat and nostrils. But here is no desertion. Along Jagiellonska Street, men and women, young and old – leaning into the wind – are hurrying, hurrying to Mass. Fixed to the church railings are Solidarity slogans, buffeted and flapping, a list of the local Independent candidates with their biographies, and a glass display-case containing photographs of Lech Walesa and other Solidarity figures. The church is crammed to the porches; the street outside is a swirl of coal-smoke and singing.

Only 300 yards away, in the cobbled town square – how many herdings of victims has this place witnessed? – a political meeting, loud with folk music, is beginning. Here, the town's lank-haired drunks, unshaven and tottering Breughel figures, gather round a beer barrel and steaming plates of sausages, to the sound of accordions.

The singers and musicians are grey with cold; the beer and sausages, in a country where sausages have always been more important than Marxist doctrines, are free for the taking. A file of men in belted raincoats from the Polish United Workers' Party, seeking not to be outdone in Przemysl, mounts the hustings.

*

Processing swiftly with a manly force, organ roaring, into the packed and chanting Franciscan Church of Cracow, these twin files of tough young priests look like a couple of football teams entering an arena. (The Pope was once Archbishop of Cracow.) 'Boycott the

Election', say the graffitti on the ancient walls of the University. Maybe; but no Communist Party will be able to beat back this elemental energy, this muscular Christianity, not in a month – or century – of such Sundays.

It is the Church Militant, fit, fierce and youthful, coming into its Polish dominion to the pealing of organs, censers swinging, the hammer-and-sickle thrown down, vanquished.

*

A grey regime figure, pipe-smoking: the former head of the central committee's Department of Propaganda, eight years editor (from 1972 to 1980) of the Party daily *Trybuna Ludu* and member of the *Sejm* for the last fifteen years, Josef Barecki was a participant in the Round Table talks with the Solidarity movement. He tells me that for personal reasons he is not standing in the coming election. In fact, though he is not saying so, many of the old guard like him have been dropped overboard by the Party, the better to face the Solidarity challenge. 'In any case, the next Parliament will not carry out high State functions,' he says, puffing on his pipe with seeming content-ment. 'It will be merely a training-ground for future co-existence between the Party and the opposition. In the meantime,' he adds, 'the government will govern.'

What about Solidarity? He tamps down his pipe with a blackened thumb, taking his time to answer. 'Solidarity is a movement of dissatisfaction, which the Pope's demagogy has encouraged. It is not a political party. In 1980 it gained a certain destructive strength, with many anarchic features. Today, we can say that it is trying to define its purpose. Does it want to be a trade union or a political party? That is the question,' he adds out of the side of his mouth, pipe clenched between his teeth, the bowl unsmoking.

'As we see it in the Party, Solidarity is divided between extremists and what we may call a serious group, or a constructive opposition,' he continues, sucking. 'If it becomes a political party, then in our opinion' (removing the pipe from his mouth) 'it should become a social democratic party. But first we must see what kind of support it gets in the election.'

This sounds exceedingly complacent, I say to him. What if Soli-darity routs the Communist Party, or shows that it would have the strength to defeat the Communist Party in a fully democratic election? Barecki knocks out his pipe in the metal ashtray. 'The situation could get so difficult', he answers, chuckling briefly and poking into the bowl with a matchstick, 'that we should have to have further Round Table, or even Square Table, conversations.'

Frankly, haven't you already lost your mass base to them? 'The working class is the base both of Solidarity and the Party,' he answers. 'But the Party is changing, reforming itself to meet every challenge.' What if eclipse is approaching? He laughs, feeling his way into a pouch of pipe tobacco. 'What is forty years in history?' he replies phlegmatically. 'You have had three hundred years of development. We inherited a country ruined by war. And what were the intentions of our Party forty years ago? To try to rebuild our country without being exploited by capital. Were we wrong in our intention?'

He slowly fills his pipe, pressing down the strands of tobacco. 'No one expected', he says, revising Polish history as he goes, 'that with Stalin's interference this experiment of ours would have shining results.' Even if that is true, I say, complete failure is another matter, surely? He strikes a match, his cheeks hollowed as he draws, the smoke fragrant. 'What had to happen is happening', he says astonishingly, 'and we should accept it as positive. We are not going to man the barricades merely because our hopes have been disappointed.'

Put another way, it could be all over bar the shouting. And if Josef Barecki is a guide, there may not be much of that either.

*

'Who can tell what kind of society we will have in the future?' he had asked, musing in elegiac fashion. 'And who can say whether under Solidarity and its free market things will get any better?'

*

A resuscitated Polish capitalism, with the odour of pre-war mothballs, is back in small-time business. Andrzej Machalski, who has a neat beard and managerial manner, is a Warsaw entrepreneur. Chairman of Economic Action (a right-wing free market pressure group), he has been chosen by Lech Walesa to run the Solidarity campaign headquarters. Machalski is also himself standing for the Senate; Economic Action has a dozen candidates on the Solidarity-backed list of Independents in the election.

Talking to Machalski is Andrzej Sadowski, a rigid young man

dressed in correct inter-war fashion. Also a private entrepreneur, he is vice-chairman of Economic Action and a self-proclaimed Hayekian; the pair of them might have stepped out of a George Grosz drawing. Riffling, tight-lipped, through their papers, they briskly collate the news of obstacles and provocations being reported from the field, of 'electronic bugs' found in the wall of a campaign office in Slupsk in north-west Poland, of popular television figures and sporting heroes being chosen by the Party as pseudo-Independents, of alleged preparations for Party ballot-rigging in rural areas.

Nevertheless, they believe that Solidarity will carry all before it. 'The main thing', says Machalski, 'is to break down the Communist system. This is no time for liberal doubts about what we should be doing and saying. Our only way is by a clear-minded attack on what socialism has done to Poland.' 'Clear-mindedness is all,' added Sadowski stiffly; a would-be junker in the new Polish order.

*

The Warsaw press centre: Marta Golinska, one of its officials, is my seductive minder. 'The Church is very close to Solidarity,' she declares, as if passing on a destructive confidence. She phones Party headquarters, fixing an appointment for me. 'They are giving Solidarity a lot of backing for the election,' she says putting down the receiver and filling in a docket.

I sit behind her desk, waiting. 'Such a thing is very strange, when most of Solidarity's advisers are Jewish,' she added, writing.

*

Cardinal Glemp, primate of Poland since July 1981, from time to time makes his own contribution to this atavistic chasing of phantoms. (There are perhaps 5,000 surviving Jews in Poland.) In March 1984 he called some of Solidarity's advisers 'Trotskyists, with little in common with true Poles'; an easily-decoded slur, raised to the purple. The same phrase was used of the Jews in the time of Stalin.

*

The new Polish extremism is many-sided, even pluralist in its own fashion. On the walls of Jerozolimskie Avenue, in the heartless centre of Warsaw, felt-pen swastikas decorate the cheeks of Lech Walesa. 'To legalize Faszyzm' has been written, in Polish English, across his forehead.

*

In a red check shirt and greasy jeans, still-underground 'Gregory' – squat, bearded, and with his hair so cropped as to leave only a tuft or top-knot – calls himself a conservative and nationalist, and publishes a right-wing journal with a circulation of 3,000. He is in favour both of a boycott of the elections and the modernization of Western missile systems.

Why are you still underground? I ask him. Aren't you less at risk these days? 'That is what the regime wants you to think,' he says darkly. The purpose of his (still illegal) activities and publications is to 'elevate people's thoughts above their daily biological problems'. He tells me that forty years of Communist rule have 'left the Poles with mental preoccupations only about what to eat and which queue to stand in. We are so inhibited intellectually, so scared by our economic problems, that most people can hardly think at all any longer.'

As for higher thinking about history, ethics, the nation, it has been 'buried under slogans'. Today, 'Gregory' declares, 'the new slogan is "The Free Market is Good for You". Such a slogan is as bad as, and similar to, the old slogans about planning or the Party. Before it was Party, Party, today it is Money, Money, Money.'

What can you do about it? I ask him, distracted by his top-knot. 'We have to fight slogan-consciousness, left and right, and intellectualize the understanding of our problems,' he says earnestly. In the meantime, he disapproves of the 'election show' – 'just a game', he called it – disapproves of the 'shallow love-of-Poland Solidarity message', and disapproves of the 'new deals being done over Poland by the Big Powers'.

He believes, almost pleading with me, that Poland is facing a new Orwellian catastrophe; that the 'glasnost business' is merely disinformation directed at the West; that the Communists have 'bought the opposition' and will retain the real power, while the 'magic of words' convinces everybody else that there has been a genuine liberalization. But what is all this masquerade for? I ask him. 'To avoid a bloody national uprising,' he answered.

'Can you give me some hope that the Americans will keep Star Wars?' he asked me agitatedly.

*

Party headquarters, 8.30 a.m., Warsaw: last residuum of power. The politburo is meeting later this morning. Professor Marian

Orzechowski, the 67-year-old former foreign minister, is a neat grey man in a grey suit who speaks fluent English. A framed sketch of Lenin hangs on the wall of his bunker-office. Head of the central committee's Secretariat for Ideology, he turns out to be yet another of Mrs Thatcher's admirers in eastern Europe's high places. 'Abstracting from her system of values, one has to admit that she is very effective,' he says.

Has Marxism now lost its ideological hegemony in Poland? I ask him, matching lingo to place and person. 'There never was an hegemony of Marxism in Poland,' he answers unexpectedly. 'What happened was that everything which was ideologically opposed to us was simply crushed by administrative methods'; that is, by the police. 'There are no secrets any more,' he added. It is also no secret that only ten weeks ago Orzechowski was insisting that the Party would not renounce its 'leading role' and was working towards an 'ideological rebirth'.

'In any case, how could such hegemony have been a realistic goal for us, in a society which is 95 per cent Catholic? Even if we say that certain socialist values – social justice, equality of oppor-tunity, humanism – have taken root in Poland, that is a different matter.'

It is also Party (and personal) revisionism with a vengeance. You sound as if you are ideologically on the run, I say to him. 'What we are doing is going down to the level of the ordinary man,' he responds smoothly. 'It is not a question of being on the run. It is a matter of speaking about the market, about prices, about access to goods and so on. We are de-ideologizing our language, we are becoming more pragmatic, we are addressing problems at the level of daily life.' Because you are on the run? 'Because socialism-without-goods is attractive to no one.' Yes, but isn't socialism itself being rejected?

He is unruffled. 'The Poles speak with a double-tongue on such questions. They praise the market, but they are opposed to privatiz-ation. They praise capitalism, and they are opposed to inequality and exploitation.' His is a polished manner, and his arguments ready. 'On the other side, we have problems with people who think we are being disloyal to socialism because we too are speaking of private enterprise. It is a shock to them.' But it is bound to be, surely, if you are suggesting that private enterprise and the market system are compatible with the aims of a Communist Party? 'We don't want the old monopoly of wisdom. Today, we have to fight the idea of the leading role of the Party.'

But aren't you losing it anyway? Aren't you completely on the defensive? Where are your choices? 'With regard to Solidarity', he replies, as sleekly as ever, 'we are acting in some regards out of choice, in other regards under pressure.' How out of choice? 'We too have a strong reforming trend in the Party,' he answers with a pinched smile. Yes, but how can you get out of the political fix you are in?

He barely moves a muscle. 'It is the most difficult era of turmoil and change in the history of socialism. But the Church is now very moderate and reserved in what it is saying. For nearly ten years Poland has been in a state of convulsion.' His voice is silky, his calm frozen. 'Everyone knows, inside and outside the Party, that we must all be careful. Many dangerous tendencies – religious intolerance, obscurantism, personal hatreds, extremism, including in our own Party – lie below the surface,' he says softly.

'People are impatient for change, here and now. But talk of making sacrifices could provoke strong reactions especially among the workers, who will have to bear the main costs of the reform process. If demagogy and populism got out of hand in conditions of growing economic failure, neither the State, nor the Church, nor Solidarity would be able to control it.'

You mean people can be frightened into accepting the continuance of Party power? He ignores the question, smiling faintly. 'Even the electrician from Gdansk has changed very much in the recent period. Of all those I have been observing in these last eight years [since Solidarity was declared illegal and Walesa himself imprisoned], he has gone through the largest changes.' In what way? 'He is a man of great charisma and in-born political talent, who has developed the ability to select the most important aspects of every problem,' said the Party's chief ideologist, with a sphinx-like stillness of manner.

'That is what I see in the electrician,' Professor Orzechowski murmured; standing up as an aide arrived to summon him to the politburo meeting.

*

Orzechowski had claimed that a healthy Europe was impossible with a 'sick Poland'. The pressures of western creditors and the IMF on Poland to reform according to their prescriptions he described as blackmail. 'Even without such pressures we would still do what we are doing,' he declared – as if Poland were acting from sovereign choice, not defeated necessity. 'Does not every social organism go through changes? Then why not socialism also?' he enquired.

*

'Don't ask me too many questions at once', the stocky, moustached fellow bantered with the crowd – some standing on window-ledges – at the end of his speech in the assembly hall of the huge Huta Warszawa steel-mill: 'I have no pen, I don't write, I'm a worker.'

Outside were chimneys, gantries and metal-grey walkways, and at the plant's entrance a flower-bedecked monument to Father Jerzy Popieluszko, the mill's chaplain before his murder in October 1984. Many in the divided audience seemed not much amused by Lech Walesa's remark, nor very friendly. There had already been restlessness, and some shouting, as Walesa had declared, clutching the hand-mike to his mouth like a fairground barker, that 'I haven't come here to look like a future president. Without you, I am zero.

'I have come to the top, I have the Nobel Prize [awarded in 1984], I want more' – his words quick and impulsive – 'but it is you who must lead and improve me. This is not a democracy, we are still intruders, there is a great battle before us, Poland is still not free, but the election is a real chance, a first step for us. Afterwards, we shall either throw Walesa out [laughing hoarsely into the microphone], or work together for the Poland we dream of.'

This steel-mill, with a workforce which is among the most class-conscious and militant in Warsaw, is regarded as one of the centres of opposition to the Walesa faction in the Solidarity movement. Fearful of unemployment, opposed to the free market, hostile to Solidarity's intellectuals, against participating in the election, they seemed more than suspicious – or jealous, in working-class fashion – of Walesa. In the volleys of ferocious questions which were fired at him, the ugly, repressed mood of a lynch-mob rose straightaway to the surface.

'How can you sign agreements with people who persecuted our union?' a shabby, grey-haired steelworker in a bomber-jacket bellowed – a Jacobin *enragé* or *sans-culottes*, who might have stepped from the pages of the French Revolution. 'Why are you running around helping them to get western credits? What is it for? So that they can remain in power over us?' [Uproar.] The questioner's voice was breaking with anger; a sudden swirl of ill-tempered jostling and pushing – with cries of 'Leave him alone!' and 'Let him speak!' – eddied around him, as if a fight were coming.

'I say "no" to witch-hunting,' Walesa shouted back, fists clenched and jumping ahead of the audience. 'I say "no" to civil war, "no" to chopping off heads. We must not fight, we must struggle to change the system. Poles from Poland can reach agreement with each other. Nothing will be gained', Walesa yelled, arms raised high in the air and seeming to vibrate with the effort to quell the audience, 'if we hang everybody from the lamp-posts.'

In the anger, applause, shock and laughter which greeted this *coup de théâtre*, Walesa, head tilted back, took a long swig from a bottle of mineral water. This was stage-craft, and well-managed. A heckler – shouting 'Traitor!' – struck again as he was drinking. Walesa, wiping his chin, rounded on him: 'Shut your mouth, and a plague upon you!' At this, there was fierce applause from the platform and from Walesa's partisans in the audience.

'So, if you know, you tell us what socialism is,' a friendlier voice called out. 'I'll tell you what socialism is,' Walesa answered. 'Theoreticians will complain about my approach, but I am a worker, I was a worker, and I will always be a worker.' [A sudden, watchful silence.] 'The bakery with the freshest, crispest rolls is socialism.' [Loud laughter.] 'A system which allows anyone to run for president, that is socialism.' [Silence.] 'And unions which genuinely defend the rights of workers, that, to Lech Walesa, is socialism.'

There was some applause for this, but the respite for Walesa was brief. Renewed heckling (mainly about low wages and rising prices) culminated in the assertion, from a thuggish thirty-year-old in a leather jacket, that Walesa had entered into a 'secret agreement' with the government.

'I'm being criticized by you now', Walesa responded wearily, 'but once I was near-holy. There are no secret agreements with anybody. But I can feel the distrust in you.' [Shouting.] 'If you don't like what I am doing, why don't you take things in your own hands?' [More shouting.] 'Let us not insult one another, let us not shock one another. Don't behave like this at meetings, I plead with you! You shout, "Let us get rid of Communism!" It is all very well as a slogan. But how can we get rid of it?' he asked huskily. 'With slings? With bows and arrows?' [Loud applause from his supporters.] 'You say to yourselves, "Everybody needs money, except Walesa. He has got everything, he has lots of greenies, what has he to worry about?"'

At this there was a scatter of laughter; but the general mood was sullen. 'I am not a hero,' Walesa continued impressively. 'I jumped out of nowhere. Should I rather have sat weeping? I have given twenty years of my life in this struggle for a democratic Poland. In abnormal times, I pulled the wagon.'

★

This was a good, strong proletarian metaphor, and for some in the audience well-chosen. 'I admire you', shouted a voice in the crowd, 'but where do you get your optimism about the elections, as if you did not know who rules Poland? Will people who got their power with the help of the Red Army agree to give up their positions?' 'Cracow wasn't built in a day', Walesa answered, with bluff good humour. 'Are we supposed not to use the opportunity which has been given us? Are we going to be laughed at for doing nothing?'

But the rest, the *enragés* – or *agents provocateurs* – were not quieted, continuing to complain bitterly, and refusing to be silenced, about their low wages (around £15 per month at the unofficial rate of exchange in Warsaw) and about rising prices. 'You, up there', shouted a steelworker – grey-faced with vengefulness and poor diet, and pointing first at the platform, then at the floor – 'how can you see what is happening to us, down here?!' [Over half of Polish household expenditure is on food, and one in four workers is said to be under-nourished.] 'What can I do, can I be everywhere?' Walesa answered, as the first few members of the audience began leaving.

'It is not fast enough, and there are so many things to take care of', he continued, 'but I am nearly unconscious I am so tired. If you want more money, they can simply print more money. I ask you to put aside these arguments about wages.' [At this there was bedlam, in which Walesa could be heard saying to the platform party, 'They are Communist provocateurs, who want martial law!'] 'The right to strike is from a different era,' Walesa bellowed. 'The government says it is wrong, and we say it is wrong. In order to avoid civil war, prices will rise, and it will be worse before it gets better!' [Uproar.] There was renewed scuffling in the crowd, fierce heckling and perhaps a punch thrown.

'Shut up, leave him alone, and listen!' Walesa shouted. 'Strikes do not suit the new reality we live in! We have to have priorities, we have to work together in an organized fashion, we have to behave like civilized people, not like a bunch of primitives!' There was a loud ovation. 'I may be mistaken about my methods, peaceful or militant, but this is a country which has been ruined. The Wild West was dangerous, but the Wild East is dangerous too. I am asking everywhere for help for Poland, so that together we can rescue our country, and build the same system that Europe has. I have lifted the burden I could lift. Aren't you satisfied? What else could I have done?' Walesa asked the audience.

Shame seemed to spread quickly through the crowd, and the hall fell silent, Walesa coughing with his mouth open, crudely genial. A voice from the floor cried out, 'There is no unity among us. Why don't we trust each other?'

'The situation has made us what we are,' Walesa responded quickly. 'It is a tragedy, the tragedy of the working class, the world over.' The silence was profound, and Walesa the master of it. The nerve of class had been touched at its rawest.

'And tell me, please', Walesa went on, seizing the initiative, 'how are we going to get rid of Communism from this beautiful, unloved country of ours, which belongs to no one? Not by demagogy, which will destroy our organization, not by shouting, not by hatred. Only by thinking for ourselves, by having interesting things to say, by work, by solidarity, by organization, so that we cannot be cheated by them.

'Poland does not belong to the secret police and the politburo. Poland has to be taken into our hands. Legality is in us now,' he says, pointing high into the air. 'Together we have to take back the power which was taken from us. I appeal to you, the jokes have ended, the situation is serious, more serious than you think. Don't run away from the election. The call for a boycott is stupid, directed against us. The Communist system has lost, it has ruined Poland, but no new system has been created. We have one or two generations of work before us. We are a talented people, and the West will help us when the situation is stable. But if you prefer, let us have martial law once more, and let us forget all about it.'

A few more in the audience were leaving, discomfited or scornful, all passion spent. The rest shifted uneasily in their places, weary at the prospect of more decades of underpaid, hard labour. 'I apologize if I have offended you,' Walesa added. 'That is the way I have been taught. My language is awful, my grammar is awful, but I am a worker. I am not any better than you. My finger nails', he said, holding up his hands, 'are still dirty.'

The applause was of recognition and acceptance of these class signals. Proletarian class consciousness – international in its modes of feeling and expression, and variously heroic or foolish in ways almost beyond middle-class understanding – had spoken. Taking a swig from the bottle, Walesa left the platform, giving the V-for-victory sign, arms held high above his head like a boxer.

★

Translator of Heine, ex-inmate of the Nazi concentration camp at Stutthof and old-time socialist journalist, Ludwik Krasucki is the near-toothless (and dentureless) deputy editor of the Party's dreary theoretical journal *Nowe Drogi*. A lively man in his mid-sixties, he thinks that left-wing ideas in Poland are compromised. If Poland is to continue to develop 'in a left-wing way', despite the Solidarity whirlwind, then the Party must 'condemn its past errors and excesses' – which Krasucki has doubtless celebrated in his time with the best of them.

Now he is a man transformed; all gums and swallowed vocables, but enthusiastic in self-denunciation. 'We have created a sclerotic, over-centralized society, with too much nationalization, lacking in the normal forms of economic life, lacking in natural economic mechanisms,' he mumbles, meaning the market. 'We must stay with our left-wing philosophy, we must retain a strong State sector, but what we have overdone must be liquidated'; that venerable Communist term again, but (today) toothless.

What went wrong? 'Many things,' he answers. 'Our big enemy was a primitive kind of egalitarian thinking. We did much too much in order to be thought left-wing. We overdid it. Though socialism is founded on good humanist ideas, we liquidated all spontaneous forms of political and economic life, and arrived at a totalitarian system. Our biggest problem now is to stay left in thinking and action, when it is we who created such a deep illness in socialism.'

This is, at last, a well-formulated version of the universal dilemma. Can the Party be rescued? I ask him. 'It is a very complex situation. On the one hand, we understand the problems, but on the other we cannot any longer say what we mean with short slogans. Everyone is looking for strong personalities, easy solutions and nice round words about the situation,' he says, pointing to the heart of the matter. 'But as a Party, how can we make a coherent programme out of liquidating this, changing that and staying with the other? In addition, on the one side are the hard, unpopular decisions which must be taken, and on the other the expectations of the popular masses, with their primitive demands for quick answers, as in Germany in 1933. In the meantime, nobody knows if there will be street-fighting. Nobody knows.'

What is the way out of this mess, then? 'There is only one, a complicated coalition with Solidarity, going step by step with them in order to win time for the changes. We are in play with Walesa. It is of course a kind of political circus. But we in Poland are much better at *circenses* than *panem*,' he adds, making an indistinct mulch of his consonants, sibilants and vowels.

'At least Walesa is giving us the possibility of manoeuvre. It is lucky for us that we have this play, this game, of democracy, that we have this reserve in Walesa. At the moment we in the Party are still in a fairly good mood, we still feel we are going forward, with the Pope, with Walesa, with Jaruzelski [telling them off on his fingers] all inside the coach together.'

And if you lose the election? 'The Party will have no more reserves left,' Krasucki answered, lower lip closing over upper.

*

At *Trybuna Ludu*, the Party's decaying daily paper – grotesquely named after the nineteenth-century periodical published in Paris by Adam Mickiewicz, Poland's national poet – the empty blather of ideological conversation carries on regardless. This is Polish Marxism's dying fall, but you would not guess it from these still-earnest fellows.

'Our task at the moment', says one scribe – as if his Party and his pen were any longer charged with determining the future – 'is to separate realistic reform demands from populist ones.' 'Our main economic thesis now', declares another, dim-sighted in pebble glasses, 'is that wages should be based on the effectiveness of production.' Deathly, here, the sense of ending; of a fruitless forty-year journey, which has left these passengers stranded in the political desert.

But surely the truth is that it is Solidarity which is now setting your agenda, I put to one of the paper's senior editors, responsible for ideological questions. 'We cannot ignore the positive role of Solidarity,' he answers, an already typeset strip of words at the ready. 'They have put a lot of pressure on the Party in relation to the practical realization of socialism.' What on earth do you mean? 'They have forced the Party to go into greater depth in its actions in order to strengthen the reform process.'

This is asylum conversation, in mid-revolution. Don't you even recognize that you are facing a profound ideological challenge from the Solidarity movement? 'It is hard to talk of Solidarity's ideology as such,' says one of his colleagues, whose threadbare patch on the paper is Party Organization. 'We don't find anything original in it at all. In fact, Solidarity has so many ideological positions – elements of socialism, Thatcherism, et cetera – that it is very difficult to say what it represents. There are figures with social democratic tendencies, figures with merely nationalist sentiments, figures with clearly capitalist values and so on. It is a very eclectic organization,' they say together, laughing privately with one another.

Could Solidarity not finish the Party for ever? The very room, dim as Dimitrov's Bulgarian vault, seems to shrug off my question. 'It has one postulate for one audience, another for another,' said the Ideology Man. 'With such eclecticism', says the Party Affairs Man, 'they are hoping to attract everybody.'

Yes, but surely Walesa, not the Party, is making the political running in Poland? 'Lech Walesa is a very unusual figure. We have not been able to find a person of similar character anywhere in the socialist countries. We sincerely hope the election will allow people like that to surface.' Like what? 'Like Walesa,' the Ideology Man answers.

'Competence is becoming the main issue in the current process of democratization of public life,' says the Party Affairs Man, energetic in manner but with another pre-set strip of words. 'What we need are people who have a wider view of the country and its interest,' says the Ideology Man. 'Today, one has to admit that educated people have wider horizons.' Whose horizons are less wide? I ask them. 'Let us say average workers and peasants.' You mean being competent and being an average worker or peasant are mutually exclusive? 'We don't agree at all,' they say, laughing to one another, having themselves suggested it.

But what do you need new people for? 'Each stage of the social process brings new people with it,' one of the two hacks doggedly replies, unwilling – or unable – to answer the question. 'Each one of us is re-educating himself,' says the other, glassy-eyed. The pair of them seem lost in the void, tribunes of the people, perishing from inanition.

★

Pultusk, a market town 65 miles north of Warsaw, in the voivodeship of Ciechanów. In the cobbled town-square there are straw flecked horse droppings; and pale children play in the bedraggled courtyards, hens pecking. A three course meal costs 12 pence here, at the unofficial exchange rate; the police station is painted in apple-green pastel; and there is not a sign of Solidarity or of the election.

In the main street, with its steeply raked red-tiled roofs and faded shop frontages, a lurching drunk is trying, ham-fisted, to force a bottle of beer into the inside pocket of his shabby jacket. He staggers, knees buckling; swaying, as he struggles with his torn lining. Around the corner, a middle-aged man sits slumped, head on knees, in front of a wooden hen-hut. An hour later, he is lying on his side in the dirt, sleeping.

9

East Germany, December 1989: The fall of Jericho

This is where a Jericho has fallen, but it could be Coney Island, under glimmering neon and to the sound of hammers and chisels. Grimy Trabants, bulging with fur-hatted East Germans returning from a day's western shopping, chug to a halt at Checkpoint Charlie, exhausts belching. On the far side of the 'anti-fascist defence wall', as East Germany used to call it, state socialism is foundering, its leaders under house arrest. And here the citizens of a bust dream-world continue to file out in clumping shoes from their newly opened prison, past the amusement arcades, saunas, beer-houses and second-hand car lots of our own Utopia.

'Joe – The Place To Go!' says the cafe hoarding, as lank village youths from the East German sticks, thin-legged in their cheap trousers, head moneyless towards the flesh-pots. On bomb-site waste ground, amid pools of standing water, crowds are huddled at the Polish day-migrants' flea-market; 'Merry Christmas!' say the backs of the Coca-Cola trucks to the visitors from another planet.

*

Since Hungary opened its borders at midnight on 9 September, event upon event has swept away the foundations of the old order. As East Germans immediately began to leave for the West through Budapest (via Prague and Warsaw also), and demonstrations gathered strength in East German cities, the new Solidarity-led Polish government was presented to the *Sejm* on 13 September and accepted by a landslide, with only 13 Communist abstentions.

The following day the opposition New Forum was established in East Germany, and in the next few weeks its support and the scale of demonstrations demanding greater freedoms increased together.

On 7 October, there were violent clashes between police and demonstrators in Dresden where the crowds shouted 'Gorby, help us!' On 18 October, the East German leader Erich Honecker – who had described the unrest as 'nothing more than Don Quixote's futile charge against the steadily turning sails of a windmill – resigned 'at his own request'; the Hungarian People's Republic was abolished; and the Polish council of ministers set itself a two-year deadline for the conversion of Poland into a free market economy.

On 23 October, Hungary's new constitution established an 'independent democratic legal State' in which the 'values of bourgeois democracy and democratic socialism' would 'prevail in equal measure'; on the same day Egon Krenz replaced the fallen Honecker as head of state and general secretary of the Socialist Unity Party

(SED), the East German Communist Party. A fortnight later, the 42-strong East German council of ministers resigned and Hans Modrow, the reformist first party secretary for Dresden, became prime minister. On 9 November, East Germany abolished travel restrictions, opened the Berlin Wall, and millions of East Germans poured into West Germany in what was described as the culmination of East Germany's 'October Revolution'.

The next day Todor Zhivkov resigned in Bulgaria, as the East German Party's central committee announced a comprehensive re-form programme, including 'free, general, democratic and secret elections'. On 17 November, Modrow's new coalition government (in which 11 of its 28 members were non-Party) was sworn in in East Berlin, and Prague demonstrators – chanting 'Jakes Out!' and demanding free elections – were attacked by the police with ferocious ardour; a week later most of the Czech praesidium, including General Secretary Milos Jakes, as well as the entire secretariat of the Czech central committee, resigned.

As hundreds of thousands of people continued to take to the streets in East Germany, Czechoslovakia and Bulgaria with demands for more radical changes, and West German Chancellor Kohl proposed a 'con-federation' of the two Germanys in a speech to the Bundestag, the Czech federal assembly (Jakes included) voted unanimously to dis-card the 'leading role' of the Party; on 1 December, the East German *Volkskammer* followed suit, by 420 votes to none, with 5 abstentions. On the same day, in Moscow, President Gorbachev described Czechoslovakia's 1968 Prague Spring as 'right then, and right now'; and, simultaneously, an East German parliamentary com-mission revealed to a stunned country the huge scale of the fallen leadership's corruption. The next day the first arrests of former East German leaders – including Günter Mittag, the politburo's economic chief – were carried out, and Erich Honecker was expelled from the Party.

The entire East German politburo and central committee then resigned, and an 'interim working committee' was set up to prepare for a special Party Congress, as crowds outside Party headquarters in East Berlin called for revenge, and the first attacks on State Security (Stasi) personnel and buildings began to be reported. It was an-nounced too that the heraldic Prussian Iron Cross and Eagle would be restored to the Goddess of Victory above the Brandenburg Gate; and the Museum of German History in East Berlin closed the exhibition rooms dealing with the entire period from 1949, when the East German State was founded.

On 6 December Egon Krenz, Honecker's successor, himself resigned to be replaced by a 'liberal democrat' Manfred Gerlach – the Warsaw Pact's first non-Communist head of state – and it was announced that the special Party Congress would be brought forward a week in an effort to staunch the crisis.

*

'Jeez,' says a callow Jewish New Yorker with an open-neck button-down shirt, his notebook at the ready in the East Berlin press centre. They are putting up the latest news on the bulletin board: of 'Mafia-style organizations', of State Security premises sealed off from vengeful citizens, of calls on the people to keep calm, of yet another act in this Twilight of the Gods in eastern Europe. 'Jeez,' he says again, shaking his head and laughing out loud over the amounts of foreign currency allegedly salted away in Swiss bank accounts by former paragons of socialist virtue. His laughter is of excitement, laced with exhilaration.

'We feel so defrauded,' my young interpreter says quietly, standing beside me at the notice board. 'My brother is fourteen only, but he too is disappointed,' she whispers. She is pale and earnest. For her this is no laughing matter.

*

'The most stable socialist State in eastern Europe', says one of the text-books I used to read on the German Democratic Republic; 'the prospect of popular dissatisfaction spilling over into mass unrest is exceedingly remote', says another. In the early 1980s, Erich Honecker, now stuck with his loot and under guard at the Party leaders' luxurious residential estate at Wandlitz, would even speak of an eventual 'socialist transformation of West Germany, led by the working class of the Federal Republic'. Further back in the 1950s, Walter Ulbricht, the GDR's founding father, believed that 'by 1961' the country would have 'overtaken West Germany's consumption levels', and thus 'demonstrated the superiority of the socialist system'.

This former 'Soviet Zone' of the defeated German Reich was born in darkness, was founded as a separate State in October 1949, and has lived for forty years in twilight. Not even the scale of its recent exodus is new. By the time the Berlin Wall was built in August 1961, 2.68 million people (of a total population in 1949 of only 18.79 million) had already left the country by flight or legal emigration: an average loss of over 200,000 people a year, in a nation with one of the lowest birthrates (and highest divorce rates) in the world.

Indeed, long before today's haemorrhage of workers to the West, a loss which has hit the transport and hospital services particularly, it was necessary for the authorities to bring in tens of thousands of its own *gästarbeiter* from third world Communist countries – Vietnam, Cuba, Mozambique and others – to keep vital sectors of the economy going.

True, there are no bread queues, rents are low, basic foodstuffs are cheap, welfare services are extensive and meat consumption, always the first measure of well-being, is on a par with that of the Federal Republic. But oranges and bananas remain for most people the fruits of a distant Eden, except at Christmas; and the country's pollution, which now demands the cancellation of league football matches when the air becomes too poisonous to breathe, is a disaster for the whole of Europe. Despite having 40 per cent of its industrial capacity destroyed in the war (and 80 per cent of Berlin in ruins) East Germany has worked its way into the list of the world's ten leading industrial nations. But the grey urban dereliction, which begins half a mile from the East Berlin city centre, is well up to the norm for eastern Europe. No wonder that, according to new findings by the Potsdam Institute of Sociology, only 30 per cent of East Germans think that socialism is an 'historic advance on capitalism, despite the latter's own crises'.

Nevertheless, it must be said that by 1989 East Germany had survived longer as a nation-State than the Weimar Republic and Hitler's Third Reich put together. East Germany's policy of *abgrenzung* – or 'demarcation' from West Germany – had been formally recognized by most States; reunification and the creation of a neutral Germany, once Stalin's aim, had become a taboo subject, East and West; and East Germany's doctrine of 'resistance to incorporation by imperialism' had seemingly become an article of faith for the whole nation. Or as Egon Krenz put it as late as 18 November 1989, 'we have created a practical alternative to the reign of German imperialism . . . It remains the undeniable accomplishment of European post-war development.' Above all, the existence of the two Germanys served both as the explanation for, and the justification of, a divided Europe, and provided a large part of the *raison d'être* for both the Warsaw Pact and Nato.

Yet East Germany was founded on an historical and political quagmire. The insurrection of East Berlin workers in June 1953, protesting at work norms and crushed by Soviet tanks, was an early token of it. (It was accompanied by deaths and followed by executions; long periods of imprisonment were also meted out to over one thousand of the demonstrators.) Even before that, in June 1945, the all-German Communist Party (KPD) had declared in its manifesto for the first Soviet Zone elections that the 'interests of the German people' demanded in the Soviet Zone 'a democratic regime, a parliamentary democratic republic, with all democratic rights and liberties for its citizens'. And in the last free provincial elections which were held in Greater Berlin in October 1946, the Social Democratic Party secured 48.7 per cent of the vote, the Christian Democratic Union 22.2 per cent, and the Communist Party only 19.8 per cent.

An East German Party (SED) report published before the June 1953 uprising disclosed, for 'inner Party' consumption, a 'general indifference to the work of the SED, open hostility among the workers towards the measures taken by the Party, the government and the mass organizations, and hopelessness and apathy among the functionaries of the factory and district branches'. Ulbricht had promised a 'true human community' in East Germany, which would be based on the 'economic and social benefits of the scientific and technical revolutions', and in which the 'socialist personality' would 'flourish'; Honecker, shortly before his fall, had in his turn declared that socialism 'provides the only society in which a person can be a person, and in which work and initiative are not exploited'.

Instead, East Germany got '98' and '99' per cent turnouts (as late as May 1989) in rigged elections, the constant flight of its citizens, the persecution of Party reformists – the Wolfgang Harich group in the mid 1950s, Robert Havemann in 1976, Rudolf Bahro in 1978 and many others – and the accretion of unaccountable power in the hands of what was to turn out to be a prodigiously corrupt mafia.

★

At the crowded bowling alley in East Berlin's Rathausstrasse, sweating young lads in their jeans and trainers sip their post-game beers, to the thump of flying bowls and the clatter of skittles. Yes, they assumed that the top Party men were corrupt. Everybody here assumed it, of course. 'But not on such a scale,' says Andreas, a fresh faced nineteen-year-old telephone repair man. 'Not millions and millions of dollars,' says Rajk, an eighteen-year-old Berlin toolmaker. To them the situation is bewildering. 'We don't know where we are going,' say the voices around me, the practised bowlers clasping the bowls stylishly above their heads, before swinging into their two or three-step run-ups.

'Suddenly they opened the borders, and now we don't know what to think.' They have lost friends, brothers, relatives, who have gone – as they may go themselves – to a Shangri-La of super-stereos and gleaming Japanese motor-cycles. The bowls hurtle down the parallel alleys, bodies straining, arms flying. Rajk's best friend has gone West too. 'He dreamed of buying the things he wanted,' Rajk says wistfully in the racket.

And when he has got those things, what then? I asked him. He shrugged his shoulders. It was the wrong question to ask, and the wrong moment, as the thundering bowls smashed into their targets.

*

The East German Communist regime, as it founders, has been tying itself in familiar ideological knots, while simultaneously struggling with the incubus of past corruption. Even the 'straightforward' Hans Modrow – who was trained as a locksmith but who needs the skills of a Houdini to get out of this mess – has called for a 'socialist spirit of free enterprise', whatever that means. He has also been urging an 'end to the political division of Europe' while setting his face against German reunification.

Meanwhile, ambivalent friends of the regime like the writer Stefan Heym – who has described Erich Honecker as a 'tragic figure', no less – have been appealing for East Germany to 'remain the socialist alternative to West German capitalism', and to return to the 'anti-fascist and humanist ideals with which we once began'.

The political turmoil and the speed of change have become convulsive. It is only a short time ago that Egon Krenz, the then just-appointed Party general secretary, was telling his ousted predecessor, 'Dear Erich, we are convinced that our Party can continue to rely on you in the future.' The Party, Krenz also told its central committee on 18 October – with his own time running out swiftly – 'has always led all changes in society. And it will remain so this time . . . We will continue to practise democratic centralism as Lenin defines it.'

Six weeks later, the Party's 'leading role' had been near-unanimously abolished and Krenz himself was in oblivion.

'For us', Krenz went on, 'socialism on German soil is not negotiable . . . What is to be done in the German Democratic Republic and what is not to be done, what reforms we will carry out – these are things that will be decided in the GDR and only in the GDR'; a proposition untenable at the time he put it forward, and made more so with each passing moment. And as the water rose to Krenz's nostrils in the third week of November, the man who as recently as June 1989 had praised the Chinese for 'restoring order' in Tiananmen Square, was now declaring himself 'available only for a socialism with a human face'.

Since then, socialism of every kind has been forgotten, temporarily or permanently, by the East Germans, as the extent of the personal enrichment of their former Party leaders has dawned on an impoverished people.

*

'The wound is so deep', he says; 'Party members are disgusted.' There are fierce feelings in the streets and taverns in this chaos. Kurt Hagewald, a thirty-four-year-old building engineer, Party organizer and ex-branch secretary in the Free German Youth (the Communist youth movement), complains bitterly, in classic Party fashion, that there is no clear line to follow, as the Party collapses.

We are in a crowded bar in the vast Stalinist Alexanderplatz, a mere half-mile or so from the tat and sleaze of Checkpoint Charlie. As it happens, Hagewald has been 'over there' – or down the road – today, taking his friend Udo Siegel, also a Party member, to see the sights. 'There is a lot of glittering light,' says Hagewald; 'glittering buildings,' says Siegel. 'Some people are attracted by it. But they are buying things they can buy here,' say the two Party men, shaking their heads over their glasses.

Siegel, who is a 'cultural organizer' with East German workers employed on an oil pipeline construction site at Perm in the Soviet Urals, has just returned home on brief furlough to see West Berlin for the first time, and to understand what has happened in his absence.

Hagewald says that he joined the Party inspired by what his grandfather had told him of the 'anti-fascist struggle' and the role of the Communists in it. Now his ideals of a lifetime are in ruins – 'the very word Communist has been devalued' – as revelations of Party crookery and thieving flood the suddenly liberated media. 'The corruption would have been a bad thing even in the capitalist system. But we saw our leaders as comrades,' he says, thin-lipped and angry. 'Now we know that we were the beggars and they travelled the world like princes. They were drinking wine while we had water,' he adds, downing another brandy.

'The old Communists must be turning in their graves. In the past everything was clear, even if it was wrong. Now there is no leadership, nothing. A lot of new political groups are emerging, but nobody knows who is behind them. No one has a clear direction.' The city is also buzzing with rumours of occupations of buildings, including ministries, and of attacks on police and Party members. 'In my Party branch, we are all like rabbits before a snake. No one is taking initiatives, no one.'

Can the Party survive? 'No, this Party cannot recover. To save our skins we opened the Wall, and now we cannot close it.' It is as good a summary of events as any. For Hagewald, who says he would join 'any Party which pursued the high ideals of socialism', the dilemmas are overpowering. 'It is not possible to go on without the help of the Federal Republic, but there must be a limit to what we concede to capitalism and consumption. Marxism-Leninism has lost, but we cannot become social democratic.' Why not? 'Because such a party [the newly re-formed SDP of East Germany] exists already.' So where to turn? 'With the borders open, very few people are interested in left ideas any more. Now we could go to the right. In this country there will always be some soil for this, lumpen elements. This is the danger.'

He shakes his head in bewilderment, flushed with drink. 'If 150,000 people in Leipzig demand reunification there could be trouble. To begin with [in the early demonstrations] they were singing the Internationale and shouting "We Are The People!" Now they are shouting "Reds Out!" and 'We Are One People!" I never thought to live through such a revolution.' 'We believed we were the alternative to capitalism, but the leaders betrayed us. They did not trust us,' adds Siegel, the more benign of the two, who has missed the last weeks' turmoils.

Do you want the Party to recover? 'It should be dissolved,' Hagewald answers. The alcohol is making him gradually meaner, his eyes narrowed. 'They were shit Communists and they have brought us only shit,' he declares, knocking back another drink. 'We might all have to become Christians,' he says. 'At least it would be better than being run by these gangsters.'

But you must have known about the corruption, the rackets, the social-fascist mafia at the head of the Party? 'We ordinary members bear the blame because we didn't have the courage to fight it,' he answers. 'Those who didn't open their mouths for years can't open them now. For decades we made fun of the Party among ourselves. We made jokes about it, but only in private. Those who spoke openly were denounced to the Stasi [the secret police] and declared to be enemies of the State.' He has given up on the old Party secrecy; we were total strangers little more than half an hour ago. But this is a revolution: a Party man is stripping off, doing an ideological bunk right here in front of me. The game must really be over.

Scared of violence himself, Hagewald – Siegel too – wants to see retribution against Honecker, and the 'rest of them in the so-called Socialist Unity Party'. They will have to be 'punished', Hagewald says, for 'making Marxism a laughing stock', for 'making a mockery of us', for setting non-Party workers on his building site and in Berlin factories jeering in their own brutal fashion at him and his fellow Party organizers. What are they jeering at? 'They are jeering at us because we are Communists,' Hagewald answers bitterly. (Next day, the Party announced its 'opposition' to the 'sentiments of contempt and hatred being expressed against Party members', the majority of whom it described as 'people of goodwill, who have worked hard to build another, better Germany'.)

They both think that 'anti-Communism' will now develop in East Germany, and that more violence could be coming. 'Someone will lose his nerve and start shooting' says Hagewald. Surveying the wreck of their socialist aspirations, the pair of them say they will 'get out' of the Party if the special Congress provides no adequate explanations of what has happened. Beyond that, what? 'There must be one Party leading the reform process. There must be some clear line,' they answer, Leninists to the last, despite everything. 'We cannot take power away from the State machine without something to substitute for it.'

Outside the windows of the bar there are scurrying, rainswept figures. 'The Titanic has sunk,' says Hagewald, fingering his glass and turning maudlin. 'Now we are in the icy water.'

★

Udo Siegel has his own view of what is going on in the Soviet Union. 'Since perestroika began I have seen things get worse in Perm. Perestroika is making reforms from above, but at the same time it is giving too much power to the people. In the Soviet Union they have forgotten how to work. They spend the whole time talking.'

And the opening of the Wall in your absence? 'Two years ago, people were shot dead crossing the Wall. Three months ago, they were drowning [trying to swim to freedom]. Two months ago, they were storming the railway station in Dresden [trying to get aboard refugee trains on their way to the Federal Republic]. Today, they are crossing freely, and getting greetings money. Who can understand it?'

What about those who have gone over and stayed there? 'Fifty per cent of them we could do without. A third will fail, and they can't help us here either. A third will get along there, more or less. A third will manage.' What about those who return to East Germany? 'They should spend a year in a camp before they get their jobs back,' he answers.

*

At the Party's Academy of Sciences they are talking, astonishingly, of closing down entirely. Not even a death-bed acceptance of the 'need to learn from capitalism' – on the ground that 'capitalism can rightly be regarded as more progressive than socialism at certain moments in history' – will be enough to save them in this revolutionary sea-change.

'The Academy could be dissolved,' says one of its luminaries in the social sciences, Dr Frank Adler; 'I don't know if we will survive.' Closure would be a particular irony for him, a reasonably free-thinking Party sociologist, since his own subject was regarded as heresy by Party conservatives until only a few weeks ago. Adler is even contemplating a future of job discrimination against former Party members. (In other words, they may get a taste of their own medicine.)

'At the moment', he says, 'we feel as if we are back where we were in 1946, and are preparing for intellectual opposition to a new order.' Representing what and whom? 'The Marxist minority,' he answers. He acknowledges that even critical intellectuals like him 'failed to question the actual structures themselves', and expresses 'deep disappointment' that socialism has been 'discredited throughout eastern Europe'. He even asserts, in elegiac fashion, that 'there never was any real chance for socialism in Hungary and Poland'; a month ago he would not have dreamed of uttering such an opinion, or not to me.

Nevertheless, he remains loyal to what remains of the Party, says that 'at least our bloody socialist societies are less interested in armaments than your western capitalist countries are', and bravely believes there is 'still a chance' of creating what he calls 'an alternative kind of society here'. There is some fight remaining in him. 'Forty or fifty people with hunting lodges' cannot be compared, he reckons, with the 'thousands of parasites in western countries'; there is a 'lot of hypocrisy' in our reports of East German corruption.

He thinks there is something positive, even creative, in the present confusion. As reports come in of crowds occupying civic buildings and Stasi offices in Dresden, Rostock and other cities – to prevent the destruction of incriminating files – it is a sign to Adler that at least East Germans are 'no longer afraid. They are overcoming the German mentality, the lack of civic courage,' he says, clinging to a spar of the wreckage.

*

Where did things go wrong originally? I had asked Adler. 'Over the question of opposition within the socialist system,' he said promptly, as if this were a long-held position. 'We needed opposition as a normal thing. Instead, it was assumed that East German socialism would be destroyed by opposition, particularly in our difficult situation *vis-à-vis* the Federal Republic. Our system was failing to satisfy material consumer needs and other needs also, but we would argue in a typically German way that it was the lesser of two evils.

'Moreover, since the justification of a second German State rested on its being different, and since we always saw ourselves as a more socially conscious society than the Federal Republic, without marginalized groups, without long-term unemployment, without western types of parasitism' (that word again), 'it hampered us from recognizing that there was no future in the way we were going. People did not see it, or, if they did, they kept quiet.'

In these parts, it is an old failing.

*

Thousands of men of the élite Felix Dzherzhinski Guards – or *wachregiment* – protected the overthrown leadership of the Party, its huge properties and possessions. Their faces are frightened and angry; tunics unbuttoned, many of them are unshaven, standing about in disorder in their squalid, cockroach-infested Berlin barracks. They shout – like defiant but cornered SS men – that they were 'only obeying orders'. This is a grim television programme; hand-held cameras shakily panning over their dishevelment and panic, recording another astounding collapse of the old Prusso-socialist order.

'I can't go out any longer in the street in this uniform,' says one distraught squaddy. 'People are stubbing out their cigarettes in our faces,' says another, eyes blazing. 'We want people who look down on us to know that we are no different than they are,' says a third. Men in uniform of any kind are being set upon. 'What do you do', pleads a fourth, 'if you are asked to protect buildings and you don't know what is in them?' Now they are a rabble, who 'want to go home', back to Leipzig, back to Halle, back to their villages, anywhere to get away from this turmoil.

*

The feared and hated Office of State Security, or Stasi, has had a name change. It is now temporarily called the Office of National Security, or Nasi; pronounced, near enough, 'Nazi'. And here, at a hastily convened press conference, is its temporary new minister, the silver-haired (and silver-tongued) Lieutenant-General Wolfgang Schwanitz – now called 'Dr' Schwanitz – in an apparatchik's blue suit, a Party badge still in the lapel of his jacket.

Before hundreds of pressmen, he reads out with Teutonic method a list of all the 'regulations and orders' – together with their serial numbers, and the dates of their promulgation – under which the Stasi acted, and which have now been abolished.

He has closed the stable door, but the beasts of the apocalypse have already bolted. Members of the security police and their families are 'in great danger of their lives and healths', Schwanitz announces, clutching a white handkerchief, his voice tense but steady. 'Dissatisfaction at the disclosures of corruption has led to spontaneous acts by certain [unspecified] social groups and individuals', as a result of which 'some Stasi' – or Nasi – 'offices are unable to function'. There have been, amongst other things, windows smashed and, elsewhere, the occupation of buildings, as crowds have sought to pre-empt moves by local *gauleiters* to destroy the records of four decades of police oppression.

'The government', Dr Schwanitz declares, 'thanks the many citizens who have helped to limit the damage and who are defending respect for the law and the Constitution.' Answering questions, he reveals unashamedly that he has himself 'given orders about what to destroy and what not to destroy. But we are not destroying essential documents, only copies,' he says to incredulous laughter.

He is particularly concerned at acts of violence against his 'colleagues', now being reported from different East German cities; colleagues who had 'always believed they were doing the right thing', and who were 'not responsible for the deeds of former State leaders'. 'They too must make a new beginning', Schwanitz adds; 'it is a bitter thing for them also.' Random and unjustified attacks on the Stasi 'threaten to drive us into chaos. They remind us of very bad times,' he adds obliquely.

The analogy is a just one. Yet another Reich is collapsing on German soil, this one like nine-pins. The old regime's security thugs will, he says, be investigated one by one, some being redeployed into socially useful occupations, some pensioned off, and some retained in a 'new structure' for what sound like benign policing duties. A kind of latter-day denazification is in progress, as Stalinism gets its winding-up order from the people.

*

At East Berlin's wan suburban station of Ostkreuz, with its rickety wooden overbridge, cast-iron roof stanchions and dark cobbled platform, a Harry Lime could still be standing, coat collar turned up against the wind. When the train doors close, the rattling warning bell in the carriage is of another epoch.

*

I have come to see Rudolf Hirsch, the distinguished East German Jewish writer – historian, novelist, essayist, court reporter. Now in his eighties, he genially, or jokingly, attributes his longevity to being a Communist. Nearly sixty years in the Party, he left Germany for Palestine in 1937, where he remained 'in political exile' (working in a sandal factory) until early 1949 when he returned to what was still the Soviet Occupation Zone of Germany.

Why did you come back? I ask him. An avuncular figure, he seems puzzled by the question. 'Because I was a German Communist, not a Zionist. This is my culture, I can think only in German, and the Soviet Zone and later the German Democratic Republic represented to me the denial of racism, the expropriation of war criminals' – in 1945 and 1946 the agricultural and industrial property of former Nazi activists was seized without compensation – 'and the rejection of German xenophobia. I had bad memories of Berlin, but I thought I too could help to change the world.'

Is what is going on now a revolution, or a counter-revolution? 'I don't know,' he answers. 'In one respect, we can say it is a revolution against the old structures. But what we had here was not socialism, so how can I say that it is a counter-revolution?' What system did you have? 'It had the appearance of socialism, public ownership and so on. But it was *dirigismus*, not socialism.' When did you discover that it was not socialism? 'I thought that many things were wrong here from the beginning. But if you are going to work here, if you are going to fight here . . . ' He does not complete the sentence.

He became a freelance reporter, making the courts his beat in a legal system where the 'old type of Nazi justice was no longer accepted. In West Germany', he says, 'they kept the old Nazi judges and lawyers. Here it was different. But I was critical. I tried to write against abuses,' he insists. What kind of abuses? 'In social matters, injustices of the abortion law, domestic violence and so on' – the stuff of the legal reporter. 'Sometimes the authorities would call me in and they would argue, in effect, that since such things *could* not exist in a socialist society therefore they *did* not exist. That was their way of thinking.'

His friendly animation, as he perches on the edge of his armchair, is awkward: perhaps this is his essay at an *apologia pro vita sua*. And the workers' insurrection of June 1953? Didn't that strike you at the time as a warning of future rejection of the socialist system? 'No,' says Hirsch, roundly, but at ideological sixes and sevens. 'It was a provocation organized by the State Security Bureau, acting in co-operation with Beria,' Stalin's secret police chief. 'It had its own logic. Their plan was to provoke the workers to violence against the authorities.' Why? 'In order to instal a new government which would begin a process of political collaboration with the Federal Republic. Their aim was a unified, neutral Germany'; and however far-fetched Hirsch's 'explanation' (or evasion) of June 1953, this indeed was one of the dreams of Soviet foreign policy in the 1950s.

Has Gorbachev set something similar in motion, to achieve a similar outcome – that of a united neutral Germany, half detached from western Europe? 'No, no, no!' says Hirsch. 'The new policies of the Soviet Party have existed for five years. This is not an East Berlin workers' uprising, this is a general upheaval in the socialist system. No one can manipulate it in such a fashion.'

I say that in East Germany it seems more like the complete moral collapse of a delinquent regime than a 'political upheaval'. He is silent. Aren't you shocked by it? 'It is terrible', he eventually answers – briefly holding his temples and becoming more Jewish – 'that such things could be done by comrades who fought the fascists. Hermann Axen [the regime's fallen ideology chief] was even in Auschwitz.' His eyes rove the room, his ebullience vanished. He tolls off the names – Honecker, Stoph, Mittag, Tisch, Mielke, Albrecht, Axen, Schalck-Golodkowski and the others – as if they were the names of sins, and this the very Day of Atonement. 'A band of gangsters,' he adds hoarsely.

At least one or two of the dozen are said to be Jews, I continue. 'I do not think about such things,' the old man says. 'I myself have never said that I was not of Jewish origin, but who is a Jew and who is not is unimportant to me.' This cannot be true; on his walls and bookshelves are many Jewish memorabilia. Schalck is said to be Jewish, I say. 'I don't know if he is Jewish. He is not known to be a Jew. But Axen is of Jewish origin', he declares, involved despite himself, 'but nobody in the general population knows it'; six weeks before his fall Axen was dutifully describing western reports that 'tens of thousands' of East Germans wanted to leave the country as a 'slander'.

As an old Communist, could you have imagined the scale of the corruption? Honecker's private Baltic island, and the rest of it? 'No.' How could it happen? 'The fact that criticism was not allowed aggravated the situation,' Hirsch answers wearily. 'This led to serious deformations,' he adds, using an old formulation from the Stalinist lexicon. 'When men cannot be criticized they need strong characters if they are not to be seduced by their own power.' Did you ever think of getting out of East Germany? 'I could have gone any time. It was the easier way, and many writers chose it,' he says, sighing.

'But for me, going over to the West was not the answer. Karl Kraus [the Austrian satirical writer] told me that if a writer's books were prohibited by the censor the writer himself was to blame for not understanding how to elude his clutches.' Hirsch says that he knew the censors 'personally'. They were 'intelligent men with a good literary education, not stupid fellows. One of them, Klaus Hopke, knew that we also would go the way of glasnost. To stay here was the harder path, but I too knew that change would have to come,' he adds, comfortable in his quiet suburban house in Friedrichshafen. Just down the road is the Felix Dzherzhinski regimental barracks.

'After the curtain rose in Hungary, the Wall could not remain. People voted with their feet. Bismarck once said that any *dummkopf*, any blockhead, could govern with a state of emergency. If you keep your borders closed for twenty-eight years, that is also a state of emergency.' Yes, but you too lived under it. 'I found some anti-fascist principles here which made life worth living.'

His wife, also a Party member, comes into the room to listen. After this collapse, how on earth are young East Germans going to be Communists, or even socialists, in the future? I ask him. Around him are the books of a lifetime, his Marxist and German-Jewish lodestars, his Brecht, his Heine. 'It is a question which is hard to face,' he answers. 'Perhaps we will have to recognize that we failed.' (Perhaps?) 'But can economies which are based on profit save the world?' he asks me, in the ancient way of talmudic – or messianic – disputation, sitting forward and tapping me on the knee. That is an evasion, I say to him, when the first issue is to face what has happened to socialism. 'An idea which has existed since the time of the Apostles cannot be driven from the world', his wife says, 'however much it has been damaged.'

Hirsch himself, hands placed together beneath his chin as if in prayer, looks at me, an old man scrutinizing a younger. 'It is a great defeat, a terrible defeat, the greatest defeat socialism has ever suffered. Old Party comrades who fought in Spain, who were in Buchenwald, who were in Auschwitz are now in prison. We don't even know where.' Is it *just* that they should be made scapegoats, when everyone is guilty? I ask. 'It is correct,' Hirsch answers, the German – or Prussian – in him taking precedence over the Jewish; I had not asked him if it was 'correct'. 'It is correct', he repeats, 'even if they are old men, and even if they will not live long.'

Why is it correct? 'Because they made terrible mistakes. They have produced a crisis of the State of unknown dimensions. They have made us vulnerable to glittering offers from the Federal Republic. They have made the images of capitalism more attractive than ever.' He leans back in his chair, looking towards the window and its lace curtains. 'People are afraid now. Winter is coming.' In the West, I tell him, people are saying, 'We have won the Cold War.' 'You have,' says Hirsch, blankly.

Aren't you glad at the changes? He is silent; or tiring. Do they depress or elate you? 'Neither,' he answers. 'It is a big chance for changes. But who knows where they will lead us?' What if you get a lumpen-populism, anti-socialist, anti-capitalist, based on the working class and with a strong grassroots leader? 'Mercy!' said Hirsch, clutching his temples.

*

Walking away from Rudolf Hirsch's house down the quiet suburban street – the poisoned air acrid – I see a well-enough dressed man in a brown cord cap rummaging through a refuse container. Propped up against a nearby tree is his bicycle, its handlebars laden with plastic bags. As I approach, he is shaking a tin can to his ear; as I pass, he places it carefully on a small heap of salvaged items on the pavement.

*

The special Party Congress, summoned in emergency and brought forward a further week as the political crisis deepens, is assembling in East Berlin's huge Dynamo Sports Hall. It is approaching 7 p.m. on 8 December 1989; street demonstrations in East Germany are also held after working hours. Outside, the banners read 'Save Our Ideals! Reform the Party!' Inside, the 2,800 delegates, rank upon rank, are already in their places, orderly to the last man and woman. The world's press photographers, made of different stuff, swarm and jostle around Hans Modrow, the new head of government and (in this Wagnerian *götterdämmerung*) one of the last hopes of the country. 'If they do not stop this, they will be flung out!' Wolfgang Berghofer, the new 'moderate' mayor of Dresden and Congress chairman, shouts into the microphone, his zeal rasping, to a savage answering roar from the audience.

Under a giant 40-foot high Party slogan of a clasped, red handshake, and with rumours of yet more arrests in circulation, this stadium roar sounds like the thunder of Valhalla; but a tense, hysterical order is

restored in an unnerving instant. 'We are here to elect a new leadership', declares Berghofer in the dead, massed silence, 'a leadership
with the legitimacy and right to direct the Party, and to restore
its capacity for action. We have to find among ourselves a new
understanding of our Party as a radically reformed Party. It is only
by reform that we will find the strength to survive this crisis. If we
destroy the Party, we will destroy hope for a just and humane society.
If we destroy the Party, we will help to destroy the country.' There
is another despairing roar of approval; around me, there are both
pallid and flushed faces, eyes dead and eyes shining, with alarm or
fervour.

A moment's pause, a swift introduction, and Hans Modrow,
blue-suited and with diffident sauntering gait, walks to the speaker's
rostrum to a fierce standing ovation. A couple of hundred army
delegates in uniform, beribboned and bemedalled, rise opposite me
as one man, hands moving in unison and sitting down together in an
immediate silence.

'We must settle accounts with the past,' says Modrow briskly, after
the briefest preamble, the crowd straight-backed in its seats. 'But
this is also the Party of Marx and Engels, of Rosa Luxemburg and
Karl Liebknecht, of Wilhelm Pieck [first president of the GDR] and
Ernst Thälmann [pre-war leader of the KPD, murdered in 1944 by
the Nazis].' Modrow's earnest, intellectual demeanour is deceptive.
'They created the foundations of our Party', he shouts out, his voice
rising sharply to an abrasive climax, 'and we cannot and will not
permit it to break down and go under!'

There is an orgasmic storm of cheering; the stadium is throbbing.
'We have to clean up everything, so that all of us in the Party can
again look the people of this country in the eye. The election of a
new leadership will be the beginning of this process. Above all, every
case of abuse of power and corruption must be dealt with. But law
and order must be maintained and there must be no violence.
Everyday life must go on as normal. There must be no attacks on
people', he cries with a sudden harsh intensity, his voice skilfully
whipping the crowd towards the end of his sentence, 'just for belonging to the Party!'

In the cannonade of answering applause, silenced at a gesture,
Modrow pushes his spectacles back up his nose, studious as ever,
every swift stridency as swiftly abated. It is a bravura performance,
and in its own way intimidating. 'The most important priorities are

public order, work, and the stabilization of the State. Our partners, and not only the Soviet Union, expect the GDR to remain a sovereign nation. There can be no selling out to the Federal Republic. We should not even speak about reunification.' The roar engulfs him. 'A sovereign GDR is a precondition for the security of Europe. Reunification is not on the agenda,' he shouts above the tempest.

'The GDR too must be part of the common European home, a demilitarized, ecological humanist Europe. We are at the beginning of a new era in the history of our country. But our Party needs a new face,' he says, arriving at his peroration. 'We for our part must learn to listen. And you, for yours, must accept that the time for waiting for a sign "from the top" is over.' Yet around me, the delegates – desperate for reassurance and half-rising from their seats – seem to be urging authority upon Modrow as he returns to his place on the platform.

There will no longer be a politburo but a council, no longer a Party general secretary – a chairman, rather – and no longer even a Communist Party. The name, at least, of everything is changing. And, paradox on paradox, a disciplined Stalinist organization is trying suddenly to make 'democracy' its Prussian order of the day, and commanding its members to think freely. The mood is uneasy: toleration and open-mindedness are being forced upon bred-in-the-bone authoritarians.

During a confused card-vote on a procedural matter, a delegate – breaking ranks – shouts out with unfamiliar daring, 'This is democracy. Voting takes longer!' and is greeted with roars of well-drilled laughter.

*

The Party's choice as its new chairman to replace the fallen Honecker and his successor Egon Krenz – the latter consigned in disgrace to a back row of the Sports Hall – is a balding Jewish lawyer in rimless spectacles, Dr Gregor Gysi. He comes to the rostrum to demand a 'full break' with 'Stalinist administrative methods', which have led to 'corruption, economic failure, ecological crisis and abuse of power'.

Gysi's manner is oddly casual, understated; what he is saying would have been a seditious 'provocation' only a few weeks ago. Though East Germany must not, he says, 'surrender to big capital', western societies are themselves 'not pure capitalist systems'; 'in them,

working people have made significant advances'. Such an assertion
in public from an East German Party leader is unheard of, even if
everyone in the hall has always known it. A 'third way' (of course)
must be found for the country and the Party, non-Stalinist, non-
capitalist, anti-fascist and so on.

What way? 'The way of democratic development and social justice',
a way which also draws on the 'cultural inheritance of humanity'.
What is needed is a 'modern socialist Party' – it has taken fifteen
minutes for the word 'socialism' to cross Gysi's lips – a party which,
heresy of heresies, is 'not a party of a class' and whose leaders are
democratically elected.

But Gysi has other fish to fry. A member of the Party's commission
of inquiry into corruption, he comes, in lawyerly undertone – the
hall deathly silent – to the question of the hour, the issue which has
wrecked 'the Party of Marx and Engels, Luxemburg and Liebknecht'.
'The picture we have got so far', he says, 'is frightening', though
'restricted to a certain number of people'. He will mention no
one by name; it is as if the corrupt were already non-persons, in
time-honoured fashion.

'Everything', he continues quietly, 'started with small matters, the
need for security, for special housing and living conditions. Some
abused the general privileges of all Party members, others had special
privileges in addition. Some extended their privileges to members of
their families – their children, grandchildren and so on – others did
not. There were special Party hotels reserved to the leadership, but
family members also used them. Government aircraft were used for
private flights, holidays and so on. There was a kind of court around
the leading figures, whose members sought a lifestyle for themselves
comparable to that of the Party leaders. We have not yet finished our
investigations. Each individual case will be inquired into.'

The delegates around me are glassy-eyed, the packed amphitheatre
silent. 'The most frightening aspect of all', Gysi goes on, 'is that there
was no method of controlling the corruption. The rights of the Party's
[watchdog] Control Commission had themselves been restricted over
the years. In effect, it had no rights of control at all. The general
secretary [Honecker] and the head of the finance section of the
politburo [Mittag] each had the right to sign a decision' – or draw a
cheque – 'without a second signature. They also each had the right
to destroy documents at their individual discretion.'

There is a freezing wave of shocked or embarrassed laughter, and the mood of a lynching. 'I will give no figures,' Gysi says; but it is the figures – in billions of dollars – for which East Germany is waiting. 'We all know now that the close link between Party and State must be dissolved. It is no way to establish order. This chaos has to stop. Everybody who was a member of the politburo violated the Party's statutes, the egoism of one at war with the egoism of another.

'It was the result of the isolation of the politburo from the people. Its members led their own lives in their own circles. All their violations of the law will be prosecuted under the criminal law of the German Democratic Republic. Two more heads of central committee departments have been arrested. If it is necessary to arrest others, they will be arrested.'

But this cleansing of the Augean stables has come too late. In due course, Gysi, the mild-mannered Jewish lawyer wielding the broom, will himself be swept away by the people.

★

There is a crowd below my hotel window moving up the Friedrichstrasse, whistling, drumming, shouting, bearing banners. I join them. '*Wir Sind Ein Volk!*' – 'We Are One People!' – they chant, at the crossing with the Unter-den-Linden, where home-going shoppers wait obediently for the lights to change in their favour. 'Free Elections!' the demonstrators demand, opposite the East Berlin offices of Intourist. 'A Confederation of the Germanys!' they yell, surging past the house where Engels lived in the early 1840s.

They follow their new leaders, as enchanted youth once followed the Pied Piper. Many of the children in the procession are carrying candles, their faces shining.

10

Czechoslovakia, December 1989: 'A free existence'

In the Czech fortress town of Terezin – once known as Theresienstadt – there are two historic memorials. One is the demented Heinrich Jöckel's concentration camp, with its SS barracks, its dread cell blocks, its places of torture and execution. Down the road is the collapsing Communist regime's silent National Security Corps museum, with its lone cloakroom attendant and heroic bronzes. Here are police uniforms, Party memorabilia, and 'seized' caches of Radio Free Europe propaganda; 'spies'' transmitters and wads of foreign banknotes are neatly displayed in glass cases. A quarter of a mile separates the two places; a seamless web of lunacy joins them.

★

The end has come quickly. On 10 November 1989, the day after the Berlin Wall was opened, Jiri Hajek, Dubcek's foreign minister, was discounting the possibility of major political reforms in Czechoslovakia, as Zhivkov fell in Bulgaria. On 12 November, Milos Jakes was still calling on Czech youth to 'boost the activities of the Party'. Two days later, Prime Minister Ladislav Adamec partially relaxed travel restrictions. The next day Prague police dispersed a small crowd of about 500 people which was calling for 'dialogue with the authorities'. A mere forty-eight hours later, on 17 November – or Bloody Friday, as it came to be called – a 30,000-strong demonstration, chanting for Jakes's removal, shouting 'Forty years is enough' and demanding free elections, was attacked by the security police; many of the demonstrators were hurt in vicious beatings, and Dubcek himself was arrested.

It turned out to be the beginning of the end for the regime, as the scale of daily demonstrations in Wenceslas Square swiftly mounted, with students and actors in the thick of the tumult. On 19 November, the opposition Civic Forum was founded under the leadership of Vaclav Havel. The next day Prime Minister Adamec received a delegation of opposition figures, Havel addressed the crowds in Wenceslas Square, and Cardinal Tomasek called for 'democratic government' in Czechoslovakia. As the number of demonstrators in Prague reached an estimated quarter of a million, Jakes continued to denounce the 'ruthless manipulators' of popular feeling, and politburo member Miroslav Stepan warned that the People's Militia was standing by. Jan Carnogursky went on trial in Bratislava on multiple charges of subversion and incitement; one of the charges related to a demand for free elections.

On 23 November an even larger crowd of perhaps half a million people occupied the centre of Prague, Carnogursky was acquitted – though he remained in custody on appeal by the prosecution – Czech army officers were publicly declaring their readiness to 'defend the achievements of socialism', and a political struggle had broken out inside the Czech media.

The majority of the 13-member Czech praesidium, including Milos Jakes, but excluding two of its leading hardliners, Miroslav Stepan and Jan Fojtik, resigned on 24 November, together with the Party's central committee secretariat, although Gustav Husak remained president. 'We have underestimated completely the processes taking place in Poland, Hungary and especially in East Germany, and their effect and influence on our society,' declared Jakes; he was replaced as Party general secretary by former railwayman Karel Urbanek. But on 25 November the crowds calling for an end to Communist rule were as vast as ever, Havel described the resignations as a 'fraud', and President Husak announced a 'presidential pardon' for Carnogursky and certain other imprisoned dissidents.

As Civic Forum called on the people for 'increased pressure', Prime Minister Adamec, invited to address the half-million demonstrators at Prague's Letna Field, declared that the Czech Communist Party would be judged by its ability to 'overcome the shortcomings of the past'. (Only four weeks before, on an official visit to Austria, Adamec had described Havel as a 'nobody, simply a zero'.) On 27 November, Civic Forum gave President Husak a fortnight to resign, as the biggest industrial strike since the war brought the country to a standstill; Miroslav Stepan and Jan Fojtik – the Party's hated chief of ideology – resigned from the praesidium, and Prime Minister

Adamec promised to form a 'broad coalition government' within a week. The Ministry of Culture lifted a twenty-year ban on thousands of books, including the plays of Havel and the novels of Kundera.

On 29 November the Czech Federal Assembly unanimously abolished both the constitutional guarantee of the leading role of the Party and the ideological primacy of Marxism-Leninism in education. The following day East Germany expressed regret for its participation in the 1968 invasion of Czechoslovakia. The day after that, 1 December, new Party General Secretary Urbanek also 'repudiated' the invasion, and Gorbachev did likewise in Moscow. On 2 December *Rude Pravo* published an interview with Vaclav Havel.

However, the 'broad coalition government' promised a week earlier by Prime Minister Adamec turned out to contain 15 Party and 5 non-Party members, and was rejected as 'unacceptable' by Civic Forum. Hundreds of thousands again took to the streets in protest, as the Warsaw Pact formally – and unanimously – condemned the 1968 invasion of Czechoslovakia. The Party and government were driven into agreement with Civic Forum that a new list of ministers, with a different balance between Party and opposition, would have to be presented to the people. On 7 December Prime Minister Adamec resigned and Milos Jakes was expelled from the Party.

Now, Czechoslovakia is awaiting the announcement of a new government and the resignation of President Husak.

*

'All those dark ages', physicist Pavel Bratinka calls the four decades of state socialism in Czechoslovakia, or rule by plebeian baseness. It is ten months since I met him last; ten months more of stoking, but ten months in which the knot of national oppression has unravelled.

Today, he is in the process of founding a new 'liberal-conservative' party, the Citizens' Democratic Alliance, and expects to stand for the Federal Assembly. His footsteps no longer dogged by plainclothesmen, he is at long last establishing what he calls 'a free existence'. Surrounded by his family, he is jovial at his table in a way I have never seen him.

The end of what he calls the *ancien régime* is a matter for blissful feelings. All over Prague there is this carousing, as the left world I myself once inhabited crashes in ruins. It is also a time for turncoats, a time when yesterday's dyed-in-the-wool Party men become overnight reformers. Bratinka says that his own father-in-law, an establishment apparatchik, 'could find no good word for me for years'. Now, as the wheel of fortune turns, the old man is effusive in praise of Vaclav Havel. In a similar fashion, western leftists of varying stripe are swarming about Prague, preposterously celebrating an anti-socialist revolution, as if it were what they had always wanted.

*

President Husak, installed in power nearly twenty-one years ago by Warsaw Pact tanks, is resigning. It is 9 December 1989. His mouth works in strange disorder, his eyes behind the pebble lenses roving unsteadily to right and left of the camera. 'I didn't even manage to write a speech,' he confides to the viewers, clutching a sheaf of papers from which he is reading. It is one more falsehood.

An emperor without clothes, he claims to approve of the new coalition government which is about to be announced; a prisoner of events, he claims that he has prevented a constitutional crisis. 'Much has been said in the last days about our past,' he stumbles on. 'There were good and bad things in it. The analysis of it and the analysis of me too', he says with a wintry smile, 'cannot be done out of hand. It must be done thoroughly.' But he has no power to command it.

This is a dying fall, without jargon. 'I have believed in socialism from my earliest years,' he says, taking his kind of socialism down with him. 'There are no better ideas than socialist ideas in the world today. If there are', he declares, blinking distractedly, 'I do not see them.'

My hosts' two young daughters are giggling on the sofa. 'I hope you solve your problems', he adds, mouth still working, 'so that you may have a happy Christmas.' The national anthem plays, and old Husak has gone for ever.

*

At humble workplaces across Prague, where the punished intelligentsia spent the long post-Dubcek years of 'socialist construction' in menial tasks, the theological cleaner or academic stoker is suddenly a hero. 'Three days ago', says Bratinka, 'a carpenter who works at my place suddenly came up to me and said he wanted to "speak about God". During all the time we worked together, I never got the slightest hint that he was interested in religion.' These are moments for a Tolstoy. All over the city there are spontaneous meetings at which Communist intellectuals, defrocked two decades ago for their heresies, explain to the proletariat that the 'dictatorship of the proletariat' is over.

★

The attentive crowd in Wenceslas Square is huge, the national tricolours blowing stiffly in an icy wind. It is 10 December 1989. Vaclav Havel, in a rough basso voice hoarse with talk and smoking, reads out the names of the government – 12 of the 21 are non-Party members – from a balcony high above the hundreds of thousands. A Cup Final stadium roar, rolling like thunder, greets the name of each non-Communist elevated to office. Even small children, riding on their fathers' shoulders, are clapping.

'It has been a revolution', Havel declares to the giant assembly, 'against violence, dirt, intrigue, lawlessness, mafia, privilege and persecution.' All round the square, there are heads at windows, witnessing the historic retaking of the country from the Communist apparatus. Except for ironic purposes, even the word 'comrade' has been abolished. 'Citizens' they now call each other, as hats are doffed for the national anthem. In a freezing wind, the huge crowd sings with passion, bare-headed.

Jan Carnogursky, fresh from detention, has become first deputy prime minister. In anorak and jeans, he pushes his way through the applause into Civic Forum's temporary offices. The Communist world has turned upside down, 'reactionaries' – or even 'clerical fascists' – like Carnogursky have become the instruments of a democratic revolution, and, as Heine's 'dark hero' dies, a whole nation has begun breathing.

★

Liberal capitalist economic ideas have sprung almost fully-formed from state socialism's ruins. Tomas Jezek, who was a Marxist in his student days, is one of the new government's principal economic advisers. A free-market follower of Hayek and Friedman, he claims that his highly-placed Communist friends are actually *relieved* that the old socialist order is ending. According to him, many of the Party's leaders had 'lost their remaining socialist illusions' as early as the beginning of the 1980s. It was the time when the Party's house-trained economists had begun to discover that the compromise efforts to combine elements of the free market with the retention of central planning were not going to work either.

Now the Party itself is going for a Burton, and not even Dubcek's socialism-with-a-human-face has many takers. Indeed, men like Jezek believe that 'socialism can be defined as ignorance of economic science'. He also says that the 'more able' civil servants with whom the new government will have to work are 'democratic or liberal by conviction'.

Private ownership for him is not a question of ideology. 'We need it for practical reasons, just as we need a free market in order to adapt our stagnant economy to the constantly changing conditions around us. Words like socialism are for us without meaning.' Outside in the street, banner-waving students are heading towards the city centre. 'All our textbooks on economics are being thrown away,' he says, and new ones – containing what he calls 'standard knowledge' – are to be imported from West Germany to replace them. The summer's school history exams are also to be cancelled; 'socialist history' is being abandoned.

For Marxism-Leninism this is a complete débâcle. What are you ultimately trying to achieve? I asked him. 'We want to be normal human beings,' he answered.

*

The bells are pealing in baroque Prague for the end of forty-two years of Communist rule, and intellectuals are standing up, putting down their hods, setting aside their shovels. But who will do their work? The proletariat of course, who else? 'There will be a big shortage of stokers in the coming period,' Bratinka said. 'A lot of the apparatchiks may have to be content with different work in future.' But what satisfaction will you get, as a Christian, from their humiliation? 'I never felt humiliated myself by being a stoker. If Communists feel humiliated by proletarian labour, that will be their problem,' he replied briskly.

11

Romania, January 1990:
The storm

Freezing Otopeni airport is crowded with paratroopers; young country lads with pink ears in tin helmets. The shoemaker has fallen in a hail of bullets, and now an unlikely figure in a blue dressing-gown is checking the passports. *'Romania Libera!'* and 'Down with Communism!' read the drear, grey walls; but here, among the fresh, open expressions are some of the same old shifty eyes and unshaven faces.

At the road-blocks along the dim road into Bucharest, they look as if they mean business, their Kalashnikovs thrust at the taxi windows. The national tricolour – with a ragged hole where, before, there were the insignia of the 'socialist republic' – flutters stiffly in the wind at the roadside guard-post. A mere five weeks before his execution the cobbler, in a flush of romantic ardour, was describing socialism as 'humanity's Prince Charming'. Now, there is a kind of grim fever of quickly-obeyed orders, revving engines, and slamming car-boots. This is liberation, but in the old icy wind, teeth still chatter.

*

When Kadar fell in Hungary in May 1988, Ceausescu had just unveiled his plan to flatten 7,000 villages for his new agro-industrial centres; when Tadeusz Mazowiecki was nominated prime minister of Poland in August 1989, the Romanian Party paper denounced the choice as 'against the interests of the Polish people'; and, as other regimes tumbled in November, the Romanian dictator was being described by his son and heir, Nicu, as the 'brilliant genius of the nation'. Would he too take the path of reform? 'Yes', declared Ceausescu, 'when there are pears on the poplars and the reeds bear flowers.'

Now, bearded revolutionaries have seized his palaces and villas, fingered his silk pyjamas, and tossed his wife's 'diamond-encrusted shoes' around her bedroom. 'I recognize neither defeat nor anything,' said little Nicolae – accusing his accusers of 'provocation' in the usual fashion, and with his delusions intact to the last moment. 'We want to die together, we do not want mercy,' said the stone-hearted Elena, scientist to the nation, as they were led away to a savage Christmas Day execution. 'No, dear, don't stand up', she had said to her husband, as the unknown, unnamed tribunal, meeting in secret, rose to consider its verdict; 'we are human beings.'

He lay huddled in the lea of a wall, his tie askew, his head shattered. In Teheran the previous week he had been telling his hosts that the situation in Romania – his 'worker-revolutionary democracy' – was 'good, stable and balanced'; political and economic guidelines until the year 2010 had been approved (unanimously) by his November Party Congress. Five days after his return from Iran, he was facing a firing squad.

★

As you set out on foot towards Palace Square, just like the last time, the fur-hatted figures queuing in the icy wind are the same; the women road-cleaners shovelling snow might have been at these very street corners; the passing mixture of *belle époque* and bunker is just as you remember. Except that here, tended by solemn children in tricolour armbands, there are caps and a bloody handkerchief hanging from the railings, candles burning before them; the multi-coloured rivulets of wax are frozen into the ice on the rutted pavement.

A block further, and the upper storey of the building on the right has broken shutters and gaping windows; the next is blackened by the updraught of smoke and extinguished fire; the next is pocked and battered – especially around its balconies and windows – by a fierce barrage directed at snipers' positions; the next, its charred roof-timbers fallen, is gutted. ('*Asa Vor Arde Criminali*' – 'This Is The Way Criminals Will Burn' – is written on a wall.)

In Palace Square, olive-green armoured personnel carriers stand in the snow, their cannon raised to the snipers' now-silent roof-top eyries. There are hundreds of discarded wine bottles; two plush chairs and a torn velvet curtain lie in a heap of smouldering detritus. Gottereau's nineteenth-century library, the columns and mouldings of its elegant façade consumed by fire, is ruined; its half-million volumes have gone up in smoke, early printed books and manuscripts of De Maupassant and Handel among them. Inside, there is a chaos of masonry, twisted and melted metal book-racks, and blackened scraps of drifting paper, light as air. But Galeron's domed Athenaeum stands unscathed, amid the burned-out and bullet-smashed wreckage.

There are dark faces in conical lambswool hats – men from the country – staring, or murmuring, at the ruins; and under the trees people peering, open-mouthed, into a vertical shaft entrance to the Securitate's system of underground tunnels. Look down and you can see a door, wedged open in a foot of black, slushy water. '*Craciun Fara Porci*!' – 'Christmas Without Pigs!' – 'Down with the Paranoiac!', and 'Down with the Bootmaker!' say the slogans, painted in the heat of battle.

And here is the balcony of the Party headquarters, stripped bare of its red insignia, from which the stricken dictator made his last arm-waving denunciation, on 21 December 1989, of the 'enemies of the people'. 'Party of Demagogy!' and '*Vox Populi, Vox Dei!*', read the answering graffiti at the entrance to the abandoned Holy of Holies, a forlorn curtain flapping at a broken window. What pent-up rage there was in the fusillade of words – 'Hitler, Stalin, Ceausescu!' – and the hail of bullets: on that *dies irae* which devoured the little grey man from Scornicesti, his wife, thousands of citizens and the socialist republic of Romania together.

*

As everywhere in eastern Europe, the end came swiftly. But it was as long in hidden gestation as elsewhere in the 'socialist system'. In November 1987, there were bread riots in Brasov, and an attack on Party headquarters, with portraits of Ceausescu being pitched into the streets and set on fire. The reprisals included arrests, beatings, 'disappearances'. In the same month Professor Silviu Brucan, a former Romanian ambassador to the United Nations and ex-editor of the Party daily, declared (in a statement bravely given to a British journalist for publication) that Romania's 'cup of privations' was 'full'.

In December 1987 there were reports of student protests in the once-Hungarian city of Timisoara, on Romania's western border; and of daring damage done to a statue of Lenin in Brasov. During 1988, subterranean contacts between malcontents of all kinds, Party and non-Party, deepened. By March 1989, six senior Party figures,

including Corneliu Manescu, the former foreign minister, had cour-
ageously sent an open letter to the dictator, telling him that socialism
had been 'discredited' by his policies.

In July 1989, the Hungarian pastor Laszlo Tökes – who was
soon to become the unexpected catalyst of the dénouement – was
incautiously criticizing the Ceausescu regime on Hungarian television. And in September, more than three months before the revolution, an hitherto unknown group made a now hotly-debated
appearance. Calling itself the 'National Salvation Front', it declared,
in a document said to have been 'smuggled out of Romania', that
the country was 'on the brink of ruin'. Denouncing Ceausescu's
'disgusting and noxious personality cult', it called on the Party to
remove the dictator at its forthcoming Congress in November. Oust-
ing Ceausescu, said the statement, was 'the only way of avoiding a
major social conflict and bloodshed'. (Today, it is strongly denied in
Bucharest, by previously trustworthy sources, that any 'National
Salvation Front' was in existence until a body with this name was
formed in the midst of the December revolution. The Front of
September is variously dismissed as a fiction concocted by Radio Free
Europe to embarrass Ceausescu, and a devious ploy by the regime's
own myrmidons to rally support for the dictator; while the identity
of name is written off as a 'mere coincidence'. The mystery of it
remains unresolved.)

At the end of October, Pastor Tökes locked himself inside his
church in Timisoara in defiance of an attempt by the authorities to
evict him from his living; the attempt was the subject of a formal
protest to Ceausescu from Hungary's new President Szuros. The
response to the protest was of a familiar kind: Tökes was physically
attacked by four masked men of the local Securitate in a further effort
to terrorize him out of his intransigence. Three weeks later, on 24
November, Ceausescu was elected *nem. con.* at the 14th Party Congress to a further five-year term as Romania's leader. The scene had
been set for a showdown.

Indeed, at the time of the Congress, as demonstrations were
engulfing the regime in Czechoslovakia, Ceausescu had sealed Romania's western border with Hungary, and put the police and Securitate on to the streets of Bucharest in inordinate numbers. During his
six-hour speech, he received sixty standing ovations – haughtily
overseen by his wife, Elena – followed by a volley of eulogies from
sycophants; he was an 'outstanding champion of the Communist and

working class movement', and so on. Nevertheless, there were clear signs of unease and pressure in the Ceausescu camp, as the speed of change in the other East European countries accelerated. Thus, on 1 December, within a fortnight of his triumphant Congress, Ceausescu could be heard declaring that the Romanian Parliament 'should play a larger role', and criticizing his own Party politburo for its 'work-style' and 'administrative shortcomings'. On 14 December, with only eight days to go before his overthrow, a new effort had begun to evict the humble pastor Tökes from his parish.

Three days later, as Ceausescu left for a brief visit to Teheran, all hell broke out in Timisoara. The small initial crowd of two hundred ethnic Hungarian parishioners seeking to protect Tökes had grown to many thousands, including Romanians. It brought 'columns of troops' and even tanks to the city, to break up a protest which was now demanding free elections, and suicidally denouncing the dictator. There was a massacre in Timisoara on 17 December; of how many people is uncertain. And as trouble and killing spread to other areas of Transylvania, troops were also pre-emptively brought on to the streets of Bucharest.

★

When Ceausescu returned to Romania on 20 December, and fatally denounced as 'fascists, spies and hooligans' – 'paid with a handful of dollars' – those responsible for the growing trouble, the situation was explosive. Fifty thousand were on the streets of Timisoara; the first troops there had already mutinied and gone over to the insurrection; and a local revolutionary committee backed by a people's militia had declared itself the sovereign authority in the city.

The following day Ceausescu tried to address the nation from the balcony of the Party headquarters in Bucharest, offering the people wage and pension increases, and increased ex gratia payments to pregnant women. At first the crowd was silent. Then a chorus of jeering, with the name of Timisoara being chanted in a roaring crescendo, drove Ceausescu back into the Party building. During that day, the gathering crowds were in various places fired on by the army; several young people were crushed by armoured cars; and the first sporadic clashes between army and Securitate were reported, as the people occupied the city by sheer force of numbers.

On 22 December, much of the army went over to the people, the Party headquarters was stormed by unarmed students and workers, the Ceausescus fled, the National Salvation Front announced its existence and fierce battles raged (and were gradually won) for control of the television station, telephone exchange, Otopeni airport and presidential palace. By nightfall, the Ceausescus had been caught in Boteni and taken to the military base at Tirgoviste. On 23 and 24 December, heavy fighting between army and Securitate continued in Bucharest, with murderous sniping from the rooftops, upper floors, and balconies of city centre buildings; bodies – many of them of young people caught in the cross-fire – lay in the streets where they had fallen. New political parties, or old political parties re-born, were now coming into being, including what was to become the National Peasant-Christian Democratic Party.

On 25 December, after a hurried trial before a military tribunal, the Ceausescus were executed. The next day, the fifty-six-year-old Ion Iliescu, once the Romanian Communist Party's central committee secretary for ideology, was named as provisional president, and Petre Roman chosen to head a Communist-dominated National Salvation Front government, pending free elections in April. 'No More Communism!' shouted the crowds in Palace Square, as the lethal sniping diminished and a committee was appointed to rewrite the constitution.

During the following week, and into the turn of the year, there was a cascade of decrees aimed at abolishing large swathes of the Communist legacy: including the birth squads which spied on pregnant women to prevent abortion, collective farms, food and oil exports, the 'socialist republic' of Romania, the razing of villages, food rationing, the ban on foreign travel, the prohibition of marriage to foreigners, and the Securitate. 'We openly admit', declared a group of unreliably penitent Romanian Communist Party members on 30 December, 'that in the dark dictatorship period the RCP compromised itself before history and the people . . . We will always reproach ourselves for not taking action in time to stop the escalation of dictatorship and arbitrariness.'

The RCP was alternatively declared to be already 'dead', to be regrouping as a social democratic party, and to be 'about to be dissolved entirely' at a special Party Congress.

On 2 January 1990, the whole of Ceausescu's former politburo was arrested.

★

The ice-blocks of chicken heads and feet have gone, but they are still queuing in the street outside the Unic Supermarket in Boulevard Balcescu. Now, there are breaded chicken legs, sausages and scraggy cuts of fresh meat; and a hundred people waiting in the cold for oranges, rare as hen's teeth in the previous order.

There are also eighty people in a patient line at the news-stand, in a temperature well below zero, awaiting the arrival of the day's *Romania Libera*, first fruit of a freed press. As you pass there is even the sound, still cautious, of open conversation and casual street-banter; four decades of whispering and eavesdropping are over.

*

'After forty years', says my young interpreter, 'there is a national trauma. We are still sick from it.' Her friend – a recently qualified doctor – spent four days almost continuously on his feet in the operating theatre at the Bucharest municipal hospital, working on the wounded, or dying. (The Securitate, he says to me, used dum-dum and fragmentation bullets.)

'Now I don't know what to do with myself, I am so happy and grief-stricken,' she says. At the pavement shrines where passers-by pause, heads bowed for a moment, there are heaps of posies – fresh red carnations, often – coins in saucers, fruit, loaves of bread, and martyrs' crosses. The candles commemorating this new Passion are so many that you might warm your hands at them.

*

Beards, anoraks, fur hats, fists at the table and, in a crowded smoke-stale room, a shambles of discordant voices: image of the political aftermath of the Romanian revolution, all dark intensity, exhaustion and disorder. This is the headquarters of the National Peasant-Christian Democratic Party. The carpet has been trampled sodden.

'Frati Romani!' begins the Party's typewritten address to the people; the hated word 'comrade' has been banished. A re-creation of the old National Peasant Party which governed Romania from 1928 to 1931, and which in 1947 had 2 million members, it does not recognize the provisional government – since it is 'too close to the old order' – and seeks a 'democracy in Romania without a trace of Communism'. It also wants the distribution of all land to the peasants and the 'moral rehabilitation of the nation'.

'During the dictatorship, we always dreamed of a moral Christian life,' says Ion Radoi, president of the Party's youth movement. A tall, handsome man in his mid-twenties, he has bushy black hair and the eyes (and pallor) of a sombre icon, or an El Greco. 'We dreamed of liberty, truth, equality and the preservation of city and country life as they used to be,' he continues; some of his ramshackle committee are sitting on the table, others crowding in the jammed doorway. It is a dream of an imagined golden age, before proletarian dictatorship settled like a pall upon Romania.

'Now we want the old social classes to assume their previous functions,' he tells the motley around him: part lumpen street-people, part embryo bourgeois, eyes shining, or blazing. Yes, young Radoi wants the old class system restored, not to put too fine a point on it. But then this is an anti-Communist, and anti-socialist, revolution; and these are some of the victors.

'Unless we get all our rights, and unless these things happen', he goes on, a mild-seeming fellow in crumpled jeans and pale blue pullover, 'there will be other revolutions. Youth has nothing to lose, except its lives.' The room applauds him, hands thudding together. 'This is an imperative imposed by the blood shed by our heroes. There has been no perestroika here. Here there was a revolution.'

Other faces are paler still, with this fever; clamant voices begin to interrupt him. They say they have no money, no 'democratic experience', and no access to the new media, which are 'in the grip of the National Salvation Front'; in fact, the TV station is still defended by tanks, drawn up in a semi-circle at its entrance.

Nurtured on the long years of rumour, falsehood and paranoia, few in the crowded room believe that the old order is really dead and buried. Dimitru Iacob, a pentecostal preacher in a fur hat, thinks that the Communists are not only still lurking everywhere in the National Salvation Front and army, but want to 'impose the old system again'. Head held high and speaking with urgent compulsion, he believes they would like to 'go on manipulating the people through terror'. In the doorway, there is pushing and shoving. 'Communism', shouts Victor Negara, an engineer, 'was atheist at its very basis. It was' – 'It is!' others call out in muddy desperation – 'implicitly totalitarian. Now the National Salvation Front has also been imposed on us, without a referendum. It is made up of old Communists', he cries, his mouth taut and trembling, 'it does not represent the forces of the Romanian nation.'

There is more tormented shouting: for and against revenge, and about the sacrifices of youth in the street-fighting, sacrifices which they fear will go unrequited. Voices, striving with each other for a hearing, demand 'something like Nuremberg', or an 'international court martial' for the 'monsters of the old regime'. Here is a dense, anti-Communist hatred. 'We want morally good people', says Ion Radoi – obtaining silence – 'to lead our country. We do not want to avenge ourselves. Let us not be extremist.'

'God will be with us, as long as we deserve it,' says a youth with a thin beard, who might have stepped from the pages of Dostoevsky. 'He loves us,' he says intently; a blood brother of the Karamazovs, reborn in Romania's moral tempest.

*

Such doubts and fears are not surprising. The 10-man 'executive bureau' of the National Salvation Front, under its Communist president Ion Iliescu, is an inner circle as select as any politburo; the council of ministers, ostensibly governing Romania, is subject to it. Moreover, Sergiu Celac, the new foreign minister and a former Party member, has gone out of his way to insist that the revolution 'would not have succeeded without the help of members of the Communist Party'; and four generals have senior places in the government, between them running the ministries of National Economy, Defence and the Interior.

Most of the Communist apparatus is still in place. 'We have to carry on our activity within superseded structures, but there are no alternative ones for the time being,' declare Front spokesmen. The language of official pronouncements has the old ring to it also, the revolution notwithstanding. The new prime minister, Petre Roman – a former administrator at Bucharest Polytechnic and ex-Party member – can still speak of 'steps being taken to normalize activities in all areas, to work out and fulfil the Plan for the first three months of the year', and so forth.

Hatred for the old order is being expressed, for the time being, in the old order's lingo. 'Coming out of the underground pits and tunnels, armed to the teeth and with a ferocious thirst for blood', Rada Budeanu writes in the official publication *Lumea*, 'the hysterical bandits [of the Securitate], rats of the dictatorship's last moments, committed their last treason. In the past, they betrayed the people. Now they betrayed the secret of Ceausescu's subterranean strongholds.' It is standard Party invective; adept hands can turn it in any direction, and on any opponent.

'By the unflinching will of the masses', announced President Iliescu in his New Year message to a battered nation, 'and by the resolute action of the youth, the personal dictatorship of Ceausescu has been overthrown . . . No attempt by the remains of the old regime is capable of turning back the wheel of history. The popular revolution has triumphed . . . In the next period we will have to surmount numerous hardships, and overcome many difficulties . . . We must promote democracy in all spheres of social life, and a genuine participation of the masses in decision-making and in their control of the leading factors. In promoting these ideas', declared the Party's former ideology chief, 'we are not the slaves of any ideology, or the servants of any prefabricated model'; only of its dead language.

*

Rubble is being tipped out of upper windows, icicles hanging from the eaves above them; it falls in clouds of grey dust on to the frozen pavements. Everywhere in the vicinity of Palace Square there is broken glass; the blue sparks of the welder; the sound of hammering and compressor engines; stooping demolition workers. Two or three blocks away, there is barely a sign of the revolution, save for the flickering candles and the walls' maledictions.

*

The Romanian revolution may have begun in Timisoara with a Hungarian pastor's defiance, but it is the Bucharest fighting which is being given pride of place in the official versions of what happened. Indeed, the 2 million Hungarians in Romania have little to gain from all the talk of a '2,000-year-old Christian and peasant foundation of the Romanian nation': it points, in the long run, only to further tribulation for the Hungarians.

The new 26-man provisional government (there are no women) contains no ethnic Hungarians; Constantin Oancea, named as deputy foreign minister, dealt harshly with Romanian-Hungarian State relations under Ceausescu; the army's garrison commander in Timisoara is even denying that his men fired on the people. Differences between the national communities have also surfaced over the question of whether Romania has any genuine 'democratic tradition' on which to base its political future. 'It has not,' say many Hungarians,

Pastor Tökes included, showing an historic contempt for the Romanians' Balkan wildness. 'It has,' insist angered Romanians, national danders aroused by the revival of old insults. As for the most cruelly exaggerated estimates of deaths in the revolution, especially in Timisoara, many were based on over-eager Hungarian sources.

Geza Domokos is one of the leaders of the new Democratic Union of Hungarians in Romania. It aims to defend Hungarian minority interests in what Domokos optimistically calls the 'new democratic Romania'. A mannerly, silver-haired figure, he describes the revolution as a 'triumph of reason'. Of course, it was true that Ceausescu had sought, in his own Machiavellian interests, to sow discord between ethnic Romanian and ethnic Hungarian; true that he had sought to extirpate the Hungarian mother-tongue culture; true that 'distrust of Hungarians' had acquired 'some roots in the minds of the Romanian people'.

But 'the blood we shed together in the revolution was a beautiful thing' – yes, a beautiful thing – on which to found a new relation. Now, closed Hungarian institutions would be reopened, old Hungarian place-names would be restored, and ethnic Hungarians at last find their rightful places in the new political order.

Meanwhile there are no Hungarians in the provisional government, and '500 to 800' people a day are joining his Democratic Union. 'It is good for the Romanians to know', Domokos declares sleekly, 'that we were among the first to challenge the dictator.' It is also polite advance warning of the oldest kind of trouble in central Europe.

*

Ceausescu's titanic new palace, a pharaonic pile five years in the building and still unfinished, stands huge and silent. A colossus nearly half a mile long, with a gigantic Corinthian portico and '4,000' empty rooms, its thunderous mass, its marbled halls, its crystal tonnage and its Transylvanian gold are fit for a Thor or Wotan. Built by thousands of workers at a cost of billions of Romanian *lei*, it is constructed of reinforced concrete, special steels – those used in the construction of nuclear power stations – and megatons of marble.

Churches, monasteries, a synagogue, the old Jewish quarter, and thousands of houses were demolished to make way for it; old Nicolae has left his thumb-print on Romania for ever. Here, a dynasty of gods was to luxuriate in its own Marxist-Leninist Valhalla; and here, even on the very day of the Apocalypse or Armageddon, a vast subterranean refuge would shelter the eternal progeny of the boot-maker.

Bucharest's greatest bunker, it is today merely a whited sepulchre, glistening and deserted under a sparkling winter sun; the giant mausoleum of the *epoca Ceausescu*. Stand still beneath its crushing façade, and there is only the distant sound of traffic.

*

Here comes smiling Eduard Shevardnadze, surrounded by Kalash-nikovs and tin helmets; the Soviet Union is about to lose the imported meat and vegetables – representing a massive 15 per cent of total Soviet consumption – which has emptied the Romanian larder for years, and left its people famished.

'The Romanian revolution', Shevardnadze declares to a battery of microphones and in a niagara of leads and cables, 'is a phenomenon of European and world importance. Never before have I experienced such emotions as I have today,' he says, pink-faced, his white hair fluffy. He describes what has occurred as 'Romania's resurgence as a democratic State'; the atmosphere in Bucharest – where Securitate agents are being silently executed – is now 'absolutely purified'; the Soviet people have felt 'great enthusiasm' for what he calls 'this spontaneous popular revolution, in the real sense of the word'.

But what about the slogan 'Down with Communism!' which now covers the city? For a moment Shevardnadze discovers a technical problem with his simultaneous translation, grimacing in the brief silence as if he had not quite understood the question. 'In respect of any dictatorship', he replies carefully, 'whatever its basis, we have the same standpoint. That is why we started our own revolution, which is called perestroika. Perestroika means the democratization of relations in our country.' ('Throw Away Your Party Cards!' say the Bucharest graffitti.) Yes, but what about 'Down With Communism!'? 'Dictatorship of any kind', answers the Soviet foreign minister, with the same side-step, 'cannot be accepted. Have I answered your question?' he says, pointing simultaneously at a raised hand in the mêlée.

He has bulging eyes, a maroon tie, a dark blue suit, and smiles at the chorus of shouted questions. And what, asks an American, if the Romanians were to reject Communism, and all the rest of the Marxist-Leninist caboodle, in the coming elections? (They already have.) 'I am not a prophet,' Shevardnadze answers blandly. 'It is a matter for Romanians which specific parties lead Romania in the future.' Yes, but wouldn't the creation of a functioning multi-party system in Romania – of all places – make it even more difficult for the Soviet Union to resist such an outcome? Shevardnadze's head-set again gives him minor trouble. 'Whether or not the Romanians have a multi-party system is a question for Romanians.' But surely, foreign minister, the cumulative effect of the changes in eastern Europe must be to push the Soviet Union towards a multi-party system?

The wall of television cameras, red lights winking, stares him down; he is near lost in a forest of clipboard. 'Everything is interdependent,' Shevardnadze replies genially, smiling at the men around him as if the question were simple-minded. 'Our perestroika, our revolution, is a revolution of democratization,' he says doggedly. Yes, but . . . 'To a certain degree', he adds, suddenly raising his voice, 'of course, our perestroika has contributed to the unleashing of changes in eastern Europe.'

The wired-up ruck in front of him does not move; nor the men with Kalashnikovs, idly fingering their weapons. The benign statesman of a doomed system is completely surrounded.

*

When I last spoke to the architect Mariana Celac in November 1987, whispering in her kitchen with the radio on, she had said that she hoped we would meet again in 'more normal circumstances'. Today, she is a member of the 150-strong National Salvation Front and describes the events of the revolution as a 'medieval horror'.

'On the evening of 20 December [1989], I saw Ceausescu on television after he had returned from Iran, denouncing the protesters of Timisoara as "fascists". There was a line of people, including his wife, standing to one side of him. While I was watching, I was thinking to myself, "The countdown has started." The next day at the office, the others were listening to his speech in Palace Square at the moment when trouble started in the crowd, and the transmission was suddenly interrupted. When it resumed, he made his money offer' – 'a dirty business', she calls it, with uncharacteristic harshness – 'of increased pensions, of 1,000 *lei* to pregnant women, and so on. I decided there and then to go out into the streets. A woman in the building helped me to find a way out by a rear entrance; there were security guards on the front trying to keep people in, though later they gave up and disappeared. I left the building alone.'

Why did you leave alone? I asked her. 'I left alone because I was completely isolated at the office. People were friendly enough on the surface, but very few of them used to speak to me out of fear for their own positions. In the distance, after I had got out, I heard an extraordinary sound. It was not shouting, it was not the sound of slogans. It was like the roar of the sea in a storm. I walked towards it as if a force outside me were directing my footsteps. I did not feel myself to be an individual with a will of my own. It was absolutely clear to me that I had to go in the direction of the sound, and no other. When I got to Strada Batistei there was a line of militia men across the end of the street, facing the crowd in the Boulevard Balcescu beyond, and with their backs to me. They were wearing helmets and green overalls, and carrying riot shields.

'I tapped one of them on the shoulder, and he let me through into the crowd. There were tens of thousands of people gathered there, packing University Square and the Boulevard. Some were talking to the soldiers, there were people with children – in the side streets they were still shopping – the atmosphere was composed, but no one was moving. The sound of the sea, the low roaring, was around me. I hear the sound now in my head; the sensations I had at the time return and overwhelm me. Above, in the afternoon, helicopters began to circle, and as they did the sound of the sea grew into an enormous crescendo, very shrill, with the sounds of whistling added to the roaring. As the helicopters came over, again and again, the whole crowd would crouch and rise up together, like a great wave, with their arms raised to the heavens. "No violence! no violence!" people were crying, "no violence! no violence!" To the soldiers, they were saying, "We are the same people as you"; and the young were saying, "We are young, and you are young. Don't let blood be shed, don't use your weapons against us!'

Was there fear in the crowd? I asked her. 'No, no, there was no fear. But it was not courage either. There was what I would call a determination going beyond self-preservation; a determination to have done once and for all with the dictator. The crowd was ready to stand on one spot, on the spot where it was, for hours and hours. People were speaking to each other, but no one would use the name of the Ceausescus. It was always 'him', 'her', 'they', 'the illiterate', 'the shoemaker'. At dusk, the whole of the Boulevard was packed and the crowd unmoving, but it had been split into sections by lines of militia. As it became darker, the feeling grew that they had been given orders to disperse the people.

'The first to die in this part of the city died at this time, at nightfall. They were crushed – perhaps accidentally – by armed personnel carriers, which had begun to move forward in order to drive the crowd from where it was standing. I heard the sound of cracking glass in the distance; people in the crush were being pushed through windows. Figures appeared suddenly in the darkness with blood on their faces. As they came towards us, the whole crowd began to cry out to itself, "Don't go away! don't go away! don't go away!"' Was anyone in charge, was anyone giving instructions? 'No one, no one. The crowd was generating its own field of force. It was unnecessary for anyone to give instructions. And how could they? The crowd was vast, and there were no microphones, no loudspeakers. If anyone spoke, the most they could do – in the corner of University Square, for example – was to stand on a table and address the people closest to them.

'It became night, and people stood their ground, waiting, waiting. They all knew in these very moments, standing in the dark together, that there was no other way for the country than getting rid of the dictator, that these were the final days, that the Party was a huge corpse which would have to be disposed of. I remained where I was until 11 o'clock. By then people around me were saying that twenty or thirty had died in the city, including twelve or thirteen young people who had been shot in front of the School of Music.' Was the crowd angered or frightened to hear it? 'When rumours of deaths came, two here, three there, there was no anger and no panic. Only the cry, "Stay strong! Don't go away! Don't leave here!"

'But I had to leave at 11 and went home, by the streets which run parallel to the Boulevard Balcescu, in order to reassure my mother. As I reached home, I passed a group of about two hundred young people heading towards the outskirts of the city and the industrial areas. They were shouting, "Come with us! Don't be afraid! Come with us! Come with us!" I stayed with my mother a short while, met my brother [Sergiu Celac, the new foreign minister] and then set off back towards the city centre, to spend the night at a friend's house. The clearing of the streets with water cannon and the shooting had begun.

'The sky, as I walked, was lit by tracer bullets, with crowds running from the direction of the Boulevard and down the side streets, the firing behind them. They were being fired at as they ran, but it was mostly over their heads. People were crouching in doorways and entrances, quickly learning the sense of when to make a run for it. The sound of shooting was terrible, but there was also a feeling of carnival, of a feast, but with real bullets. I eventually reached the safety of my friend's house, and by 1.30 a.m. the shooting had stopped. The streets had been cleared.

'The Securitate spent the night painting over the wall slogans, as we discovered in the morning.'

★

'You know', she says – interrupting her story – 'in all those hours, I felt that different rules of existence had come into being. When I was a child, I recall trying to understand what the infinite was. My explanation was this. The infinite is an interesting place, where extraordinary or unique things happen. Parallel lines meet and a number divided by zero actually has a value. I got this same feeling in the revolution: that the city was being governed by a different logic of life and action from the normal. Even the weather was unusual. It was 7° centigrade at night and went up to 18° in the daytime. You could stay out for hours on end, even all night, without freezing. It played its part in the revolution.'

★

'On the night of 21–22 December, I slept till 6 a.m., and went early to the office. There I heard that five great columns of people, led by students, were on their way towards the city. One of these columns had been formed by the group of two hundred which I had chanced to see the night before on its way to the suburbs and the factories. I heard that each column had received flowers and bread throughout the night's journey of many kilometres, and had gathered up tens of thousands of people behind them.

'I left the office very quickly, though there were attempts to stop me. It was 22 December. By about 9 a.m. the whole of the centre of the city was occupied. People were killed in the main boulevards and squares, including Piata Romana and Piata Cosmonautilor. In Boulevard Magheru, where I found myself, there were tanks in position. They were surrounded by the crowd. There was also a new slogan which I had not heard before: "Don't be afraid! Don't be afraid! Ceausescu will fall!" People were talking to the crews of the tanks, and some of the crowd, children included, were trying to climb on to them, but they were being dislodged, sometimes with violence. At around 11 a.m. a new chant started, "Ole, ole, ole, Ceausescu is no more." It was not yet true. New slogans were also being painted on the walls, including for the first time, "Ceausescu, assassin".

'It was also at mid-morning that I began to notice in the crowd certain very excited individuals, people in a state of extreme exultation. They looked as if a wave of energy was overwhelming their wills.' Who were they, organizers? 'They were, let us say, tribunes. They were people, I felt, who had probably spent the whole of the previous day talking to the soldiers. Among them, I believe it was the best, the most eloquent, the most convincing, who now appeared as the leaders of the crowd.

'I had been in Boulevard Magheru for nearly four hours, when I witnessed a great turning-point of the revolution. At a certain moment, some time before noon, a tank crew near me accepted gifts of bread and flowers. When that happened, the tank was immediately overwhelmed by children, on whose heads the tank crew placed their helmets; but the tank crew stationed at only a few metres, distance continued to beat people away. At this point, I heard the leaders of the crowd telling the crews of two other nearby tanks to go to the TV station.

'There was twenty minutes of hesitation. Then they suddenly switched on their engines, to a roar from the crowd. The tanks began to turn in their tracks in clouds of exhaust fumes. At that moment I was looking at the members of the crews in their turrets from a very close distance, and have never in my life seen such relief on human faces. It was as if a spell had come over them. Some, two or three of these young boys, were actually weeping as the crowd pressed bread and cigarettes, or whatever they had, upon them. The other tanks near me also started up their engines, turned, and went off in the direction of Palace Square and the headquarters of the central committee. Two more tanks followed from further down the Boulevard, and the crowd followed behind them in tens of thousands.

'It was half-past twelve when I reached Communist Party headquarters. In front of the building, complete strangers were embracing. According to the people around me, the dictator was still inside. On the roof I could see a small white helicopter with its rotor turning.

From somewhere, a truck appeared with loudspeakers and other equipment on it, and edged its way to the front of the central committee building. Fifteen minutes later, a section of the crowd in front of me, ordinary citizens who were unarmed, forced the doors of the building. There was no shooting, nothing.

'Within only a few seconds, some of them appeared on the balcony where Ceausescu, the day before, had tried to address the people. I could see the white helicopter still on the roof, its rotor turning; despite the noise of the dense crowd, I could hear it also. At this moment, a portrait of Ceausescu was thrown from one of the windows, and a couple of books were flung from the balcony. That is all. I remember thinking that great historical events develop from such symbolic gestures. The small white helicopter's rotor blades were still turning; I think that for fifteen or twenty minutes part of the crowd and the Ceausescus were in the building together. The helicopter then took off – at the time I believed it had gone off empty. Some people appeared on the very top of the building. They were waving to the crowd and holding up the Romanian tricolour with the centre cut out of it. I now believe that they were members of the personal guard of the dictator.

'Meanwhile, the loudspeakers must have been connected up, since within minutes the first names of a temporary new committee of government were being read out from the balcony. It was then that an agent of the Securitate was seized by the crowd in front of the central committee building; he would have been lynched had students on top of a bus not seen it, and begun shouting "No violence! No violence!" During all these events part of me was completely overwhelmed by sheer astonishment, by pleasure, even by enchantment. Another part of me was deliberately detached from what, for us, was insane disorder. I recall consciously trying to keep at least part of my personality outside the events, in order to remain lucid and to remember.'

Were you saying to yourself, or thinking, this is a revolution? 'On one level, it remained, despite the deaths, a Romanian carnival. On another, I knew it was a revolution. That is, I knew there was no way back.'

*

And your years of darkness? I asked her. What of them, now? 'Oh,' she said, 'I tried so hard, and it cost me so much energy not to adopt the psychology of the prisoner, to live as far as possible as if I were free. I tried not to develop a siege mentality during all those years, and not to identify who was reporting on me. I am trying to maintain the same stand now. I don't want to know who the people were who did what they did for Ceausescu.' Why not? 'Because I want to face the past and its burdens now, in the same way as I tried to face them then, as a free person with my own free feelings.'

What about the execution of the Ceausescus? She hesitates. 'I am against the death penalty, against meeting violence with violence. But my feeling was that it was the only solution.' You didn't feel pity for them? 'Absolutely not. But, looking at myself now, I am astonished that I did not feel it. I was under the same spell as everyone else of collective anger and general indignation, which demanded some supreme satisfaction. I surprised myself. Then, afterwards, a feeling of intense sadness came that a human matter had been settled in such inhuman fashion.

'I feel bad about it now. It was a medieval spectacle. But when it happened, people wanted them to suffer. I even heard people talking in the street about putting them in a cage and displaying them in public. Now, I have a feeling of disgusted rejection of the execution. For years we passed, all of us together, through an experience which had something deeply evil, even satanic, about it. Now that it is over, we have an opportunity to be normal.'

Are things normal? 'They are more normal than they were,' she answered, her eyes weary.

*

In the warmth of the Intercontinental Hotel, there are ogling Romanian girls in red nail-varnish and black leather, laughing to see the western journalistic sport. Outside the bar windows, and set in the inhospitable ice, the fitful candles flicker.

*

Son of a miner, Janos Fazekas is a tough, burly fellow with a mean glance and the basso voice of a Comic Cuts villain. Sixty-three, overweight and out of condition, he slowly climbs the stairs to his flat in carpet slippers. A member of the dictator's politburo from 1965, and deputy prime minister into the bargain, Fazekas fell from grace in the spring of 1982, though he remained in the central committee until the whole shebang collapsed a couple of weeks ago.

Breathless, he lowers his bulk into a chair, pudgily smoothing out the tablecloth in front of him.

An ethnic Hungarian, he is all phlegm and bile on the subject of the late *Conducator* of Romania. Within the first moments of our conversation, he is denouncing Ceausescu and his wife as 'sly', 'diabolical' and 'wily'; and accusing them of every crime in the old Party book, from dim infractions of this or that Party statute, to letting the Securitate loose on all those who crossed them, Fazekas included.

It is rough stuff. 'He was totally uncultivated,' declares Fazekas of Ceausescu; he himself is a thick-set, big-fisted proletarian who plainly knows a thing or two about bare-knuckle Marxism. 'For years I fought to make him understand what scientific socialism is, but he never grasped it,' says Fazekas, sinking an early morning glass of the local schnapps, and wiping his moustaches.

'You, who are not a Communist, must surely know more about Marxism than Ceausescu,' he continues bullishly. 'He was an anarchist, a careerist, a parvenu, feudal, an absolutist, a dictator, and a tyrant.' (And that's just to begin with.) 'But whoever claims that nobody dared say anything to him is lying. When I was deputy prime minister, there were about ten of us in the [40 to 45-strong] politburo who were against him. I was one of those who consistently told him what I thought of him.' I ponder this assertion, as Fazekas bangs on about it; he certainly looks rough enough to have tried a fall even with a Ceausescu.

'For example, in 1982', Fazekas is saying, 'Ceausescu kicked out Prime Minister Verdets and named Constantin Dascalescu to replace him. I stood up in the politburo and opposed the decision in front of Ceausescu. This I am telling someone publicly for the first time. I said that Dascalescu was a man without culture or experience. I said that our Five-Year Plans were fanciful and unrealistic, and could be carried out by no one, and certainly not by Dascalescu. I said that I would vote against Ceausescu's proposals.

'I then asked Ceausescu, to his face, "Why don't you do a little resigning? What about giving up the office of president, and some of your other jobs also? If you had less burdens, you could become prime minister yourself and try to implement this impossible Five-Year Plan of yours, which you want other people to carry out for you."'

Sitting at his table, the obese Fazekas begins bellowingly to recount the ensuing confrontation, real or imagined, with the dictator. 'He was infuriated, like a madman, half rising out of his chair and trying to stop me. "Fazekas", he yelled, "you sound like the voice of Radio Free Europe!" When Ceausescu used to shout at politburo meetings it was always a sign that he felt threatened, a sign of fear that his authority was being challenged. Everybody fell silent. Those who thought, like me, that the Ministry doorman would have been a better choice than Dascalescu said nothing. They even avoided looking at me.

'I had little to lose, and I knew that as a Hungarian I was isolated. In fact I was surprised that Ceausescu had not sacked me before, after other battles with him. Already since 1980 I had been denied the right to travel abroad, even to the Soviet Union. I was deputy prime minister, but I was not allowed, on the orders of Ceausescu, to attend diplomatic receptions. Despite my position, the Securitate constantly watched me.'

How do you know? I ask him. The liquor bottle clinks unsteadily at the lip of his glass, the schnapps spilling on the tablecloth. 'There were microphones,' he says, waving vaguely at the walls of the room. How did you find out? He shrugs at the question; the whole subject is commonplace, barely worth discussing. 'I used to work for the Communist youth movement. Many of the activists went into the army or Securitate, and remained my friends. In 1970, at the time when I was deputy prime minister, I asked some of them to come over here with a detector. They found the microphones without difficulty. I took them to Ceausescu, and threw them on the table.

'He told me that he would enquire into it, but instead the surveillance increased after I had complained about it. When Valentin Ceausescu, his eldest son, who used to live next door, moved out three or four years ago, his whole house was turned into a Securitate listening post.' Why? 'Because many senior Party leaders lived around here,' Fazekas answers, offering me the bottle.

*

And who could count the thefts, the murders, the disappearances? There is a brief but ugly silence at the table; it is as if the whole room, with everything in it, were about to be sucked into the void of Ceausescu's vicious endeavour, a void which Fazekas himself inhabited for a lifetime. 'He was a violent Romanian chauvinist, anti-Soviet and anti-semitic,' Janos Fazekas continues; the cobbler was a man of parts.

21 East German refugees camping in the garden of the West German Embassy, Prague, October 1989

22 Prague workers leaving the CKD engineering works on the day of the Czech general strike, 27 November 1989

23   Part of the crowd in Wenceslas Square, Prague, calling for an end to the Communist regime, 22 November 1989

24   Vaclav Havel embraces Alexander Dubcek as news of the resignation of the majority of the Czech Praesidium reaches a Civic Forum meeting at the Magic Lantern theatre, Prague, 24 November 1989

'The army, the Securitate, the Ministry of Justice, Ceausescu threw all the Jews out of them. If you were a Jew, you could not be an officer in the army.' But why did Ceausescu have diplomatic relations with Israel? 'It was his greed and cunning. He knew that international capital is mostly in the hands of Jews' – ah, Fazekas also – 'and he wanted to sell his Romanian Jews to Israel. He exported them for cash per head, like he sold the ethnic Germans one by one to the Federal Republic, and kept the money in his bank accounts. The only reason he opposed the swinish invasion of Czechoslovakia was that he wanted to go on tricking western countries to support him.'

What about Elena Ceausescu? 'She was demented, an hysteric and a violent anti-Hungarian. You could say she had the same role here as Madame Mao in the Chinese Cultural Revolution. She was afraid of me, because she could not win me over as easily as the others.' (Comrade Fazekas is not that winning either.) What kind of personality did she have? 'She had no personality.' Was she worse than him? 'They were both the same.' Do you regret their deaths? 'No. Death was too easy for them. They should have been made to work,' he adds briefly. 'Above all, Nicolae was terrified of the people. That is why he developed his diabolical organization. It was the most perfect system of dictatorship in eastern Europe. But the moment had to come, especially for us Hungarians. If it had not started in Timisoara, it would have started somewhere else, sooner or later.' How do you know? 'Because the Hungarians in Romania supported the reforms in Hungary, but Ceausescu continued to starve the people.'

Fazekas looks as mean-eyed as ever; a man who was once to be reckoned with. You were the son of a miner and a life-long Communist, I say to him. (He is on his guard, an old heavy-puncher.) Hasn't your life ended in the same ruins as Ceausescu's? 'I will not give up my faith in "scientific socialism", he says, sounding rock-steady. 'I will not change my ideological beliefs as I would change my shirt' – tugging roughly at it – 'or my trousers. There are many anti-Communists now in Romania. Those who were unfairly arrested or tortured [sic], we cannot expect to defend a Communist or socialist party. But among the dead in the revolution', he declares, with fists clenched and voice again resonating, 'there were also many members of the Party. In every multi-party system, there is room for a Communist Party, provided that it is democratic.'

How can any Communist Party be democratic? Low-browed and

bull-necked, he weighs me up like a Sumo wrestler. 'If it abandons democratic centralism, the dictatorship of the proletariat and the class struggle, it can be democratic.' (This is the new orthodoxy, the orthodoxy of sweet reason: even the old Kung-fu mobsters are learning it.) Yes, but if it abandons all that, what else *is* there? The long-winded answer is that Fazekas is among those wanting to reconstitute the Romanian Communist Party as a 'left socialist party'. Such a party would aim to 'attract intellectuals and youth'. But first Fazekas and his gang must crush those calling for the Party's complete dissolution; as if they were in the room, he shouts them down as 'servants of the Ceausescu clan' and 'mediocre opportunists'. Then, with 'many democratic parties in place', including a cleaned-up Communist Party – and Fazekas in the van of it – 'we can solve all our problems in a civilized manner'.

He sits, punch-drunk, at the table; the present beyond his grasp, and his past leaden.

*

It is hard to keep a foothold on these frozen pavements. As darkness falls and fog begins to shroud the boulevards, every ear seems to be cocked for the phantom sniper. At key buildings, the black hulks of silent tanks – can anyone be inside them in this weather? – still keep their guard in the darkness. But the soldiers on patrol in Boulevard Magheru (they reappeared in force for Shevardnadze's visit) are at their ease now. As you pass, they are talking in low voices, smoking, or stamping their frozen feet in the shelter of doorways.

The stunned, bloodied city is settling to its liberation; quietly licking its wounds, and waiting – as cheerful as can be – for the cold tomorrow.

*

Last time, he had not wanted to show himself at his door when we parted. Today, with the approach road to his Ministry under armed guard, Andrei Plesu is minister of culture. A former art historian, he was hounded out of his academic job in Bucharest and then banished to a north Moldavian village for his dissenting opinions. Not wearing a tie, he laughs in his grandiose ministerial room, back from exile near Bacau less than three weeks ago. 'I can't cope with it. I can't function,' he says, beaming; 'I am busy all day, doing nothing.'

On his gross desk there is a bank of telephones; when one of them rings, he makes two wrong choices. It is a call from Bucharest's chief of police, seeking permission – which Plesu refuses – to frisk each member of the audience as the theatres and cinemas re-open. 'I am afraid I am looking very important,' he giggles, as he puts down the receiver.

Plesu describes the pre-revolutionary 'administration of culture' under Ceausescu as an 'anti-Ministry, the organized effort to stop the functioning of our culture'. With the fall of Ceausescu, there was an immediate ideological void; political decisions needed to be taken at once, within moments, and it was to the long-time opponents of the dictator – men like Plesu – that the revolution, and the revolutionary crowd, gave legitimacy. He himself returned from his village exile on 22 December, in the thick of the firing.

'It is tremendously stimulating intellectually to have witnessed the fall of Communism in Romania,' he says, a genial and portly figure. 'But now I have to remove a corpse, with the help of 140 functionaries who spent years working against culture. Praising Ceausescu was their main function. They were not serving ideology, they were the embodiments of it. But I cannot disown them yet because I need them. They understand the functioning of this huge machine and I do not. I simply cannot work with them, but to sack them would be risky. They would probably accuse me of conducting a Stalinist purge,' he says, laughing.

'I have a secretary who, when I press a buzzer, comes running into here in a sort of terror,' the new Romanian minister of culture continues, leaning against his desk. 'I have told her several times, "Look, please don't be afraid of me. There is a new person in charge here. Things have changed. There has been a revolution." It is tragic. The other day, I asked for something to eat, a cup of tea and a sandwich. When they brought it in, I offered to pay for it. They were totally dumbfounded.'

The bleak room is of tennis-court proportions; twelve ugly chairs stand at a glass-topped ministerial table. Plesu sees me looking at them. 'I feel very depressed in this Stalinist room,' he says gloomily. 'I don't think I will be able to stand it.'

*

Next day, I visited Plesu at home, where (two years before) we had had an illegal conversation, *sotto voce*, which he had failed – also illegally – to report to the Securitate. Now the house is alive with conviviality and laughter; non-relatives can even stay the night.

But, as in the heady aftermath of the French Revolution, there are many new battles to fight. 'At the last meeting of the National Salvation Front', Plesu reveals, 'there was a fierce conflict about culture. Delegates from the provinces had also been invited to attend, perhaps eighty of them. Even without their presence, the Front contains many people who prefer to talk about cheese and meat, rather than intellectual questions, in the name of being "practical". This type asks, "Why should we bother our heads at such a moment of material difficulty with the problem of political language, spirituality, or culture?" The provincial delegates actually began to shout us down when a few of us tried to talk about the ideological and cultural problems the revolution is facing.'

It sounds like the battles in the French Convention, or the conflicts in the first Soviets of the Bolsheviks. 'They kept on intervening. Their problems were "real", one of them said, while ours would be better as a television programme. I became almost afraid of their vehemence, and tried to get the prime minister, Petre Roman, to react and defend us. I told him it was outrageous that there was no specific item on the agenda dealing with cultural problems. But even he, a civilized person, said that such matters would have to "wait for another moment."'

What kind of people were doing the shouting? I ask Plesu. 'Anthropologically', he answers – these are fierce times – 'they were the old type of provincial people, very brutal. We were pushed into a minority at this meeting in the face of an old-fashioned, backward kind of proletarianism. All this could be a very dangerous portent, especially when so many of the intellectuals coming to the surface are themselves technocrats. Their intelligences are technical; spiritual and cultural matters make them uneasy. "Do your job", the prime minister says to me; "I am not interfering."

'But when I, as minister of culture, say to them, "Look, we must discuss religion", or "There ought to be a representative of the church on the National Salvation Front", they just laugh and say, "Do you mean this too is one of our problems?" On top of this, there is the danger represented by the National Peasant Party. Their nationalism, their old-fashioned patriotic rhetoric and their anti-semitism are no use to us either. They have no notion of tolerance and no feeling for Europe. They are potentially a great danger.

'Then there are the new moral problems which the revolution

has created. For example, we have got people saying now, even in intellectual circles, that they don't want the Romanian émigrés back yet, because "they didn't suffer with us". And this from people many of whom did not "suffer" themselves under Ceausescu!

'The trouble is that everybody wants to feel that he was a victim, even if he wasn't.' (What wonders there are in a revolution!) 'So everyone has acquired a dissident biography, which is morally very embarrassing to deal with. Then there are the people who are going around whispering that there are "too many Jews in the Front". Both Professor Silviu Brucan, a king-making member of the 10-man executive bureau of the Front, and Prime Minister Roman, are Jews. So was Corneliu Bogdan, who died 48 hours after being appointed secretary of state at the Foreign Ministry. Between them, they represent a tiny proportion of the revolution's leading figures.

'A neighbour of mine who has joined the National Peasant Party', Plesu continues, 'came to me the other day and said, "You are in the government now, but be careful. The Jews are coming back in Romania." I had to say to this wretched fellow, "Look, Ceausescu was not a Jew, he was an evil Romanian. And, yes, Brucan is a Jew, but hasn't he done a great deal for your freedom?" I could see that what I was saying made no difference. My neighbour's is a kind of abstract prejudice, with its own circular logic. But it is coming into the open now, and is a great danger.'

Plesu is a dark, bearded man with a loving, generous manner; he could be the morally-anguished protagonist of one of Chekhov's tragi-comic short stories. 'I will tell you something else as a friend, and you may think what you wish of it. In the last months of the Ceausescu regime, I began to be visited regularly by a Securitate man, who for seven years had been keeping a watch on me. He would sit here talking quite openly. At first he would say to me, "In the end, you will see it is we who are right." But gradually he started trying to give me the impression that he was protecting me, rather than keeping me under surveillance. One day he said, "You can't imagine, Mr Plesu, what I am doing to keep you alive."

'It began to get very complicated. He would come to me and say, for example, "You have met foreigners again. Don't do it." He even went to the lengths of getting copies of books I have written, and once asked me to sign one of them with a personal dedication to him. It was a book on ethics,' Plesu says, laughing. 'I thought for a while, and then wrote on the title page "To Mr Manuescu, whose ethics, I hope, will one day approach mine." Some days I would think he was trying to play the good angel. But I still do not know whether he would have shot me if he had been given the order to do so.

'After I had been nominated minister of culture, I got a phone call at home from the army. The army, as you know, has taken over the functions of the Securitate, which we have abolished by decree. The voice on the phone said that I would now need to be protected in the usual fashion, as a member of the government. Someone would be sent over to the Ministry to talk to me about it. When he came into the room, I could not believe it. It was Manuescu. What is more, I discovered that after the revolution of 22 December, he had been promoted. He actually stood before me in my room, telling me that I needed to be careful, that there could be people around who were hostile to the revolution, that it was his job to keep an eye on those who might want to harm me, and so on.

'I was almost speechless. "These counter-revolutionaries you have come here to warn me about", I said to Manuescu, "are the very people you were working with only a few days ago." He was not particularly put out, but I was completely astounded that he was still at work protecting the system. He, of course, is claiming to me now that he did not report to his superiors the things he discovered about me. But we have had a revolution, the Securitate was absorbed by the army, I am now a member of the government, and here I am being protected by the very man who watched me in the time of Ceausescu. The person whose task for seven years was *me*, is now, according to him, at my service.

'I still don't know, and cannot find out, what he is really doing. "We are not here to do anything against you," he said to me. "Every normal country has a security system, Mr Plesu, and we are the professionals." It's a bit complicated,' the new minister of culture added.

★

The old heroic slogans have been torn down, the Leader's works swept from the bookshelves, the portraits banished. Bucharest has been picked bare of Communism and Ceausescu. Their names survive only as bloody imprecations, daubed curses. On the walls of the frozen city, a painted boot – sardonic hieroglyph of out-and-out rejection – derides them both. *Vox populi* has spoken; and neither could answer.

Afterword

There have been many changes of fortune for those who appear in this book. In Poland, the candidates whom I listened to in Jaroslav – Ulma and Musial, Trelka and Onyskiewicz – were swept into the Senate and *Sejm* by a landslide in the June 1989 election. In Bulgaria, Zhelyu Zhelev – to whose dingy apartment I was accompanied by a security police recording-van – became president of the Union of Democratic Forces. The Transylvanian philosopher Gaspar Tamas, who in 1987 told me with gusto that Marxism was 'obsolete' and in January that the Hungarian Communist Party was 'decomposing', became leader of the Free Democratic Alliance and was elected to the Hungarian parliament in January 1990.

In Czechoslovakia, Jan Carnogursky, with whom I discussed the allegation that his father was a fascist, became first deputy prime minister and Vaclav Havel, sanctified in St Vitus's Cathedral by Cardinal Tomasek, became president of the Republic. Father Vaclav Maly and Jan Urban acted as leading spokesmen for Civic Forum at the height of the Czech revolution. As the old regime collapsed, the rough-voiced Vanek Silhan, who declared to me that 'only art' could do justice to the history of Czechoslovakia after 1968, was addressing mass meetings of anxious industrial workers. Milan Simecka, the political philosopher turned labourer, thought he was 'living through a dream' in Bratislava. As for the men in Pavel Bratinka's stokers' hut, they marched to Prague's Wenceslas Square in a body on the day of the revolutionary general strike in November, leaving one man behind to keep their furnace fire burning.

In the dismal Romanian city of Cluj-Napoca, where in 1987 a frightened woman had said that there were 'only the stars in the sky

and the moon to see with', dozens were gunned down by the Securitate
as the Ceausescu regime disintegrated.

★

What pleasure there was for the libertarian of left or right as the
medal-hung, and usually corrupt, Communist mighty fell one by
one from their various thrones into outer darkness! Hungary's Kadar
was ousted amid scenes of pandemonium at a Party congress in May
1989 as he tried to shout down his opponents. East Germany's
Honecker went in October, Bulgaria's Zhivkov in November, Husak
and Ceausescu in December. Honecker and Zhivkov asked to be
'relieved of their duties' and were expelled from their respective
parties; Ceausescu was executed. 'I have done everything to create a
decent and rich life for the people in the country, like in no other
country in the world,' he could be heard saying, as his executioners
fingered their triggers.

Communists found themselves overtaken by reforms they had
themselves promoted. Party reformers ate their ideological hats, only
to be swept aside as insufficiently reformist. Yesterday's Stalinists
turned today's progressives, and last month's dissident pariahs became this month's celebrated men of power. They could even be
discovered working together, hatchets buried – or half-buried – for
the salvation of the nation. In the thick of disorder, those still faithful
to the tumbling *anciens régimes* continued to preach their virtues.

And what extravagances, wondrous minor extravagances, there
were as Communism foundered. In Hungary, the red star was
dropped from the national coat of arms (on Communist orders) as an
'alien symbol'. The Slovenian Communist Party switched its colours
from red to blue-and-yellow. Even the Italian Communist Party
abandoned its hammer and sickle. In Hungary in September 1989
Rupert Murdoch acquired a 50 per cent equity in Peter Töke's
Reform weekly; two months later Robert Maxwell followed suit, with
a 40 per cent stake in the daily *Magyar Hirlap*. Radio Free Europe
opened a Budapest office, and the Party daily *Nepszabadsag* abandoned the slogan 'Workers of the World Unite!' which for decades
had stood at its masthead.

Of the hundred senators in the new Polish Upper House after the
June 1989 elections, 99 were from Solidarity, and the 100th was a
millionaire private entrepreneur. Astoundingly General Jaruzelski
referred to 'what Mrs Thatcher did with the [British] miners' in

the bitter 1984-5 strike, as 'socially unpopular but economically necessary'. The Adam Smith Institute of London held seminars in Warsaw for representatives of the new administration on how to 'set up a stock exchange, launch share offers and create profits', while Lech Walesa told an AFL-CIO convention in Washington that Poland was 'seeking buyers for 80 per cent of the Polish economy'. Thousands of workers at the Ursus tractor factory in Warsaw struck to press demands that their firm be privatized as a joint stock company.

'Our inheritance is almost unmanageable,' declared Karoly Grosz, the Hungarian Party leader on May Day 1989, as he himself faced oblivion. 'We have a huge foreign debt, an empty State treasury, broad social discontent and disillusion. We have to start many things over again.' Such sentiments were to become commonplace. Failure was recognized as failure.

For the opposition, the constitutional guarantee of one-party rule was the main target for removal, the change eventually receiving almost unanimous votes of approval in national assemblies which only recently had been moribund. The designation 'People's Republic' was rejected. Party cells in workplaces were prohibited. Workers' militias, the parties' private armies, were abolished. Secret police forces were redeployed, disbanded, or – more ominously – purged and reconstituted. Communist parties changed their names, split, became 'democratic socialist', even vanished; on all sides intellectual dissidence, criticism of the regime and religious observance became lawful.

Statues of past heroes – Lenin in Budapest, and Felix Dzherzhinski (friend of Lenin and founder of the Cheka, the first Soviet secret police) in Warsaw – were brought down in clouds of dust and heaps of rubble. Party *mea culpa*s rent the air, as new converts to the cause of reform drew on old habits of self-criticism, formerly enjoined upon the Party member for doctrinal error and backsliding. The result in most cases was merely deeper humiliation, while hitherto reviled and persecuted dissidents had the bitter experience of hearing on Party lips what they had themselves been jailed for asserting for a generation.

It was spontaneous popular action, the fond instrument of so much left fancy, which throughout eastern Europe helped to give the final push to regimes with little remaining legitimacy, and to deliver the *coup de grâce* to their leaders. When the people surged into the streets in remembrance of their lost history and culture and in anger at their present conditions – demanding free elections, striking for justice, mobilizing under banners of new political parties – the manner of such 'struggle' at once reminded the western left of its own old daydreams. Yet this, embarrassingly, was popular struggle not for Communism, but against it; not for a workers' socialist Utopia, but against it.

As the events unfolded, left intellectuals in the West were, not surprisingly thrown into uttermost confusion. Emotionally predisposed to favour dissent, especially underground and persecuted forms of it, were they for or against Solidarity in Poland, the Democratic Forum in Hungary, the New Forum in East Germany, the Civic Forum in Czechoslovakia, and so on? Some beguiled by the form of the upheavals and ignoring their deeper political significance, pretended that the ferment was a token of socialist renewal; some leapt straightaway onto the passing political bandwagon. 'We are all democrats now' was their swiftly adopted slogan. Others, the majority, fell silent.

★

The pattern of the collapse of the eastern European system was remarkably constant, and of the greatest political interest. The catalyst was clearly Gorbachev's assumption of power in Moscow in March 1985 and his ending of the 'Brezhnev Doctrine', which fatally deprived eastern Europe's regimes of the assurance of Soviet assistance and intervention in the event of popular uprising. (The exception was Romania, which had no Soviet troops on its territory in the first place.) Their sovereignty was no longer to be limited, but neither was internal stability any longer to be underwritten by Soviet armour – and this in a phase of rapid economic deterioration. Apparatuses which had come to depend for their ultimate survival on the Red Army were nearing political exhaustion, but from now on they would have to find their legitimacy in popular approval; or (as in Romania) rely entirely upon the sanction of domestically organized terror.

The dilemma was an impossible one, as opposition movements in each country grew more daring. In turn, the bolder reform spirits in the threatened Communist parties would call for, or even conduct, dialogue with the opposition, while the conservatives would (typically) call for resistance to the anti-Communist or socialist forces. As pressure mounted, there would be politburo reshuffles, the dropping of hardliners, even talk of coalition; except in Romania, where events moved too quickly and overwhelmed Ceausescu in a twinkling.

In the more slowly seething ferment elsewhere, curbs on foreign travel and the media would be eased or gradually lifted. Extensions of other civil liberties would be promised, and then – often after false starts and increasing protests hesitantly enacted. Dead-letter national assemblies would be partially rejuvenated and their functions extended. Such measures would in turn spur on demands for the greater separation of State and Party, for the establishment of a legal order, for freedom of association. As Party memberships everywhere began to haemorrhage, demands would mount for the ending of the one party system.

Here, the rearguard battles would be most fiercely fought. 'Socialist pluralism', economic reform, greater participation, and the elevation to prominence in each country of existing stooge parties would be offered by drowning apparatuses as a compromise alternative to a multi-party system, free elections, and the certain defeat of ruling Communist parties.

Communists, hanging on, would in succession redefine their purposes, promote younger men, air a few skeletons in the cupboards, rehabilitate the wrongly persecuted. As the going got rougher, they might bring in liberal democratic justice ministers to uproot, or appear to uproot, the nation's socialist institutions, while publicly beginning to laud the 'democratic principles' of western Europe.

When the ideological game was up, and every point of principle on which Communism had rested had been abandoned, they would turn themselves into social democrats and dissolve the Party. A rump would retain the forlorn hope of reconstituting it under a new name and a new management, when the dust had settled.

The attempt to recover the truth about the national past, after decades of Party-imposed falsehood, everywhere accompanied the upheavals. In Hungary, for example, the 1956 counter-revolution was re-categorized in February 1989 as a 'popular uprising'. Imre Nagy was not only exhumed and re-buried, but grotesquely re-tried in June 1989, and posthumously acquitted. Taboos about the past were broken.

Similarly, in Poland, on the 50th anniversary of the outbreak of the Second World War, General Jaruzelski admitted what everyone already knew, but no one in high places had said before, that Poles had been imprisoned and had died both in Nazi camps and Siberian gulags. Likewise, the contents of the hitherto secret protocols in the Molotov-Ribbentrop pact of August 1939 – which had carved up large swathes of eastern Europe between Stalin and Hitler – at last appeared on the historical record. The real nature of the Warsaw Pact invasion of Czechoslovakia was also admitted.

What was at issue here was not merely the truth about this or that contested or obscured event, but respect for human reason, ravaged for decades (to the point of collective madness) by institutionalized lying. The cancellation of affronts to countless minds had begun.

New fears (not all of them irrational) began to raise their heads and to stalk eastern Europe – fears of a post-Soviet vacuum, of revived Balkan grievances, of restored German power, of crass mob-violence, of a return of anti-semitic feeling, of terminal economic failure. Indeed, there were many hints of what lurked beneath the Soviet surface too, including the danger of a movement of populist-led disgruntled proletarians impatient for economic improvement, conservatives hostile to perestroika, and scapegoat-hunting anti-semites.

'Get bourgeois degenerates out of the Soviets!' read a slogan at a conservative rally of Moscow workers in October 1989, championed by Igor Ligachev, the Kremlin hardliner. Many observers fastened their alarm on the shadowy *Pamyat*, the Russian nationalist movement whose lumpen 'style', strong-arm methods, and anti-semitic slogans resembled those of the Blackshirts. Others pointed, as if at an omen, to the potentially anti-reform watchdog committees of workers set up during the strikes in July 1989 in the Siberian and Donetsk coalfields; their ardours and hatreds showed themselves to be fiercely proletarian, and in the oldest, most reactionary fashion.

'The Communist Party of the Soviet Union is above all a Party of the working class,' Ligachev declared in a Supreme Soviet debate in July 1989, playing (in the name of orthodoxy) with reactionary fire. 'Socialist ideals', warned Boris Gidaspov, the Leningrad Party chief, in November 1989, were being 'deliberately confused', and citizens 'duped by sweet fairytales about people's capitalism, unlimited democracy and non-Party glasnost'.

Moreover, in each of the East European countries, long-suppressed forces – anti-secular, extreme nationalist, monarchist, fascist even – saw in the current turn of events towards pluralism merely a prelude to, or rehearsal for, some other, more desired apocalypse. 'This is only the beginning of Poland's struggle for freedom,' announced Leszek Moculski, the Polish nationalist (KPN) leader, after Solidarity's triumph at the hustings. What end this struggle might have he did not specify. At the same time, in the furthest Balkans, the

Serbian Orthodox Patriarch – speaking in the presence, and under the protection of, the Communist Slobodan Milosevic – was describing the ancient Battle of Kosovo against the infidel Turk as the 'defence of Christ against anti-Christ, light against darkness, freedom against slavery, and civilization against barbarism.' Most miserable phenomenon of all, there were some 150 court actions in East Germany in 1989 over neo-Nazi activity, much of it the work of East Berlin skinheads.

The content of the *Letter to the Polish Electorate*, published in Warsaw under Lech Walesa's name in April 1989, was one of the notable exceptions to this kind of recidivism. 'Members of national and religious minorities are to be found, in greater or less numbers, in every electoral district in Poland', the declaration read. 'Our candidates should devote the proper consideration to these fellow citizens and their concerns. (And not only in your electoral promises, gentlemen, but in your later work in Parliament!) This will be one of the most important tests of the real competence of our senators and deputies. Their task will be to inaugurate, through their skill, honesty and humanity, a new period in Polish history: a closing of the accounts of mutual guilt and injustice, and the opening of a new age, an age equal to the demands of the imminent third millennium after Christ, an age when citizens of all nationalities, cultures and religions will live together in justice on the banks of the Vistula.'

This was a rare pronouncement, made in a heady moment of collective euphoria when state socialism's burdens were about to be unloaded from the backs of the Polish people. But if a new nihilism and new depths of disillusion were to be averted, something of much more substance – above all in social and economic progress – was going to be needed.

*

In Terezin, on a cold December day with a light snow falling, I thought I saw an old European abyss open before me. Here was where Commandant Jockel would have whole families beat each other to death for sport, promising to spare (for the time being) the life of the last family survivor. There, in the snow beneath the abandoned watchtowers, were the grey compounds and silent cell blocks, the SS quarters, the camp gallows. Just ahead of me, tramping along the prescribed slaughterhouse route for visitors, was a twenty-strong school party of cheerful West German teenagers in jeans, anoraks and trainers. I could hear their voices and follow their paths in the snow, from compound to compound. 'Only with West German young people, we have sometimes problems,' the Terezin guide said, in heavily-accented English.

We entered a dark punishment block, which the school party had just vacated. Here, the inmates would be crammed twelve to a small airless dungeon, to die by suffocation. The wooden, iron-bolted, cell-doors – some fifteen of them in a dark, narrow passage – were painted dark-brown, the walls whitewashed. On each of the doors were fresh wet footprints, six and eight to each door, one upon the other, made with the soles of trainers; there were other lashing kick-marks, some of them waist-high, on the fresh whitewash. The guide shrugged her shoulders. 'Very often they kick the doors', she said, 'or make some gesture'; cleaners with mops and buckets and paint-brushes would clear the traces ('as always') of what the West German school party had done, before the camp reopened in the morning.

★

In mid-February 1990, I met Günter Grass in West Berlin. 'Let us come to the point straightaway,' he said to me. 'If we think about Germany and the German future, we have to think about Auschwitz. It stands for everything which is hostile to the idea of European unity. It was the very expression of the anti-European spirit.' Do you mean that the Germans have not yet paid a sufficient price for Auschwitz? 'I mean what I have just said, that our neighbours are right to be afraid of us, and that we have a duty to do what is acceptable not only to us, but to them also.'

Surely you cannot hear the sound of *The Tin Drum* still? 'I am not saying that there will be another Auschwitz. I am saying that it will be very bad for the future of Europe if in the middle of the continent there is a unified colossus of 80 million people' – spreading his hands wide – 'with all our economic power. If things go this way, this super-strong nation will not invade its neighbours to the East, of course not. It will buy them with the Deutschmark.'

But Poland, Czechoslovakia, Hungary, the Soviet Union and the others are in desperate need of German economic aid and involvement, I said to him. 'Look,' he declared, 'their need is not the main issue. In a couple of years' time, if there is a united Germany, distrust of us will soon begin to develop. Our neighbours have their own experience of us. When the Germans begin to sense mistrust, what do they do? It is already beginning. The German voice grows louder. It grows louder', Grass added, laughing, 'even when it tries to speak softly. Let me tell you that when the Germans feel isolated, when they feel surrounded by enemies and by suspicion it is then that they make their worst mistakes. Our terrible history shows it.'

This was a dark vision, as the pall of decades of humiliation was lifting for most other Germans. 'Errors are already multiplying in our behaviour towards the GDR' ('This poor country' he called it). 'Consider what has happened there. There has been a revolution. Yet in their very first moments of freedom, even before the East Germans themselves have had time to recognize what has been achieved, before they have had time to begin to live their own history and build something new, you already cannot hear their voices. With our huge strength', Grass exclaimed, clenching his fists, 'we are arriving en masse and turning them into beggars. In their terrible economic conditions and under our pressures, what else can they say except "Yes, let's unify!"?'

These are not popular judgments. 'A man came up to me in the train the other day, and declared to me in a loud voice, very confident of himself, "I have read everything you are saying and writing. You are a traitor!" The others in the carriage heard him, yet nobody said a word. I love my country. But I was in the Hitler Youth and I have my own experience of the German mentality.' Grass fell silent. 'I have made my decision about where I stand on this question,' he added, shrugging.

*

In the death, or suicide, of East European state socialism, what will be the nature of the moral order which succeeds it? Who will benefit, and who suffer?

Moreover, to what kind of new or reformed system do most of the reformers (ex-Party and non-Party alike) aspire? The answer was becoming quite plain when the Hungarian Republic was formally established in October 1989. The new State would, if possible, be as like a western liberal democracy as could be contrived: with a mixed economy, plural parties and a welfare system. Similar aspirations were disclosed in country after country, including in post-Ceausescu Romania. On the left, in East and West, some have pretended – in order to save ideological face – that all these attempts to establish, or in some cases re-establish, a bourgeois democratic order actually represent a triumph for the 'democratic socialist model'. There are even those who see, or have to see, in every step taken towards the capitalist market the forward march of socialist progress.

But however high-flown some of the reformulations of political purpose in eastern Europe, it is the 'values of the market' which have come increasingly to be spoken of and applauded, as each country has entered more deeply into the turbulent reform process. After decades of Bolshevik experimentation and the exploitation – in the name of socialism – of multitudes of workers, such applause is not surprising. 'The working class', Gorbachev has nevertheless insisted, 'is as determined as ever to protect its interests. It exists, and its ideology exists,' he added.

Was he right? The answer must be yes. The dissolution, in the heat of the East European upheaval, of distinctions of position between 'left', 'right' and 'centre' we can already see was temporary. The new eastern European party formations – those in the Soviet Union too – in essence reproduce the standard colours of the western political spectrum. In the wake of the disintegration of Communist authority, the ideologies of Old Far Left and Old Far Right can also be seen at their familiar business, including in the Soviet Union. Those seeking a Third Way between them are characteristically much less certain of their direction.

The tragic socialist interregnum, which from the mid-nineteenth century disrupted – and almost destroyed – the democratic legacy of the French Revolution is ending, but only in its state socialist incarnation. Socialism itself, like fascism, will not go away, and least of all in conditions of moral and economic crisis. It will not go away even when the crisis, as in eastern Europe, was of the socialists own making. Moreover, as long as Marx's most awesome and fundamental prediction remains untested – that the true socialist dawn will come only when capitalism itself founders in its final catastrophic stage of universal monopoly, gigantism and world conquest – so long will every kind of socialist hope spring eternal.

How will it end? No one knows, but gods and goddesses acquainted with the future. One thing is certain: the life of Communism, Heine's dark hero, has been taken; by Demos, the people.

D.S.
February 1990